# INEQUALITY FOR ALL

## The Challenge of Unequal Opportunity in American Schools

# INEQUALITY FOR ALL

## The Challenge of Unequal Opportunity in American Schools

WILLIAM H. SCHMIDT
CURTIS C. MCKNIGHT

TEACHERS
COLLEGE
PRESS

Teachers College, Columbia University
New York and London

KH

Published by Teachers College Press, 1234 Amsterdam Avenue, New York, NY 10027

Figures 9.1 and 9.2 adapted from *Why Schools Matter: A Cross National Comparison of Curriculum and Learning*, by W. H. Schmidt, C. C. McKnight, R. T. Houang, H. A. Wang, D. E. Wiley, L. Cogan, & R. G. Wolfe, 2001, San Francisco: Jossey-Bass. Copyright 2001 by Jossey-Bass. This material is reproduced with permission of JohnWiley & Sons.

*Library of Congress Cataloging-in-Publication Data*

Schmidt, William H. author.
  Inequality for all : the challenge of unequal opportunity in American schools /
    William Schmidt, Curtis McKnight.
      pages cm
  Includes bibliographical references and index.
  ISBN 978-0-8077-5341-5 (pbk. : alk. paper) —
  ISBN 978-0-8077-5342-2 (hardcover : alk. paper)
    1. Educational equalization—United States. 2. Educational sociology—
  United States. 3. Discrimination in education—United States. 4. Educational
  change—United States. I. McKnight, Curtis C. author. II. Title.
  LC213.2.S365 2012
  379.2'6--dc23                                                   2012017472

ISBN 978-0-8077-5341-5 (paperback)
ISBN 978-0-8077-5342-2 (hardcover)

Printed on acid-free paper
Manufactured in the United States of America

19   18   17   16   15   14   13   12          8   7   6   5   4   3   2   1

6/28/13

*For*

Keara

Xia Xia

Aidan

Finley

Alex

Emily

Brent

Dylyn

Elayna

Reegyn

*We wrote this book thinking of you
and the world you will inherit.*

# Contents

# Preface

This book is about inequality in the American educational system. It is focused, in particular, on inequality related to the coverage of important content. Schooling is about the transmission of the ideas, knowledge, skills, reasoning, and problem-solving abilities in several subject matters that a society deems important to the development of its single greatest resource: its children. The core of schooling involves the interaction of students and teachers around subject-matter content. Such interactions are termed *opportunities to learn*. So in that sense, this book is about one of the core elements of schooling—coverage of subject-matter content—and how such opportunities are distributed across the millions of U.S. schoolchildren. It is in the provision of such opportunities that the core American ideal of equality of opportunity for all should be realized. If the phrases "all men are created equal" and the right to "the pursuit of happiness" are to have any meaning, the equal distribution of educational opportunities related to subjects essential for personal and economic success must be provided to every child.

The sad reality is that the American educational system does not provide equal opportunity for all but rather perpetuates vast inequalities in content coverage. This is especially true for mathematics and science. The inequalities begin with the state and local community in which the child is to attend school and continue with the neighborhood school to which the child is assigned. This inequality of opportunity is not only an issue for children in poverty or children of color but rather one that disadvantages many, perhaps even most, children in the United States.

Such inequalities begin with differences in state standards. Content standards have been adopted by virtually all of the major developed countries in the world, as well as many developing countries. State standards have also become a mainstay of the American educational system. Recognizing the importance of content, over the last several decades U.S. states have defined content standards that stipulate which topics are to be covered at each grade level. Those standards have varied appreciably. In an effort to both improve the quality of standards and to ensure equality of opportunity, more than 40 states have joined together to define and adopt a common set of standards in mathematics and English (language arts). Those Common Core State Standards are now in the process of being implemented.

But this is not a book on the history of standards or a discussion of their pros and cons. It is neither an elaboration of the details of the Common Core State Standards for Mathematics nor is it a defense of them. Standards are a central feature of the educational system and as such they play a role in the development of inequalities of opportunity; for that reason they receive some attention in this work. However, as important as they are, even the most perfectly conceived set of educational standards will not guarantee equal access to educational content by themselves. The heart of the matter lies elsewhere.

If there is one insight to be learned from this book, one fact that needs to be remembered when considering inequality of content coverage, it is that *the greatest source of variation in opportunity to learn is not between local communities, or even schools, but between classrooms.* This simple fact points to the pernicious effects of practices such as tracking, as well as the presence of competing signals about what should be taught from textbooks, tests, and most especially standards. The many, varied, and often conflicting definitions found in such documents place a tremendous burden on teachers, who have to make the important decision of what content to cover, leading to yet another source of variation in content coverage. Let us be very clear: To say that teachers are a major source of variation in opportunity to learn is *not* to blame teachers for educational inequality. Teachers are not the problem; putting them in such a situation and failing to give them the training and support they need *is*.

The data presented in this book strongly suggest that educational inequalities pose a risk to every child. Variation in content coverage corrupts the entire U.S. educational system, in effect creating an enormous educational lottery in which every student takes part—whatever their racial, ethnic, or socioeconomic background. The system of schooling represents a game of chance that few are even aware is being played. The public, parents, and even many policymakers are usually unaware of the widespread and large variations in content coverage that occur across classrooms in America's approximately 137,000 schools.

We wrote this book because we felt it was important for the public and the education policy community to understand the nature and extent of inequalities related to opportunities to learn mathematics and science. This book focuses on mathematics and mathematics literacy, which are of ever-greater importance in today's increasingly technological world. Much has been written about inequalities in schooling, but most scholars focus on inequalities of finance and resources. Instructional content involves the core component of schooling: that which we as a society want children to learn. As with resource inequalities, public policy has a powerful role in shaping curricular inequalities, and it is long past time that policymakers, parents, and the public give inequalities in opportunity to learn the attention they merit. The Common Core State Standards are a step in the right direction toward equality of opportunity, but whether the new common standards in mathematics will be effectively implemented or continue to receive sufficient support remains to be seen. Moreover, even as these standards are implemented, there will still be a great deal of work left to do.

Economic inequalities and the growing gap in wealth are a major part of contemporary public debates regarding educational issues, and this book makes an important contribution to that dialogue. There is good reason to believe that educational inequalities are strongly related to economic inequalities, both in terms of the distribution of wealth and economic mobility. Alexander Stille (2011) states that "with educational attainment going increasingly to the children of the affluent and educated, we appear to be developing a self-perpetuating elite that reaps a greater and greater share of financial rewards" (p. SR6). Should Stille's observations accurately characterize the U.S. educational system, it would represent a fundamental betrayal of the bedrock American commitment to equality of opportunity. We hope that this book will spur efforts to make sure that these fears are not realized, and that every child from every background in every community has an equal opportunity to learn.

# Acknowledgments

Over years of both national and international research related to mathematics and science education, I began to see a pattern of inequality related to the coverage of important content. This concerned me greatly as an academic, a citizen, and a parent. The issue of inequality in American education, especially in mathematics and science, is very important to the nation in terms of economic competitiveness, as well as to individual children and their futures. As a result, I was driven to write this book, which combines years of research. I arranged a leave from Michigan State University and moved my family for a year and a half to Charlottesville, Virginia. I had the extreme luck and pleasure to rent the historic Garth House, a 250-year-old home at the foot of the Blue Ridge Mountains (in which Thomas Jefferson was said to have set foot). I wish to thank Mrs. Garth and her family for providing us true hospitality and friendship. This setting provided me with great beauty and thoughtful space in which to write this book.

The research presented in this book was supported by seven grants, and many people have been involved and need to be acknowledged. I am forever grateful to these dedicated and loyal colleagues who have contributed so much to these efforts.

Jacqueline Babcock started with me when I was first named National Research Coordinator for U.S. Third International Mathematics and Science Study (TIMSS). She has evolved into my chief of staff, organizing a group of people with diverse talents into a cohesive and productive team with high standards. During the writing she managed to make sure that all my many other responsibilities did not fall by the wayside. It is not an overstatement to say that without her involvement throughout this effort, the book would not have come to fruition.

Jennifer Cady has probably spent almost as many hours with the book as I have. She has been tireless in word processing draft after draft, editing, and tracking down references. What I am especially grateful for is her careful and thoughtful reading of the manuscript. She became not a word processor but a partner in producing this book. Its quality is a reflection of her meticulous efforts, and I am extremely grateful for her dedication, hard work, and support.

I wish to thank my long-term colleague and friend, Richard Houang, for his analytical thinking and leadership with the data and analyses. He was a key confidant and our many conversations helped me reflect on, identify, and refine many of the main ideas and analyses in the book, as well as the various methodological issues. In many ways, he is a silent author whose contributions to all of the research were monumental—something I shall never forget.

I also thank Leland Cogan for his assistance with analyses of the data, and also for many years of involvement in the design and implementation of the studies that produced the data upon which this work is founded. A sincere thank you also goes to Kathleen Wight for her extensive and unique knowledge and leadership in the coding of state standards and textbooks and in the design of questionnaires, and to Neelam Kher for her extensive help in the analyses. I also wish to acknowledge Amita Chudgar for her work with the data during her post-doc year at Michigan State University and Christina DeFouw, who always makes sure that I use the research funds in the wisest and most productive way.

Nathan Burroughs and Leland Cogan were very helpful in reading drafts and making substantive suggestions for the book. Nathan provided critical insights in my thinking, especially in the concluding chapter. I also want to acknowledge my long-term friendship and respect for my co-author, Curtis McKnight.

Finally, I want to express my thanks to Judy Brazil Schmidt. She has endured my pursuit of this project and supported me all the way, from moving to Charlottesville to its final conclusion. She has read major parts of the manuscript, pushing me to make the writing more readable and less technical so as to make it more accessible to a larger audience. She always did this with honesty and affection. Without her support this book could not have been written, but what I thank her for the most is the title: *Inequality for All*. When she suggested that to me, I knew she understood what the book was all about. Those three words sound the call for equal educational opportunities for *all* children.

—William H. Schmidt

## NOTE

The work was funded by seven grants from the National Science Foundation: Award numbers 9252935, 9550107, 9814042, 0231886, 0314866, 0120282, and 9346762. We gratefully acknowledge this support. The authors alone assume responsibility for the results and interpretations presented in the book.

# INEQUALITY FOR ALL

## CHAPTER 1

# Introduction:
# A Story and a Myth

This is a story about schooling in America and, thus, a story about children—the nation's greatest resource. It is also, at a more personal level, a story about our own children. We know that the content, skills, reasoning ability, and problem solving children develop in school are important both to their future and to the nation's; every country in the world understands this. However, in the United States, one of the wealthiest and most democratic nations on earth, the reality is that the opportunities many children have to acquire such knowledge—especially in mathematics and science—are not guaranteed. As they walk into school, children become players in a game of chance, one that is dangerously invisible to both child and parent, and one with very high stakes. Sadly, therefore, this story has no fairy-tale ending.

The opportunities of too many students are arbitrarily determined by factors outside of their control, such as the state and local community where they live, the school they attend, the teacher they have, the textbooks the school has purchased, and the tests they must take. There are no villains in this story; everyone acts with the best of intentions, if not always with the greatest of wisdom. All of these factors conspire to create a very inconsistent and uneven system, one in which chance plays a major role and, as other countries have demonstrated, chance has no place in the education of children. The telling of this as a story is not just a literacy device to make a more abstract point; it is, at its most basic level, a real story about real children.

One must consider the consequences of having chance play such a major role in education. For parents, it is the ambiguity of never fully knowing if their child will have the necessary opportunities to succeed in life. Even worse is parents' realization that they have no other realistic options. The lack of opportunities available to their children must simply be chalked up to life's bad breaks. Parents and concerned citizens often cannot see the differences in opportunities that may limit America's children and turn them into underachievers by the standards of developed countries around the world. We are telling this story to make visible the situation in which American schoolchildren find themselves. We use two metaphors to elucidate what is happening to our nation's children—a game of chance and an unlevel playing field.

For American society, the implication is that two children with very similar characteristics and backgrounds most likely will not have had the same opportunities to learn mathematics, for example, after 12 years of schooling. If that is true, imagine how different the opportunities would be for two children of dissimilar backgrounds. This lack of equality has major economic and societal implications affecting not just individual children but the nation as a whole. Such inequalities also have important legal and moral implications.

When writing this book, one of the authors was on research leave from Michigan State University and spent the year in Charlottesville, Virginia, at the University of Virginia. He lived 3 miles outside the city limits, and, as a result, schooling was provided by the county school system. It was then that the topic of this book became a real story. He was able to see the implications for his two daughters, Ava and Keara (but especially for Keara), of how what they were studying in mathematics compared with what they would have been studying if they had been at home in East Lansing, Michigan.

He was familiar with the Michigan mathematics standards, since he helped write them. Consequently, he knew that there were big differences for his daughter in the content covered in 2nd grade. These differences existed only because of the particular state in which they happened to be living that year, but the differences in opportunity were significant. Michigan, for example, called for the introduction of multiplication in 2nd grade, including memorizing the multiplication tables up to the number five. Multiplication was not even intended to be covered in 2nd grade in Virginia's mathematics standards. As a parent, he thought it was reasonable that Keara should have had the same opportunities to learn mathematics whether she was in Virginia or Michigan. She did not. He knew that when they returned to Michigan, Keara would find herself behind in 3rd grade. Her learning opportunities had changed simply because her location had changed.

Keara's experience is not unique. It reflects what much of education has been and is like in today's schools. Children find themselves in situations that are like games of chance, where ability, motivation, and effort are not the primary determinants of success. Rather, success is based on a roll of the dice. Yet the outcome of the game is not the fun of winning a trivial contest, but obtaining the knowledge, skills, problem solving, and reasoning abilities necessary for success in today's complex and technologically oriented world. The stakes of this game are indeed very high and, as such, the vicissitudes of life, those chance occurrences of which life is full, should not determine something as important as one's education—not when we have other choices.

Teachers define the parameters of the game by deciding what content will be covered in their particular classrooms. This should not be determined by arbitrary and random factors such as the district in which they teach, the textbook that happens to have been adopted, or the extent of the teacher's content knowledge provided in their teacher preparation program. The rules of the game should be the same for all students. The rules should be national, if not international, in scope because students will be playing against their peers in every country. If the parameters are allowed to vary because of chance, then the teachers become unwitting contributors to the game of chance in which students find themselves.

## POTENTIAL CONSEQUENCES RELATED TO DIFFERENCES IN CONTENT COVERAGE

The example of Keara illustrates only one small way in which inequalities arise. It does not address the long-term consequences of such differences in opportunities. Unfortunately, we do not have the type of longitudinal data that it would take to trace *individual* children across their schooling from grades 1 to 12. However, we believe it is important to understand how the inequalities in opportunities described in this book have real consequences for the lives of individual children. What follows below is not meant as just an abstract characterization of American schooling. It is a description of the opportunities real children have, or do not have, and how all of these opportunities over 12 years accumulate to have real-life consequences.

To make this inequality more concrete, we ask you to imagine situations based on the data we have for groups of children at different ages, as described in Chapters 2 through 5. Our thought experiment is hypothetical, but we use what we have learned from the data to create the individuals and the scenarios. Although the individuals are fictional, they are intended to describe actual U.S. children since the data from which we created the fictional characters are quite real.

Imagine we were able to assemble all U.S. children eligible to attend 1st grade in the beginning of the year and that we paired these children according to the typical characteristics linked to differences in learning or outcomes. Each pair of children would be of the same age, gender, race, ethnicity, socioeconomic status, level of school motivation, and general ability and would have had the same number of years of preschool, as well as sharing other characteristics related to school learning. Imagine that after pairing all of these incoming 1st-graders, we were to pick four children and follow them during the next 12 years of their schooling, recording the opportunities they had to learn mathematics. The first two children would be a pair essentially representing children whom we would expect to be equally successful in school. The other two children would also be chosen as a matched pair, except they would not be particularly motivated about school and would not have some of the socioeconomic (SES) advantages of the first pair.

First, let us follow the two students we would expect to do well in school. They come from families with similar socioeconomic backgrounds and live in similar types of communities that are in different states. Emily lives in Togala, while Carrie lives in Osko. Emily's state has official standards for school mathematics that contain ten topics that are not included in the standards for the state where Carrie lives. This will leave certain holes in Carrie's preparation, since mathematics in later years builds on the mathematics learned previously (progresses hierarchically). The omitted topics include, for example, the relationship between decimals and fractions. This means that at the official state-policy level, the fact that the two girls live in different states already makes it likely that there will be differences in what each child has a chance to learn. This perhaps is the simplest illustration of the arbitrary nature of the different opportunities these two girls, alike in so many other ways, are likely to experience.

Since Emily and Carrie have different teachers using different mathematics textbooks, we have to look beyond the state standards to what the teachers actually cover in their mathematics classes. Differences in opportunity not only exist at the level of topics being covered but also in the amount of time allocated to the study of those topics.

In the first three grades, the focus most typically is on the concept of number, focusing on understanding place value, as well as on the addition, subtraction, and multiplication of whole numbers. In our hypothetical scenario, let us say that the cumulative difference in exposure to this topic was enormous over those first 3 years for our two students. For example, Emily ended up spending 2 1/2 months longer on studying number ideas and operations.

The differences only grew as they moved into 4th grade, when there is a heavy emphasis on fractions. Emily already had some exposure to elementary fractions in 2nd grade and spent a fair amount of time in 3rd grade learning basic fractions such as 1/2, 1/4, 1/3, and 1/6. Carrie, on the other hand, had very little exposure to fractions in 3rd grade.

By the time the two girls reach 6th grade, the differences in content exposure become more serious, with lasting implications. Sixth grade serves as the transition year from elementary arithmetic to the more fundamental notions of mathematics, algebra, and geometry. Carrie, who has had few or no opportunities to learn several basic concepts (such as the relationship of decimals and fractions, the basic distributive and associative properties of numbers, and the relationships of fractions and whole numbers), has much more difficulty in 6th grade as the basic ideas of positive and negative integers are introduced. She struggles with the very basic transitional concept that all of this is part of a system, the rational number system. Fortunately, she is in a school in which this topic is given about 3 months of instruction. However, she also spends almost 2 months focusing on dividing and multiplying fractions, decimals, and whole numbers. Emily also spends about 3 months on the rational number system, including positive and negative integers and the operations associated with those, but the background she brings to this study is richer.

In Emily's school, 7th and 8th grade focus heavily on algebra and geometry, with over 10 months of instruction related to these two topics. In Carrie's school, 7th- and 8th-grade students continue to spend large amounts of time reviewing the same topics covered in 6th grade, but include about 6 months of coverage related to algebra and geometry, a full 4 months fewer than Emily's.

Both girls are capable students and plan to go to college. Carrie enters high school taking Algebra I, Geometry, and Algebra II and opts to take Statistics in 12th grade. By contrast, Emily, who took Algebra I in 8th grade, moves on to take Geometry, Algebra II, Trigonometry and Analytical Geometry, and AP (Advanced Placement) Calculus in 12th grade.

As you can see, the structure of learning opportunities for these girls ends up being quite different. It is not only reflected by the particular courses they did or did not take, but it is also reflected in the depth of knowledge within certain areas of mathematics. Carrie generally has had less mathematics opportunity than Emily. Surprisingly, however, over her 12 years of school, Carrie has had a larger exposure to geometry and geometric reasoning than Emily, especially before high school. In the end, these two girls, who were essentially equal in learning potential and motivation to learn mathematics, were exposed to different content areas with different emphases. In one way, each student was limited by the particular opportunities she had. Thus, Emily enters college with a very different set of course possibilities from Carrie's. Even these two girls, where the level of their success given their backgrounds is not really questioned, end up with very different sets of opportunities in mathematics and, as a result, different skill levels. Perhaps some of these differences could be filled in at the university level. However, in our imaginary case, as is often true, Emily went on to take a minor in mathematics while Carrie, frustrated she was assigned to a precalculus course as a result of the college course placement test, did not take any more mathematics—a decision she later regretted. In today's technologically oriented economy, Emily's job options are greater, given her strong quantitative background.

The other two children—we will call them Jason and Aidan—start out 1st grade by all accounts as students who should succeed in school but are not likely to excel given their backgrounds. As we follow them, not only is the comparison between the two of them important to observe, but also how they contrast with the two girls. During the first 3 years of schooling, the two boys find themselves spending over half of each of the 3 years studying the basic number facts of adding and multiplying, as well as the operations associated with adding and subtracting multiple digits. No time in either of their 2nd-grade classes is spent on introducing fractions. The two boys live in the same state but in different neighborhoods and in different cities. Although their state standards call for the introduction of fractions in 2nd grade, fractions are not taught in the particular communities in which both boys live. They both attend schools in what would be considered low-socioeconomic-status neighborhoods. The differences in opportunity between the two boys and the two girls are large. However, even between the two boys, the differences are notable. Jason spends about 2 weeks in 3rd grade being introduced to fractions, while Aidan spends no time in this topic area.

In sharp contrast with the girls' opportunities, as Jason and Aidan approach middle school, they continue to spend large amounts of time on the basic operations of adding, subtracting, multiplying, and dividing whole numbers. In fact, over the first 8 years of schooling, Jason spends cumulatively some 36 months on such basic whole number computational skills. This is about half of the total mathematics time he spends in school over those 8 years. Aidan spends about 25 months studying the same subjects. Over those eight grades there are roughly some 72 months in total. One can see that not only are the differences between the two boys substantial, but that the differences between these boys and the two girls who attended schools in a higher-social-class community are even larger.

By the time these two boys reach high school, Aidan still struggles with mathematics and is tracked into a course called Basic Mathematics, which continues to provide lessons on the same elementary mathematics operations. Jason, on the other hand, is put in a class called Elementary Algebra. His parents thought this was good since he was taking algebra. However, a closer examination of the Elementary Algebra course would show that it was not the equivalent of Algebra I. It was a shortened survey version of the typical Algebra I course experienced by Emily and Carrie. Consequently, Jason next takes a course called Geometry Made Easy and a statistics course, which is his last mathematics course. He goes on to college but, given his weak background in mathematics, is required to take a remedial course for no credit. As with many students taking remedial courses in college, he ends up dropping out of college. In high school, Aidan takes Algebra I, fails it, and is then put into a course called Algebra A, followed by Algebra B (breaking up the same content into two courses so it can be covered at a slower pace). Unfortunately, after having failed once, then taking 2 years to cover Algebra I in the slower-paced courses, he does not take any more mathematics. Frustrated with this and other difficulties with school, Aidan does not attend college.

Once again, the differences between Aidan and Jason are pronounced even though they have similar backgrounds. However, the differences between the two boys and the two girls are enormous. It is almost as if they lived in different countries, not in different cities.

What does this thought experiment tell us? It starkly reveals that inequalities in opportunity are pronounced not just across children with different backgrounds but even when children's characteristics are quite similar in terms of demographics, motivation, and other factors. Children have different content exposures that are quite distinct simply because of the particular communities in which they live, the schools they attend, the teachers they have, the textbooks to which they are exposed, and the types of tests they take. All of these factors create the differences that accumulate until they become enormous in scope.

The scenarios were hypothetical, but they were based upon what we have discovered from the data about real children. The characters are imaginary, but the disparities are real. The purpose of our thought experiment is not just to illustrate that there is inequality in learning opportunities, but to suggest how cumulative opportunities develop in real schools. We will present you with all-too-real numbers that show just how substantial these differences in content exposure are. These imaginary scenarios are not really imaginary at all—they are a reality that applies to many children attending schools in the United States.

A good illustration comes from a colleague at the University of Michigan. While presenting some of the data that will be presented in this book to a set of education leaders, I suggested that identical twins would not be guaranteed the same opportunities even though their genetic makeup was identical and they grew up in the same family.

The suggestion was hypothetical. However, after giving the talk, my colleague told me that this was exactly the situation that she and her twin sister had experienced. She explained that the two of them, being identical twins, did attend the same school but, as is often the case, they were put into different classrooms at the same grade level. As a result, even though they were in the same school, they had different teachers. Content choices differed across the classrooms and across the varying grades. These differences accumulated so that by the time the two of them reached the middle grades, they were placed in different mathematics tracks. This essentially determined that they would, in fact, have very different content opportunities from that point on.

## THE AMERICAN MYTH OF EDUCATIONAL EQUALITY

Around the time President Abraham Lincoln signed the Homestead Act, offering land for work in opening the land to settlement for hardworking Americans, he said in a special speech to a joint session of Congress,

> This is . . . a struggle for maintaining in the world, that form, and substance of government, whose leading object is, to elevate the condition of men—to lift artificial weights from all shoulders—to clear the paths of laudable pursuit for all—to afford all, an unfettered start, and a fair chance, in the race of life. (Lincoln, 1861/1989, p. 259)

This speech of Lincoln's was the source of President Barack Obama's use of the phrase "a fair chance in the race of life" in his Lincoln Day address in Springfield, Illinois, in February 2009. In a speech shortly before his inauguration, President Obama had struck a similar note when he said,

> What you [the American people] showed me time and again is that no matter who we are or what we look like, no matter where we come from or what faith we practice, we are a people of common hopes and common dreams, who ask only for what was promised us as Americans—that we might make of our lives what we will and see our children climb higher than we did. (Obama, 2009, p. 2)

These words of two presidents are both spun off from one of America's founding myths. That is part of what it means to be an American, why the Declaration of Independence says, "We hold these truths to be self-evident . . . that all men are created equal, that they are endowed by their Creator with certain unalienable Rights, that among these are Life, Liberty and the pursuit of Happiness." We use the word *myth* here in the sense of a story or belief that "unfolds part of the world view of a people" and explains part of their practices and beliefs (Myth, 2011). We do not use *myth* in the sense of "unfounded or false notion" (Myth, 2011).

Schooling traditionally is viewed as providing equal opportunities to succeed in American society. It is the way "up"—to a better job and a better standard of living, a way to have "a fair chance in the race of life." Because of schooling, ability and hard work can win out over circumstance. Any student who takes advantage of his or her schooling has the chance to go as far as he or she wants, regardless of family origin, wealth, and social status. This is close to the heart of the individualism that is so much a part of the American character. Failure is often perceived as the responsibility of the individual, reflecting a lack of motivation or perseverance, not a lack of opportunity that can be ascribed to the fault of society.

This book is about the disturbing reality that, although we want to believe it, the myth that there is a level playing field for all children and that schooling offers equal educational opportunities to all is likely a myth in the second sense (an unfounded or false notion—it is in this sense that we use the word *myth* in the remainder of this book). It is likely not true even for two children who live in the same neighborhood but attend different schools. It is especially not true for two children who live in neighborhoods with vastly different standards of living.

The reason children do not have the same opportunities to learn is not because someone sets out to make sure that they don't. In fact, just the opposite is true. Government, schools, principals, teachers, and all others involved in determining the education that will be provided to American children mostly act in good faith. They want all children to have the same exposure to important content. That is part of what it means to be an American, why those words were in the Declaration of Independence. This is not a story about bad intentions. It is a story about what happens in spite of our best intentions.

For many decades, our nation has been committed to ensuring that all children have the same chance for success in school. Since 2002, those ideals have been embodied in a piece of federal legislation called the No Child Left Behind Act (NCLB).[1] Regardless of what one thinks about this particular legislation, it sums up what has always been one of our core values. Yet inequalities remain. Some children *are* left behind—not always for lack of effort, talent, or ability, and not because anyone sets out to sabotage their success. These inequalities often exist for no other reasons than where these children live, which school they attend, and the classroom to which they are assigned.

When we hear the word *inequality* in the United States, many (at least those in the White middle class) tend to think of this as a word that applies to someone else. Inequality is about race or ethnicity. Inequality is about wealth or poverty. Inequality is about social class. Surely, inequality is not about children generally. Surely, it could not possibly be about our own children. We hope to show in this book that this is not so. The reality is that inequality in education is about any two American children, living anywhere in the United States.

Our sense of fairness as a nation demands that all children playing the same game have an equal chance to win. In this book, we will expose the notion of education as a great equalizer that creates a level playing field for all children for what it is—an American myth.

## THE DIFFERENCE THAT SCHOOLING MAKES

Schools provide students with opportunities to learn. The heart of such educational opportunities is the coverage of specific content deemed important by society. (We use the word *content* throughout this book to refer not only to knowledge but also to skills, reasoning ability, and problem solving.) That content comes from mathematics, science, history, literature, and other subject areas. In this book, we focus primarily on mathematics but also consider science. Schools are organizations, but schooling is the process by which students are led to learn (Bidwell & Kasarda, 1980). That process involves the instructional activities by which schools organize and deliver the content. Therefore, schools affect student learning primarily through covering content and providing learning opportunities for students. Equal educational opportunity demands that such content coverage be essentially equivalent for all American children.

What schools choose to teach is important to student learning. So is the quality of the instruction provided by the teacher—a point that will be discussed in Chapter 7. Clearly, schooling matters. Those points seem so obvious that it hardly seems necessary to make them. Surprisingly, such obvious points often have been called into question. To argue that inequalities in educational opportunities are important, we must believe that school-based opportunities matter.

There is scholarly work that has challenged the importance of schooling. Its line of inquiry suggests that what really matters for learning is the genetic makeup and inherited abilities of a student as well as his/her home environment. According to this position, schools play, at most, a secondary role in student learning. Advocates of this position believe that schooling can never overcome the effects of genetic makeup and home environment.

In 1966, James S. Coleman, as lead author, issued what became a seminal study, *Equality of Educational Opportunity*, in response to the Civil Rights Act of 1964. Drawing on sophisticated statistical analyses, the report examined whether equal educational opportunities were available to U.S. students regardless of race, religion, and national origin. The most famous conclusion of that report was that student achievement was influenced more by students' and schools' socioeconomic circumstances than by the quality of the schools.

Since that time, scholarly discussion has gone back and forth over whether this was true and is still true today. There is no question that socioeconomic status (SES) for students and schools has important impacts on the success of schooling. The claim of the Coleman report, however, was that these SES effects had a stronger impact than the quality of the school. It was essentially a very pessimistic conclusion about whether improving schools would improve the learning of children.

The Coleman report and research related to it were not the only challenges to whether schools mattered. In 1994, the book *The Bell Curve* defended the proposition that because human ability related to school learning varied in a society, there would always be some people at the low end of the distribution. For them, learning would always be very difficult and not easily overcome by schooling (Herrnstein & Murray, 1994). The authors also explored the possibility that some subgroups in American society might have systematically lower ability as a group.

Because of arguments such as these two examples and others related to them, we felt we could not begin with what would seem obviously true to most people—the assumption that schooling matters to what children learn and achieve. Social class and ability are certainly important and have considerable impact. However, are they so powerful that we must conclude that concerns about schools and what is done in them are less important to what our children will achieve?

More recent research, including that from an international perspective, clearly suggests that schooling does make a difference (Schmidt & Maier,

2009; Schmidt, McKnight, & Raizen, 1997). For example, in the Third International Mathematics and Science Study (TIMSS), cross-national differences in student achievement among some 40 countries were strongly related to the nature of the content opportunities schools in the different countries made available (Schmidt et al., 2001; Suter, 2000). Actually, the issue of what students learn is complex. For an individual student, of course, it involves his or her effort and ability. However, given equal student efforts and abilities, the learning that takes place in school involves the coverage of the content to be learned and both the student's home and school environments. To make it even more complex, content coverage and varying environmental factors likely interact with each other.

For example, we will make the argument in Chapter 3 that the socioeconomic status of the parents has not only a direct effect on student learning, as Coleman and others have suggested, but also an indirect effect. This indirect effect is through the impact that the SES of the community (in which the student lives and goes to school) has on what content schools teach. This additional indirect effect adds to the more direct effect of SES on individual students through home environments.

This might be one reason why SES and student achievement are more closely related in the United States than in many other countries. In the United States, local communities control their schools and what is taught in them, which helps create this indirect effect of SES on learning.

How much does the United States differ in this respect? For the 40 countries involved in the 1995 TIMSS, the average correlation of the SES of parents with mathematics achievement was .30 at the 8th-grade level. In the United States, that correlation was almost .40, which was greater than the correlation in 32 of the 40 countries studied. [2]

Clearly, we are not arguing that schooling alone makes a difference in what students can learn. Rather, we believe that schools matter—that the effects of schooling interact with SES and other factors to determine what students learn.

## A DEFINITION OF OPPORTUNITY TO LEARN

To help clarify the issues, we discuss the concept of *opportunity to learn (OTL)*. It will play an important role in the discussions that follow in this book. Opportunity to learn is a commonsense idea—for a student to learn something such as how to add fractions, he or she must have had an opportunity to learn that topic. This can take place out of school or in school. It can be a chance experience or a planned learning experience in school. For our purposes, opportunity to learn is defined as those opportunities related to the coverage of content that happen because of planned instructional activities in school.

What content should schooling seek to cover? One of schooling's main functions is to transmit from one generation to another the knowledge, skills, and problem-solving and reasoning abilities that society considers important. A great deal has been written about what should be transmitted and many different theories have been put forth.[3] Our position is simple. Almost all nations specify in some form the knowledge and skills to be transmitted through schooling—that which is intended to be learned. These often go by names such as *curriculum standards, learning goals, framework, syllabus,* or *national curriculum* (Schmidt, McKnight, Valverde, Houang, & Wiley, 1997). In the United States, this specification has historically been done at the state and school-district levels but not at the national level, as is done in most other countries. The recently released (2010) Common Core State Standards for language arts and mathematics represents a deviation, at least in principle, from that historical pattern. Although not sponsored by the federal government and not adopted by all states, the Common Core State Standards are in fact the United States' first standards that are truly national in scope (Common Core State Standards Initiative, n.d.; Lewin, 2010; Porter, McMaken, Hwang, & Yang, 2011; Strauss, 2010; Zehr, 2009). The Common Core State Standards for Mathematics will be discussed in greater detail in Chapter 2. More background is also given in the Preface.

What level of the educational system makes such decisions as to what content is to be intended? In most TIMSS countries, the central government creates national content standards and, as a result, every child has the opportunity to learn the same content. This creates the possibility of a level playing field (Schmidt, Houang, & Shakrani, 2009; Schmidt et al., 2001). This is more difficult in the United States, where setting standards has traditionally been done at the state level and even locally by individual school districts. All states in the United States have their own content standards that they use to define what should be learned, and states have testing programs to see how well the content of the state standards is being learned. The new Common Core State Standards comprise a set of standards developed nationally with the cooperation of over 40 states and are available for individual states to adopt. The standards are national in scale only because more than 40 states have adopted them as their state's standards. They are different from the standards of most other countries in that they were not developed by the federal government and because state adoption is voluntary.

In most states, however, legal power for determining the specific standards for what is to be taught in the schools of a certain district is left to the local community—through its school board and local school-district officials. States try to influence what local districts do, with varying degrees of success. State preferences are, for the most part, simply advisory to local school districts and their school boards. For mathematics and language arts, with the advent of the Common Core State Standards, the situation may be changing. If successful, the standards will change the calculus of who decides what—at least for the states. We will discuss this more fully in Chapter 2.

Intended OTL is defined by what content is specified in such standards, but the concept of OTL is further defined as the set of experiences that schools organize to help students acquire the knowledge, skills, and abilities that are specified in those official standards. We will call these societal goals *standards* or, more simply, *the curriculum*. The activities that schools enact to realize those standards, we will call *instructional activities*. We will consider each such set of experiences organized by teachers to transmit knowledge or skills specified in curriculum standards as an OTL.

This is a simple, straightforward conception. Other conceptions have been offered. They are often more elaborate and derive from some philosophical point of view. For our purposes, this straightforward definition will be adequate. Using this conception of OTL, we can characterize OTL for a particular content topic as present or absent, depending on whether a student had experiences in school designed to learn that particular topic. The topic need not be formally required in the curriculum. However, we would expect that for topics in the official curriculum, the probability would be high that students involved in instructional activities relevant to that curriculum would have had relevant OTLs.

Our definition of OTL is based on the same concept formally introduced by John Carroll. He originally developed OTL to help understand student learning (Carroll, 1963). Opportunity to learn, in the sense that we use it here, was also developed at about the same time by the International Association for the Assessment of Educational Achievement (IEA), which has been studying student achievement in different countries and its effects since the early 1960s. When the IEA began to study student achievement in different countries, it soon found it necessary to consider whether students had had a formal opportunity to learn a given idea or piece of content in school. In its earliest form, OTL information was gathered by asking the teachers in various countries whose achievement data would be collected whether their students had had a chance to learn the content needed to answer each of the test items. These OTL data were used to explain national differences in student achievement. Both school subject-matter content that was intended to be learned and school subject matter that was actually covered (*implemented*) in the classrooms of the students who were tested were included.[4] Later IEA studies, such as TIMSS in 1995, measured OTL by analyzing content standards, the textbooks used in instruction, and what opportunities teachers said were provided for their students to learn.

Put in the most obvious form, our definition of OTL says that for given school subjects, students are more likely to learn what they have been taught and given a formal opportunity to learn. As a result, such opportunities to learn become the most critical, and perhaps the defining, feature of schooling.

If those opportunities to learn specific content are not provided for all students, then no real claim can be made for providing a chance at equal opportunities for all students.

## THE ROLE OF INDIVIDUAL RESPONSIBILITY IN EDUCATION

Part of the American ethos is that if you work hard in school, then you are likely to succeed in life. If you do not succeed, the ethos says, it is because you did not take advantage of the opportunities you were given and did not work hard enough. Many other beliefs built into our culture support this ideal. For example, as a nation we claim that such opportunities should be equal for all.

Many believe that past abuses have for the most part been corrected. After the legal ruling in 1954 in *Brown v. Board of Education*, "separate but equal" was no longer acceptable and certainly unequal opportunities in school were not acceptable. The kind of inequality that grew out of segregation is past. "For all" should now be a reality.

Another part of the American dream is the belief that everyone who tries can achieve a good standard of living in the United States. We believe that success is up to individuals, to their talent and efforts. This is individualism, another American ideal. Nothing should stand in the way of individual talent and efforts.

Because of these ideals, schools are central to the American dream. They provide the opportunity for *upward mobility*, a change for the better, for any individual. It is up to individuals to seize the opportunities made available to them in schools and use all their talents, efforts, and energies to make the most of them. More recently, in 2002, this sense of equal opportunities and the responsibility of schools, communities, and states to make them real was formalized in legislation through the No Child Left Behind Act. The NCLB legislation had as its vision the notion that schooling should be the vehicle for everyone to "make it" in our society.

Along with the positive vision of what schools should accomplish, there is a complementary notion about individual responsibility. Many believe that those who fail to achieve or "make it" in society are to blame for their own failure. It is their individual choice not to take advantage of the opportunities provided to them. We can affect what states and schools do. We can legally mandate their responsibilities. But we cannot legislate individual success. If students do not choose to use their talents, effort, and energies, no one can make them. We can provide a level playing field for schools, but we cannot make each child play the game or play his or her hardest. If we provide a level playing field, then if children do not succeed it must be because they do not try or do not have what it takes. It is sad, but that is life. It is their fault, not society's fault.

This line of thinking is comforting to some and lets us off the hook for some of society's continuing inequalities, but it is a myth. The thinking in the book *The Bell Curve* is an example of this line of thought. At the heart of *The Bell Curve*'s argument is the crucial assumption that school-based learning opportunities are equal across the whole of society and thus are not a factor in the differences of what individuals achieve. Such differences in life are not differences in schooling but simply differences in cognitive abilities. To some, that may be a comforting hypothesis, but it is wrong.

## THE NEED TO CHALLENGE THE AMERICAN MYTH THAT SCHOOLING IS EQUAL FOR ALL

This is the myth that we wish to challenge: Differences in learning are due mainly to individuals because schooling is equal for all. Using data from several sources, we will debunk this myth and show how schooling has not been equal for all. We will focus on whether there have been and currently are differences in content coverage in mathematics and science that permeate America's schools and have the potential ultimate impact on student learning. If there are differences in opportunities to learn in school, in spite of our beliefs and ideals, then differences in outcomes for students is not simply a matter of different abilities or level of effort.

We will use mathematics for our main area of investigation. In that context, we will use OTL defined in terms of a particular content or topic, such as being able to solve linear equations. The issue of equality is whether all children are provided with an opportunity to learn a specific topic.

Unfortunately, the actual issue is much more complicated. It involves complexities such as whether different sequences of covering content are equal opportunities. It involves whether the features that help define the quality of the OTL are equal. It also involves in what school grade the OTL is provided, since even the same quality OTL provided to one student two grades later than another would be a source of inequality. In what follows, we will deal with each of these complexities.

We hold a fundamental belief: If society has determined that a particular topic is an important content area or skill for its future citizens to master, then equal educational opportunities and fairness demand that OTL for this content be made available to all children in some appropriately equal form in school. The quality of the OTL should be similar and made available under similar conditions. For example, the same OTL should be provided in a timely way (often at the same grade level) for most topics. The extent to which these things are not true implies inequalities of OTL for that topic.

The data we have gathered and present in the following chapters will clearly show that opportunities to learn have not been equal for all students in American schools—that is, some students get an opportunity and some do not. In mathematics, at least, whether this continues to be the case awaits the outcome of the implementation activities surrounding adoption of the Common Core State Standards in the 40-plus states. We also believe that the data will show that the system of U.S. schooling is itself structured in ways that do not provide opportunities to learn certain topics for minorities, the poor, and those who struggle in school generally.

By design or by accident, we as a country have structured the U.S. school system so that "the rich get richer and the poor get poorer" (in an intellectual and learning sense, but, actually, by implication, also in a strict economic sense as well). What we as a society need to know is that these differences in opportunity to learn do not only affect the poor, minorities, or the less able; they affect all children, no matter their social status or their abilities. They affect children regardless of race, income, or residence.

Inequality of learning opportunities is not just a matter of inferior schools in inner cities or rural areas. It also happens in comfortable, middle-class suburbs. Two schools in the same state located in two different communities serving children of identical family backgrounds—identical in terms of wealth, education level of parent, income, professional status, and so forth—are not guaranteed to provide the same OTL to their students.

## EQUALITY VERSUS EQUITY IN OPPORTUNITIES TO LEARN

Legally, equal OTL would imply that all children living within the jurisdiction of a particular state are entitled to instructional activities in school designed to teach each stated expectation for their appropriate grade level. For example, if a state's standards called for memorizing the multiplication tables during the 3rd grade, then all 3rd-grade children should be given the opportunity to learn the multiplication tables by 3rd grade.

*Equal* in this context implies that not only must the opportunity be provided for all children, but that it should be of a similar, if not identical, quality. Although this aspect of similar quality is extremely important, it certainly cannot take place if the coverage of the content itself (of whatever quality) is not provided. For that reason, in this book we will focus on the simpler aspect of *equal* as meaning that appropriate content coverage is provided for all children. The vision of the NCLB act recognizes this right of children, even when the attainment of that right proves problematic.

What would equivalent opportunity mean in statistical terms? It would be measured by how much the OTL for a particular topic varied in a particular grade for all children, classrooms, and schools. The United States has standards at state and local levels but not national standards, with the exception of the Common Core State Standards for English/Language Arts and Mathematics, which are only now beginning to be implemented in some states. This immediately raises the possibility of a lack of equivalent OTLs for children raised in different states (see Chapter 2).

The issue of equity in OTL is more complex. Justice in a legal sense is involved, as is the background of children, such as the SES of their parents and concepts of what is truly equal in such cases. Coleman and others have stated that for OTLs to be equal, they must in some respects be unequal. But what are some of the factors that impact the quality of OTL and hence are related to issues of equity? We will examine how OTLs, in their simplest form of content coverage, vary across children, classrooms, and grades within an educational system. If equality in this simple sense is absent, then, surely, equity in a fuller sense must be absent as well. To facilitate this discussion, we will borrow some conceptions of OTL developed by others (Berliner, 1990; Wiley & Harnischfeger, 1974). The defining elements of a learning activity according to these conceptions typically include the following:

- students
- a teacher
- instructional material
- time in which students, under the direction of the teacher, are engaged with the instructional material in activities designed to provide the opportunity to learn the content on which the activity is focused

All four of these elements can influence the quality of the OTL provided for that topic by that instructional activity. A fifth factor not modeled directly here, but one that can indirectly influence quality by its effect on the teacher and the instructional materials, is the funding available to the school. All of these factors can influence the engagement level of the students involved. This surely would affect the quality of the OTL for the students and hence the potential for learning. Some of this is under the control of the individual students; they can become engaged or not according to their interests, choices, and willingness to put forth effort. Our focus is on the other side of the picture—on what the school can control relative to an OTL.

## Teachers

First, consider the teacher involved. Much has been written about the importance of good teachers (Richardson, 2001). However, what defines a "good" teacher remains an issue of debate. Some argue that it is the teacher's personality type. Others argue that it is the pedagogical or teaching skills of a teacher (Connelly, Phillion, & He, 2008), while still others argue that it is a teacher's knowledge of the subject matter that makes him/her a good teacher. This knowledge can be divided into general subject-matter knowledge, as distinct from subject-matter knowledge specifically related to the teaching of that subject matter, or what some call *pedagogical content knowledge* (Ball & Bass, 2000; Darling-Hammond & Bransford, 2005; Shulman, 2005). Others have argued that just as important to defining a "good" teacher is the teacher's knowledge of related fields that contribute to his or her understanding children's social, emotional, and cognitive development—such as knowledge of child development, sociology of schools, and cognitive psychology, among other subjects.

Whatever combination of skills, knowledge, personality, and experience is considered important, the main point is that teachers affect the quality of an OTL by the knowledge and experience they bring to the topic (or subject). Much research has found a link between student learning and measures of teacher knowledge defined in these different ways (Floden & Meniketti, 2005; Wilson & Youngs, 2005).

## Instructional Materials

Schools usually choose instructional materials, most often textbooks. These choices are a reflection of the curriculum standards that guide their local school district. The quality of the materials directly influences the quality of the intended curriculum and hence the quality of OTLs. Materials set limits on what can be done in learning activities, or at least what can be done easily. In the absence of other factors, these materials often determine what content a teacher will cover in instruction. If the topic is in the materials, the probability is greater that it will be covered in class. If the topic is not in the materials, the probability is greater that it will not be covered in class. Textbooks and other materials do not determine what a teacher may do, but for busy, overworked teachers, they often serve as *de facto* curriculum and set strong limits on what is likely to be done and thus on the likely presence or absence of OTLs. Certainly, textbooks and instructional materials are strongly related to the OTLs that are actually provided in classrooms.

There have been many battles over textbooks. Textbooks are the face of the curriculum seen most easily by the public at large. However, it should be remembered that the textbook is not necessarily equivalent to the curriculum. The textbook is intended as a tool for the implementation of a curriculum by a teacher, although the pressure of classroom realities may, at times, make a textbook become more than that.

## Instructional Time

Although the school day and year may seem subjectively long to children, any good teacher will tell you that instructional time is a limited commodity. There are many demands on the available time, and it is hard to find enough time for everything that needs to be done. Within limits, it seems fair to say that the more time associated with the study of a particular content topic, the greater the resulting learning opportunities will be. It is worth noting that there are points beyond which more instructional time is not necessarily associated with better learning. In general, however, instructional time is a good, though rough, indicator of the amount of OTL for a particular topic.

## School Funding

School funding in the United States has been a contentious issue for some time. It has been said that differences in how schools are funded across states and districts contribute to inequality in education. Much has been written on this, especially as it relates to issues of educational equity.[5] School funding is beyond the scope of our discussion here; however, school funding seems to be clearly related to the quality of OTLs provided in schools.

School funding potentially influences the instructional materials provided and the quality of the teachers who provide instruction. Districts with higher levels of school funding can afford to hire teachers who are more qualified and retain them, and to spend more on instructional materials (including not just textbooks but supplementary materials as well, which can help enhance the quality of OTLs). Since these factors affect the quality of OTLs, differences in school funding have clear implications for the differences in OTLs. Funding also has a less direct impact on OTLs through its effect on the quality of the school environment and its motivational effects. Given the heavy reliance upon local property taxes as the main source of school funding for most school districts, and the fact that property taxes, except when more complex state funding policies are in place, are related to the wealth of a school district, this seems to be a further example of the rich getting richer and the poor getting poorer.

## THE ROLE OF OTL IN INEQUALITIES IN AMERICAN EDUCATION

School funding surely contributes to differences among schools and school districts in terms of the climate and resources they have to provide opportunities for their students. However, we argue that such funding differences are mainly important because of the way they impact and contribute to differences in opportunities to learn, the inequalities that seem likely to matter most in terms of what children learn.

This book is about how inequalities in content coverage are built into the very policies that shape schooling in America. They are embedded in the resulting organizational structures that govern American schools. Because issues of school funding and teacher quality are related to OTL, they have been the focus of public discussions on education and the target of policies meant to shape and reform U.S. education. Our purpose is to focus instead on an even more fundamental issue: the unequal distribution of OTLs across schools. These differences can be investigated and demonstrated unambiguously. We will also examine how SES, school funding, and teacher quality interact to create differences in OTL. All of these differences affect children very directly. These differences are engendering some surprising results—results that may have unpleasant implications for each of our children and, therefore, the future of our country as well as the world in which those children will live as adults.

This book portrays the scope and depth of the inequalities in mathematics and science content coverage (OTL) currently found in American schooling. The work is based on six major national and international studies (see Appendix A). Chapters 2 and 3 begin the task of identifying the etiology associated with these inequalities by looking at the major components of the system that identify the content children are expected to learn: the states and districts. Chapters 4 through 6 examine what happens in the classrooms, while Part II (Chapters 7 and 8) explores the role that textbooks, tests, and teacher knowledge play in creating learning inequalities. Finally, Part III (Chapters 9 and 10) consider the implications of such inequalities.

# Part I

# THE INEQUALITIES THAT PERMEATE THE AMERICAN EDUCATIONAL SYSTEM

## CHAPTER 2

# One Indivisible Nation?

Every time we as Americans say the Pledge of Allegiance, we pledge our allegiance not just to our flag but to our country, a country that we declare is "one nation under God, indivisible, with liberty and justice for all." The words are beautiful. The ideas are beautiful. They express our hopes and our dreams. But are they true? More particularly, are they true when it comes to education? Are we truly one indivisible nation in education and in what happens in our schools across the 50 states and in the many local communities? Is there truly liberty for all with respect to education?

There are two ways to think about the idea of liberty. It can mean that all children of citizens in our country have the same legal rights to equal educational experiences and to participation in publicly supported schools. We assume that this is true across our country "indivisibly." In short, we assume that nothing legal stands in the way of equal opportunities for all students.

There is also a more positive way to think about liberty. There is a substantive sense of the word that implies *freedom to do all that we wish to do*, not because we are unhindered by laws and regulations, but because we have the opportunities to exercise our abilities (Berlin, 1969; Taylor, 1979). In that sense, *liberty for all* would imply that each of us has an equal chance to use our abilities to reach as far toward our aspirations as we can. In education, this means that every child of American citizens not only has a legal right to attend public schools but has an equal chance to go as far as his or her effort and abilities will permit. In this sense, indivisible *liberty for all* implies that schools are meant to be equally empowering.

That is the theory. Is it the practice? We are all aware that different children live in different states and different local communities. We are aware that economically there remain barriers that might impact educational experiences. We are also aware that states and local school districts have their own standards or expectations about what children should learn. But as a nation, can we at least say that we have the same *content goals* in mathematics for children in the same grade wherever they live in our "indivisible" country?

At a minimum, for example, does the United States have common mathematics content goals for all children at least through the 8th grade, the grade after which major differentiation in school studies begins to occur? Many nations view having such common goals as their responsibility, and they have structures that develop nationally stated expectations—content standards—for all children at least through the equivalent of 8th grade. Some countries, such as Canada, are divided into regions, with standards for each region. However, even in such cases, national organizations strive to make standards similar across regions. Some countries, such as France and Germany, have common examinations given at critical points in schooling to all children. Some have official inspectors to ensure coverage of the common content goals (for example, Belgium). Such efforts aim to ensure that the standards are at least comparable and that similar and equal content coverage is provided to all students.

Is the United States one of those countries with educational structures that work to ensure equal educational opportunities through common content standards for all children in public schools? The short answer is no. In fact, combining a state-driven educational system (as defined by the U.S. Constitution) with the all-pervasive and, in many states, legally defined concept of local school control of the curriculum has produced the opposite: a fragmented system with a splintered vision of what children are expected to learn in various subject matters, including mathematics and science. The rest of this chapter presents evidence demonstrating the consequences of such a system.

But in discussing the issue of a fragmented system in terms of content coverage, we must distinguish between the two levels of governance—states and districts—due to the recent emergence of the Common Core State Standards (CCSS) for both mathematics and language arts. This recent development changes, at least potentially, the degree of fragmentation among states but not necessarily among districts within states. The National Governors Association (NGA) and the Council of Chief State School Officers (CCSSO) have led the development of those standards together with 48 states that had expressed interest in adopting them. The development of the mathematics standards involved mathematicians, mathematics educators, teachers, school administrators, and members of the public (Common Core State Standards Initiative, n.d.). This has changed the policy environment as more than 40 states have already adopted them as their own state standards. At the time of the writing of this book, the new standards were to be implemented over the next couple of years, with each state having its own plan for phasing in the new standards.

For states, the data presented in this chapter portray a large amount of variation in content goals. This paints a picture, however, that is likely to change over the next couple of years, but it is a picture of what has been, and for the moment what still is, the reality. The data especially reflect why the United States needs common standards and should encourage all states to adopt them, for without the adoption of the CCSS, the dire picture painted in the first part of this chapter will persist. If the CCSS fail to take hold, the fallback position for the states will be to continue with what is already in place.

On the other hand, data for local school districts, also presented in this chapter, suggest not just the need for common standards but also the greatest potential impediment to their implementation. Districts have traditionally enjoyed local control of curricular content even in the presence of state standards. Many states do not have the legal authority to force local districts to adopt state standards, and as a result, they must rely on state assessments as a means of enforcing them. But even in this case, this enforcement often only happens in terms of public exposure. This implies that such a culture or zeitgeist is likely to die slowly, if it dies at all. The data presented in this chapter highlight the difficulties in getting districts to adopt common standards and, more important, to actually implement them in the schools and classrooms.

This chapter has two main themes. The first serves as a detailed portrayal, informed by data, for why we as a nation so badly need the Common Core State Standards for Mathematics—an argument related to both states and districts. As we move toward common standards, it is important for us to fully understand why that is the right thing to do—why it is essential that we do this. However, this chapter is not intended as a defense of the specifics of the Common Core State Standards for Mathematics. It is only an argument that, without some reasonable set of common standards, inequalities in content coverage will be inescapable.

The second theme assumes that, in the end, the Common Core State Standards for Mathematics will be adopted by virtually all of the states, which at least theoretically ensures equality of content expectations at the state level. But as the history of the standards movement and the data presented in this chapter tell us, adoption at the state level does not necessarily translate into adoption at the district or classroom level. The data show how likely it is that these common standards will move successfully to the next rung in the structure—that of the local school district. If the variation across districts within a state proves to be large in terms of content expectations under the current No Child Left Behind (NCLB) legislation, why would we expect it to be less so with the Common Core State Standards, which has as its enforcement mechanism the same NCLB legislation or perhaps the next generation of legislation, which could have even weaker enforcement provisions (Dillon, 2011; Ravitch, 2010a)? This second theme points to the enormous challenge facing the current effort to implement the CCSS across all states and across districts within states.

## THE MOVEMENT TOWARD COMMON STANDARDS

Even before the development of the Common Core State Standards, there were indications that the United States in general seemed to believe that common content goals for all children are desirable—at least for some subjects, such as reading and mathematics, and for some grades, particularly 1st through 8th grade. Since 2001, NCLB has provided an educational vision that was developed during the administration of President George W. Bush. Apart from the mechanics of the NCLB legislation, consider for a moment the vision inherent in that approach to education. The very rhetoric of "leaving no child behind" is one of common expectations and equal educational experiences. In what sense are children not to be left behind? Presumably, they are not to be left behind each other, no matter where they are, which would seem to imply common goals.

The NCLB legislation—as implemented—has fallen short of that vision. Each state has set its own standards in reading and mathematics as well as its own program of testing to determine whether the standards are being met. Within limits, rewards and punishments are set by each state according to their own program of standards and testing. However, there is nothing in the legislation to explicitly ensure that these goals are common across states or, in many states, even common across local districts within the state. This is hardly the practice of an indivisible nation.

Other mechanisms also have worked toward making standards more common across states. The National Assesment of Educational Progress (NAEP) is given to children across the United States. These examinations are based on a framework—a definition of content goals—that the National Assessment Governing Board (NAGB) has identified as the important knowledge that all children should have and the essential skills that all children should be able to master. This framework is developed by bringing together subject-matter experts. The examination based on this framework is given to a national sample and to a sample of children in all 50 states. It is used as a benchmark against which state assessments can be compared.

Further, professional organizations in various subjects have developed and published documents defining what they believe is important for all children to learn. Such organizations include the National Council of Teachers of Mathematics (NCTM) for mathematics. For science, they include the American Association for the Advancement of Science (AAAS) and the National Academy of Science (NAS) and its National Research Council (NRC).

Recent reports have also called for national standards. One report includes endorsements from former U.S. education officials, including Michael Cohen (from the Clinton administration), Diane Ravitch (from the first Bush administration), and Chester Finn (from the Reagan administration) (Finn, Julian, & Petrilli, 2006). A second report suggests a set of lessons from other countries that can be used to develop standards and suggests the consequences of not moving to national standards (Schmidt, Houang, & Shakrani, 2009).

## THE CLASH OF TWO GREAT TRADITIONS

Two American traditions are in conflict in the matter of what is taught to our children. We have a long tradition of local control of the public schools (with some oversight by the states in which the local school districts are located). This local control includes setting the content to be studied in the schools. We also have a vision and tradition of liberty and justice for all, which, when applied to public education, argues that all American children should be afforded equitable learning opportunities for important subject matter. We use the term *equitable* here because educational contexts differ, and providing the same content in the same way would not necessarily secure equal opportunities to learn for different students. However, at a minimum, the same basic subject-matter content needs to be covered if learning opportunities are to be even somewhat equitable (for all students). If we ignore political and ideological issues about who is responsible for and should determine the curricular content of America's schools, this goal of equal content coverage for important subject matters for all students is hard to disagree with. It is difficult to imagine a plausible position asserting that children in one part of the United States should be expected to learn certain topics in mathematics, science, or reading while children in other parts of the United States are not given the same opportunities or held to the same expectations.

Equal content coverage becomes especially important in the context of the global economic situation. We are told that, economically, the world is "flat" and that all parts of it will have to compete globally now and in the future (Friedman, 2005). This means that U.S. children will be competing for future jobs not only with other U.S. children but also with children from around the world. In that context, unequal opportunities put some U.S. children, or even entire groups of children, at risk of being left behind not just other U.S. children but also children from around the world. Such inequalities would almost certainly have an impact on the entire U.S. economy and its competitiveness in the future.

## THE CONSEQUENCES OF LOCAL CONTROL OF THE CURRICULUM

Risks of this magnitude put insistence on local control of the curriculum in areas such as mathematics, even if it produces inequalities in content coverage in a more critical context. These risks make such positions even more at odds with the vision of leaving no child behind. Who would want to publicly defend the notion that a topic taught around the world in 8th grade—such as the algebraic idea of a slope—should be taught to children living in one part of the United States but not children living in another part? Who would want to defend having such a topic in the mathematics content standards of one Michigan district but not in another district within the same state? Who would want to explain this to the parents of the children in the district that did not receive such content coverage? Yet, we will see later in this chapter that the topic of slope was not intended for coverage *at all* in various districts even within the same state. We will also see in the data the same variation across districts for other important topics.

Why should this be true? The answer is that, educationally, the United States is not truly "one nation indivisible." Structurally, the United States does not have one educational system. Instead, it is made up of 50 state educational systems. These state systems are further subdivided into around 15,000 local districts, each of which is an educational system in its own right. These educational systems are essentially autonomous, in part because of the ideology of local control of schools. The issue that is raised in this chapter is not about changing the structure of our educational system, such as eliminating local school control, but about the consequences of local control of the *curriculum* specifically, in terms of equal learning opportunities for all children.

We as a nation have created the tradition of local control of curricular content. As with any decision, however, there are consequences. Some of the consequences are intended and others unintended. We believe that one of the unintended consequences of our system is that it enables variability, resulting in inequality in the distribution of educational experiences and opportunities to learn important content across U.S. school districts.

One of the terms used throughout this book is *variance* or *variability*. Variance is a statistical measure of how much variability exists (such as the number of mathematics topics covered by students). In the context of this book, we use variance as an indicator of educational equality. Our use of the term *equality* does not imply strict equality, but rough comparability. If an aspect of educational experience and practice varies greatly, this is at least highly suggestive that equality is unlikely. When there are large differences among districts in terms of content coverage, it is unlikely that the experiences of students will be comparable. We will often discuss variance and seek ways to depict it graphically in order to present evidence that there are sufficiently great differences in content coverage that equality of education is unlikely. Since we do not use the term *equality* to imply absolute equality (identical), our inferences must always be phrased in probabilistic terms.

In the next section, we look at the mathematics and science content standards for the 50 states and for a sample of local districts, including large urban districts. We do this to explore the issue of equal learning opportunities as they are guided by the content standards of these two levels of the U.S. educational system. If we see large variations across states and districts in these content standards, then it is likely that similar variations will also occur at the school level. In addition, although not the focus of this book, we will look at how state- and district-level content standards compare with the standards of other countries.

## CONTENT VARIATION IN STATE STANDARDS

To examine whether official state standards in mathematics and science and the content coverage they intend varied among states, we examined the state standards that were in place across the United States during the 2000–2001 and the 2008–2009[1] school years. Analyzing the two sets of standards provides a portrait of significant variation across the states because such standards typically remain in effect for several years—often for 5 years or more.

Many of the 2008–2009 state standards are still operative but will be phased out over the next couple of years for the 40-plus states that have adopted the Common Core State Standards. The variation shown in this chapter characterizes what has been, and for many states still is, the case, and likely will be for several more years. The data thus provide strong evidence to support the need for Common Core State Standards. Without such standards, the inequalities portrayed in this chapter will continue to impact the lives of millions of children and, through them, the nation's future.

State standards specify for each topic the grade or grades at which that topic should be covered in that state's schools. Our focus in this chapter is on 1st through 8th grades. High school standards are often specified differently in terms of requirements for certain courses. These standards will be considered in Chapters 4 and 5.

We use a coding procedure based on a framework that delineates possible topics. For example, in 1st- through 8th-grade mathematics, we used a framework built around 44 specific topics (see Appendix B) that may be taught in one or more grades. Topics include mathematics concepts such as fractions, decimals, percentages, two-dimensional geometry, proportionality, linear equations, data displays, and other topics. These 44 topics cover the full spectrum of what is typically taught in 1st through 12th grades (or their equivalents) around the world.[2]

### The Total Number of Topics Intended to Be Taught Across the States

Many aspects of intended content standards can vary from state to state. One of the most general of them is simply the number of different topics to be taught over the first eight grades taken together. Variability in the number of mathematics topics to be covered provides evidence that some states required certain topics to be covered that other states did not require.

The number of topics out of the 44 that were intended to be covered in different states ranged from a low of 24 topics in one state to a high of 42 topics in another. Thus, at the most general level, there were differences of as many as 18 mathematics topics across the first eight grades among the states' mathematics content standards.[3] The typical (median[4]) number of intended mathematics topics was 33. Two other recent reports also suggest such large variation in state standards (Porter, Polikoff, & Smithson, 2009; Reys, 2006).

Mathematics is a hierarchically organized subject. New topics build on old topics. Further aspects of a given topic build on aspects of that topic that have already been covered. Given this, students from a state that does not cover many of the topics are likely to experience one of two consequences: First, there might be gaps in their mathematics knowledge, making it more difficult for them to learn the mathematics at later stages, since an early foundation was not established; a second possibility is that at the end of high school, a typical student in that state will not have progressed as far as students in states that cover more topics.

## Intended Coverage of Specific Topics Across the States

All states intended coverage for many topics: adding, subtracting, multiplying, dividing, working with fractions, working with basic geometric shapes, algebra, and handling data. These topics are generally considered essential. However, for 30 of the 44 topics, the percentage of states specifying intended coverage varied from as little as 10% to as much as 95%. Most of these content areas were covered by 60% to 95% of the states.

One way to interpret these results is by concluding that the topics that are covered by 90% to 95% of the states are basic and that large variability for the rest of the topics does not represent a problem but simply reflects local (state) choices. However, further examination shows that the topics missing in many of the state standards are key topics, such as the properties of mathematics operations, properties of fractions and decimals, ideas of estimation, proportionality, and slope. These topics provide an important foundation for a deeper understanding of mathematics that enables a student to go beyond mathematics as just calculation to using mathematics as a basis for thinking and solving quantitative problems.

## The Grade at Which Various Topics Are Covered

A more refined analysis of which topics are covered in which grades does not have the elegant simplicity of the previous section's discussion about pointing out inevitable inequalities. However, such an analysis is essential in order to indicate further inequalities with profound implications. Here, we examine the more specific question of which topics are intended to be covered at which grade levels.

Theoretically, any of the 44 mathematics content areas could be specified for coverage at any of the first eight grades. Thus, we have many *cells* or *topic-grade combinations*—combinations of a particular grade and a topic to be taught at that grade. We determined the percentage of the 49 states (excluding Iowa) with mathematics standards that fit into each cell—that is, that intended a specific topic be covered at a specific grade. There were 44 topics and eight grades, for 352 possible combinations. If standards were the same across all states, then each of these 352 cells would be covered by either 100% or 0% of the states—that is, all or none of the states would cover a given topic at a particular grade level—a very strict definition for equality of intended content coverage across the states.

Simply equalizing the total number of topics intended to be taught over the first eight grades alone would not guarantee equal content coverage. Given the hierarchical nature of mathematics, the specific grade at which a topic is included in the curriculum is not completely arbitrary. It influences which topics precede it or follow it. The issue, then, is not just whether topics are *covered* but also in what *sequence* they are covered. State standards typically specify an intended sequence for covering mathematics topics as well as which topics are intended to be covered. Not all potential sequences or progressions of learning opportunities are desirable (as we will discuss in a later section). However, for now we look at the differences across states in the intended coverage of each of the topics at each grade level.

The percentage of states for each topic-grade combination (cell) can vary between 0 and 100. This indicates the degree of variability across states, and as a result, the degree of equality in learning opportunities. The greatest variability occurs at 50%—indicating that the topic is intended at that particular grade by half of the states but not by the other half of states. We can calculate this for each topic-grade combination. Figure 2.2 represents the variation in the percentage of states intending coverage across the 352 topic-grade combinations. (Readers unfamiliar with box and whiskers plots should review Figure 2.1.)

The point of Figure 2.2 is not the particulars—the details for a particular topic-grade combination—but rather the general pattern and what it tells us about the variation across states in intended opportunities to learn mathematics. The distribution is represented by a box plot for all 352 topic-grade combinations. Each combination represents a potential opportunity to learn a particular topic at a particular grade. These are all the possibilities using the first eight grades and the 44 content topics in our mathematics framework. Not all such combinations should exist in state standards. Instead, these indicate what *could* exist—these are simply *potentials*. The amount of variation

**Figure 2.1. How to read a box and whiskers plot.**

A box and whiskers plot, sometimes called a box plot, provides a visual summary of many important aspects of a set of values for a variable of interest. The *box* stretches from the 25th percentile to the 75th percentile, thus containing the middle half of the values in the set. This is also known as the interquartile range. The median, or 50th percentile, is shown as a line across the box. The lower "whisker" stretches from the 25th percentile to the minimum value; the upper "whisker" stretches from the 75th percentile to the maximum value.

In this example, and for most of the box plots in this book, the scale is in terms of percentage of cases. The cases may be states, dis-

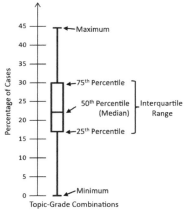

tricts, schools, or teachers. The hypothetical box plot at right summarizes the intention to teach 352 specific topic-grade combinations from states' standards. The maximum value of 45% means that for all 352 topic-grade combinations possible, the most states intending to teach a specific topic-grade combination was only 45%. Similarly, the 50th percentile represents the middle point (median) of the set of specific topic-at-specific-grade intentions in states' standards, or the typical combination that is covered by 22% of the states. Furthermore, half of all topic-grade combinations are found in more than 22% of states, while half of the topic-grade combinations in standards have agreement in fewer than 22% of the states.

**Figure 2.2. Distribution of the percentage of states that intended coverage of 352 topic-grade combinations.**

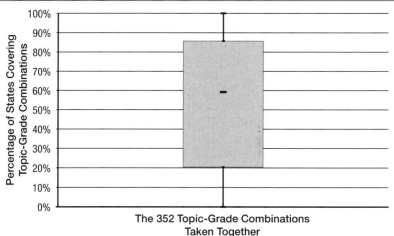

The 352 Topic-Grade Combinations
Taken Together

*Note.* For an explanation of how to interpret box and whisker plots, see Figure 2.1.

in the distribution of state percentages portrays how much or, rather, how little agreement there was across states in the opportunities provided. It provides a basis for assessing how likely it is that inequalities in learning opportunities in mathematics existed among the states.

Interpreting Figure 2.2 is central to the argument of this book and a key piece of evidence for one of its central points. It also represents a fundamental method and graphical approach used throughout the book. Thus, we devote a large amount of space to its interpretation.

A box and whisker plot provides a picture of how values for a specified variable differ among all the cases of interest. Here, the variable of interest is the percentage of states intending coverage for a topic-grade combination. The cases are the 352 potential topic-grade combinations. The box represents the middle 50% of cases, or those cases having values in the middle of the range of values for the percentage of states intending coverage. The bar in the box identifies the 50th percentile—the value at which half of the cases are below this value and the other half are above this value. In Figure 2.2, the 50th percentile is about 60%, or 29 of the 49 states. The top of the box is the 75th percentile—the point at which 75% of the 352 values are less and 25% are more. Here, the 75th percentile represents 85.7% (42 states) intending coverage. The bottom of our box identifies the 25th percentile in the distribution of the 352 values—in other words, the point at which 25% of values are below this and 75% are above. In Figure 2.2, the 25th percentile falls at 20.4% of states (10 states). The whiskers are the lines that extend up from the 75th percentile to the maximum value and the one that extends down from the 25th percentile to the minimum value.

Some topic-grade combinations are agreed on by all states, as indicated by the maximum value (the top end of the top whisker) of 100%. There are also topic-grade combinations that all states agreed on excluding. This is indicated by the minimum value (the bottom end of the lower whisker) being 0%. In fact, there are 18 such topic-grade combinations for which all states intended coverage and 20 for which no states intended coverage.

What about the rest of the topic-grade combinations? The median value indicates that it is typical for about 60% of the states (29 states) to intend to cover a particular topic at a particular grade. This alone suggests considerable variation across states, as it is close to a 50/50 split. However, for the middle half of all possible topic-grade combinations, as few as 20% of the states and as many as 85% intended coverage for various topics at specific grade levels.

Nonetheless, there is more agreement on topic-grade combinations than Figure 2.2 may suggest. Over one-fourth of the combinations are indicated for coverage by 85% or more of the states. Another one-fourth of the combinations had between 0% and 20% of the states intending coverage, which implies that 80% or more did not intend coverage.

The data on the 2000–2001 state standards portray in great detail the absence of a uniform progression of topics across grades for the coverage of mathematics in the first eight grades of schooling in the United States. In fact, they demonstrate that which topics are intended to be covered at which grade levels across states is effectively random. More recent data from 2008 to 2009, which included all 50 states, paint essentially the same picture (see Figure 2.3). Using a criterion of unanimity that all 50 states intend coverage of a given topic-grade combination, we can see that only six topic-grade combinations met this criterion. Apparently, even after the NCLB legislation came into place, little changed. In the "indivisible nation," mathematics instruction is so divisible that for 7th-graders in each of the 50 states, there was no topic that was intended for all of them to learn.

Many argue that the United States does not need the Common Core State Standards for Mathematics, suggesting that we already have *de facto* national standards. As Figure 2.3 indicates, we do not. What we do have is akin to a national lottery for determining content coverage.

## Focus and Coherence of School Topics

School subjects (mathematics, sciences, history, literature, and so on) are derived from formal bodies of knowledge—that is, academic disciplines. Formal disciplines have a structure in which some topics are more important than others as well as logically prerequisite to others. We argue that the sequencing of school topics must reflect the internal logic of the discipline from which the school subject matter derives. This is how we define the term *coherence*. Our definition of coherence is taken from Schmidt, Wang, and McKnight (2005):

> If one of the major purposes of schooling is to help students develop an understanding of the various subject matters deemed important by a society, such as mathematics and science, then the definition of "understanding" is important to examine as a way of viewing each discipline intended for schooling.
>
> Bruner . . . suggests that ". . . to understand something well is to sense wherein it is simple, wherein it is an instance of a simpler, general case. . . . In the main, however, to understand something is to sense the simpler structure that underlies a range of instances, and this is notably true in mathematics." Bruner's definition implies that the structure of the content in a discipline is important and that, for example, the goal of helping students understand mathematics is facilitated by making visible to them an emerging and progressive sense of its inherent structure. Bruner (1995, p. 334) . . . describes this as ". . . opt[ing] for depth and continuity in our teaching rather than coverage . . . to give [the student] the experience of going from a primitive and weak grasp of some subject to a stage in which he has a more refined and powerful grasp of it."

**Figure 2.3. Topic-grade combinations intended in state mathematics standards.**

| Topic | 1 | 2 | 3 | 4 | 5 | 6 | 7 | 8 |
|---|---|---|---|---|---|---|---|---|
| Whole Number Meaning | | | | | | | | |
| Whole Number Operations | | | ● | | | | | |
| Measurement Units | | | ● | | ● | | | |
| Fractions | | | | | | | | |
| Equations & Formulas | | | | | | | | |
| Data Representation & Analysis | | | ● | | ● | | | |
| 2-D Geometry Basics | | | | | | | | |
| Polygons & Circles | | | | | | | | |
| Perimeter, Area, & Volume | | | | | | ● | | |
| Rounding & Significant Figures | | | | | | | | |
| Estimating Computations | | | | | | | | |
| Properties of Whole Number Operations | | | | | | | | |
| Estimating Quantity & Size | | | | | | | | |
| Decimals | | | | | | | | |
| Relation of Fractions & Decimals | | | | | | | | |
| Properties of Fractions & Decimals | ○ | ○ | | | | | | |
| Percentages | ○ | | | | | | | |
| Proportionality Concepts | | | | | | | | |
| Proportionality Problems | | | | | | | | |
| 2-D Coordinate Geometry | | | | | | | | |
| Geometric Transformations | | | | | | | | |
| Negative Numbers, Integers, & Their Properties | | | | | | | | |
| Number Theory | | | | | | | | |
| Exponents, Roots, & Radicals | ○ | ○ | | | | | | |
| Orders of Magnitude | ○ | ○ | | | | | | |
| Measurement Estimation & Errors | | | | | | | | |
| Constructions Using Straightedge & Compass | ○ | ○ | ○ | ○ | | | | |
| 3-D Geometry | | | | | | | | |
| Congruence & Similarity | | | | | | | | |
| Rational Numbers & Their Properties | ○ | ○ | ○ | | | | | |
| Functions | | | | | | | | |
| Slope | ○ | ○ | ○ | ○ | ○ | | | |

Intended by all states ●
Intended by more than half of the top-achieving countries ▮
Intended by none of the states ○

> We define content standards in the aggregate to be coherent if they are articulated over time as a sequence of topics and performances that are consistent with the logical and, if appropriate, hierarchical nature of the disciplinary content from which the subject matter derives. This is not to suggest the existence of a single coherent sequence, only that such a sequence reflect the inherent structure of the discipline. This implies that a [coherent] set of content standards . . . must evolve from particulars (e.g., simple math facts and routine computational procedures associated with whole numbers and fractions) to deeper structures. It is these deeper structures by which the particulars are connected (such as an understanding of the rational number system and its properties). This evolution should occur both over time within a particular grade level and as the student progresses across grades. (p. 528)

This definition of coherence implies that the particular selection and sequencing of topic-grade combinations for a hierarchical subject like mathematics should not be arbitrary. Theoretically, each of the 44 mathematics topics in our framework could be intended for coverage at each of the first eight grades. Coherence implies that only some of these possibilities make sense in light of the logical structure of mathematics. Not all of the 352 combinations are desirable when coherence is considered. Many of the topic-grade combinations can be detrimental to coherence. They reflect potential learning that is out of any reasonable sequence for mastering school mathematics. These combinations could have a negative impact on student learning. The general concept of coherence described above must be defined specifically in terms of topic-grade combinations and the sequences of learning opportunities they represent.

The standards of almost 50 nations were analyzed as a part of the 1995 TIMSS. The countries included most of Eastern and Western Europe as well as Asian countries and others. These include Germany, Spain, France, Italy, Hungary, Belgium, the Netherlands, the Czech Republic, Greece, Portugal, Norway, Sweden, Denmark, Russia, the Slovak Republic, and Slovenia, as well as Japan, Hong Kong, China, South Korea, Singapore, Australia, Mexico, Canada, Venezuela, and Argentina. A model of intended coverage was developed from this work based on those countries whose 8th-grade achievement was among the best in the world. We think of this model as an international benchmark—a sort of "gold standard" that reflects a composite picture of intended mathematics-content coverage in top-achieving countries. It is not a model of what any one country does, but is based on what two-thirds or more of the top-achieving countries had in their national standards. This composite was then examined by research mathematicians who found it logically reasonable from a mathematics point of view. This, then, became our working definition of coherence.

The result is a logical sequence proceeding from the more elementary aspects of arithmetic and geometric shape in the early grades to the fundamentals of geometry and algebra in the middle (6th through 8th) grades. Of the 352 possible topic-grade combinations, only 99 define this model of coherence. This includes 32 of the 44 topics combined with a select set of grades in which those topics should be covered. The logical sequence is such that the most advanced topics are intended only for the higher grades. The more elementary topics and those that are prerequisites for advanced topics are intended for the early grades but are no longer intended for the upper (7th and 8th) grades. Figure 2.4 gives a graphical representation of the model.[5]

Two observations need to be made at this point. First, previous studies have found that the U.S. state standards and the original professional standards of the National Council of Teachers of Mathematics (NCTM) reflected a general lack of coherence in the sense described here. In fact, in many states most of the possible topic-grade combinations were present in their standards. This was especially true for those combinations involving the 32 topics in the international benchmark model of coherence. This means that many states intended to cover these topics even in grades in which such coverage was no longer likely to be effective. This is especially true for more elementary topics. They often continued to be specified for coverage in later grades. In short, no topic ever went away (Schmidt et al., 2005).

Second, recent work has shown that coherence was positively related to achievement at 4th, 7th, and 8th grades (the only grades at which appropriate testing was done). Using data from 32 countries, we found that those countries whose standards were most consistent with the model of coherence specified above were likely to have higher achievement levels. This was true even of countries that were not a part of defining that model of coherence in the first place.[6]

Before further analysis, a second concept must be described. This is the idea of *focus*, which builds on and relates to the definition of coherence. Focus has to do with the fact that instructional time is a limited resource in schools. If all topics (say, just all 32 topics involved in the model of coherence) were intended to be covered in all eight grades, then each of the topics would receive relatively small amounts of instructional time at each grade. This is as opposed to providing more time for key topics by focusing on a more limited number of topics in certain grades. This limiting of the number of topics in certain grades is what we term *focus*.

In the United States, school mathematics curricula have been characterized as being "a mile wide and an inch deep." Many topics are included at each grade, receiving a limited amount of instructional time because so many topics are included and are repeated in multiple grades, adding further to the lack of focus.[7]

**Figure 2.4. Benchmark model of coherence.**

| Topic | \| 1 | 2 | 3 | 4 | 5 | 6 | 7 | 8 |
|---|---|---|---|---|---|---|---|---|
| Whole Number Meaning | \| ● | ● | ● | ● | ● | | | |
| Whole Number Operations | \| ● | ● | ● | ● | ● | | | |
| Measurement Units | \| ● | ● | ● | ● | ● | ● | ● | |
| Fractions | \| | | ● | ● | ● | ● | | |
| Equations & Formulas | \| | | | ● | ● | ● | ● | ● |
| Data Representation & Analysis | \| | | | ● | ● | ● | | ● |
| 2-D Geometry Basics | \| | | | ● | ● | ● | ● | ● |
| Polygons & Circles | \| | | | ● | ● | ● | ● | ● |
| Perimeter, Area, & Volume | \| | | | ● | ● | ● | ● | ● |
| Rounding & Significant Figures | \| | | | ● | ● | | | |
| Estimating Computations | \| | | | ● | ● | ● | | |
| Properties of Whole Number Operations | \| | | | ● | ● | | | |
| Estimating Quantity & Size | \| | | | ● | ● | | | |
| Decimals | \| | | | ● | ● | ● | | |
| Relation of Fractions & Decimals | \| | | | ● | ● | ● | | |
| Properties of Fractions & Decimals | \| | | | | ● | ● | | |
| Percentages | \| | | | | ● | ● | | |
| Proportionality Concepts | \| | | | | ● | ● | ● | ● |
| Proportionality Problems | \| | | | | ● | ● | ● | ● |
| 2-D Coordinate Geometry | \| | | | | ● | ● | ● | ● |
| Geometric Transformations | \| | | | | | ● | ● | ● |
| Negative Numbers, Integers, & Their Properties | \| | | | | | ● | ● | |
| Number Theory | \| | | | | | | ● | ● |
| Exponents, Roots, & Radicals | \| | | | | | | ● | ● |
| Orders of Magnitude | \| | | | | | | ● | ● |
| Measurement Estimation & Errors | \| | | | | | | ● | |
| Constructions Using Straightedge & Compass | \| | | | | | | ● | ● |
| 3-D Geometry | \| | | | | | | ● | ● |
| Congruence & Similarity | \| | | | | | | | ● |
| Rational Numbers & Their Properties | \| | | | | | | | ● |
| Functions | \| | | | | | | | ● |
| Slope | \| | | | | | | | ● |

Intended by at least two-thirds of the top-achieving countries ●

### State Variation in Coherence and Focus

Looking only at the 32 topics from the coherence model described above for U.S. states, we find less variation in intended coverage than was indicated when we considered all 44 topics. At least 80% of the states intended to cover most of the 32 topics at some point in the first eight grades. This was not true for three of the 32 topics, all of which were included by the top-achieving countries but were included by only about one-third of the states. The three topics were the kind that would provide a deeper understanding of fractions, algebra, and geometry.

This analysis does not address the subtler aspects of coherence. Coherence is not really just about whether states intend for educators to cover key topics. It is also about the sequence in which a state intends the topics to be covered. The 99 topic-grade combinations that characterize the benchmark model of coherence form the criterion by which to examine the issue of coherent sequencing.

We determined the percentage of states that covered a topic at the specified grade level for each of the 99 topic-grade combinations indicated in the benchmark model of coherence. Figure 2.5 shows the variation in that percentage over the 99 topic-grade combinations. Unsurprisingly, this variation is smaller than what was seen for the 352 combinations presented in Figure 2.2.

**Figure 2.5. Distribution of the percentage of states that intended coverage of the 99 topic-grade combinations.**

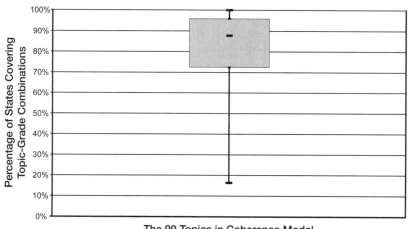

The 99 Topics in Coherence Model

*Note.* For an explanation of how to interpret box and whisker plots, see Figure 2.1.

There were none of the 99 topic-grade combinations that no states intended to cover. If there had been combinations that no states intended to cover, this would have indicated no variability across states. It would, however, have been at odds with the international benchmark. Fortunately, this did not happen.

How many states typically intended to cover each of the 99 *coherence combinations*? The typical percentage was just under 90% (44 states). Half of these coherence combinations had about 70% to 95% of the states intending to cover them. This situation is certainly less variable than what happens when we consider all 352 of the topic-grade combinations (the box and whiskers of Figure 2.5 were shorter than those for Figure 2.2, implying a smaller range of values). However, these combinations are the very essence of coherent mathematics instruction. For these combinations, it would be desirable for 100% of the states to intend coverage, but in fact, there were only 12 coherence combinations (of 99) for which all states intended coverage.

Almost half of the states did not indicate an intention to cover some of these coherence combinations. Such omissions can be especially problematic for student learning. In addition, only about 15% to 70% of the states intended to cover about one-fourth of these 99 coherence combinations. These included the properties of arithmetic operations and the properties of fractions and decimals. Understanding these properties may not be essential for simple computation. However, these topics are essential for understanding the idea of number and the "why's" of the operations of addition, subtraction, multiplication, and division, so that students learn when to use these operations and how to use them effectively. With only about half of the states intending to cover these topics, this is close to the maximum variability possible and implies that there are large inequalities nationally. The greatest inequalities among states occurred in the middle and upper grades for the more advanced topics. There was, however, extensive agreement among states on the more elementary arithmetic topics.

What about focus? If a state intends to cover more topics at a given grade level, it will intend to spend less instructional time (on average) on each topic—that is, not to focus as much. If a state intends to cover fewer topics, then it intends to place a greater average focus on each. The results for how many topics states intended to cover at each grade level are summarized in Figure 2.6. There was considerable variation. Typically, states intended to cover 15 to 20 topics in each of 1st through 4th grades and around 20 to 25 topics in each of 5th through 8th grades. How does this compare with our international benchmarks? The countries with the highest-achieving students typically intended to cover about five topics in 1st grade, about 10 to 15 topics in each of 2nd through 4th grades, and around 20 topics in each of 5th through 8th grades. Differences such as these led, in part, to our characterization elsewhere of the U.S. school mathematics curriculum as "a mile wide and an inch deep."

**Figure 2.6. Number of mathematics topics states intended to cover at each of grades 1–8.**

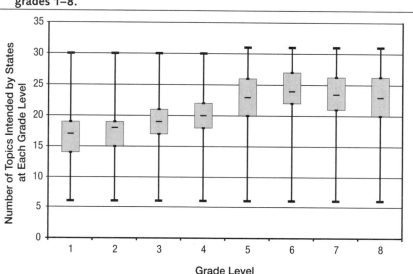

*Note.* For an explanation of how to interpret box and whisker plots, see Figure 2.1.

Within the United States, variability was large across the states. The differences were often as many as 15 to 20 topics or more, while the amount of instructional time devoted to mathematics was essentially the same in each grade and state. For example, teachers in one state were asked to cover 30 mathematics topics in 8th grade. In another state, teachers were instructed to teach only 15 topics. Instructional time is limited for teachers in both states. With less time per topic, those teachers who must cover 30 topics can hardly provide the same depth of coverage as those in a state with only 15 intended topics.

We referred earlier to a study across 30 countries that found a relationship between coherence and achievement (Schmidt & Houang, 2007). The same study also found a significant relationship between focus and achievement. Intending to cover more topics was negatively related to achievement at the country level. A country that planned to cover more topics had lower average achievement than a country that planned to cover fewer mathematics topics.

As we put together differences in focus, coherence, and intended topic coverage among the states, a clear picture emerges. Large inequalities in opportunities to learn mathematics in school have existed and currently do exist among different states. Until the Common Core State Standards are consistently implemented, the state in which one grows up and attends school will play a more important role than it should or needs to. Differences in state-level mathematics achievement results from the U.S. National Assessment of Educational Progress (NAEP) have been large (National Center for Education Statistics, 2009, 2010). Given the differences across states in intended content coverage, this hardly seems surprising if we accept that content coverage influences student learning. Although other factors (e.g., SES) will continue to shape student achievement, the variability in content coverage amounts to an unnecessary and easily rectified source of inequality. Should the movement toward Common Core State Standards fail, what has been portrayed in Figures 2.1 and 2.4 will continue. They represent the default position.

## CONTENT VARIATION ACROSS LOCAL DISTRICTS

We have examined how learning opportunities vary by state. Few states have standards that are mandatory for all school districts. In effect, school districts often have their own versions of standards (sometimes called *scope* and *sequence charts* at the district level). At a minimum, districts may have their own interpretation of their state's standards, often tied to and adapted for the textbooks used in that district. The ultimate question of intention, then, may well be, what do local districts intend to cover in mathematics, and do these intentions vary among districts within the same state? There are around 15,000 local school districts in the United States. Some are quite large in geographical area while others are quite small. Some encompass a single small suburb surrounding a major U.S. city. Others, such as Hawaii, encompass the entire state.

Since state standards are usually advisory to districts rather than mandatory, we examined the intended mathematics content coverage in district standards for a sample of 101 school districts. These districts are not a random sample of the whole United States. However, there is sufficient variety in the districts sampled to provide something of a microcosm of the whole set of districts for the United States, a microcosm that would be refined only slightly with a national random sample of school districts. If anything, this more limited sample will likely underestimate the variation that would be found in a random sample of the whole United States. The bulk of these districts come from Michigan, Ohio, and California. Others come from Illinois, Washington, Delaware, New Jersey, Colorado, North Carolina, Pennsylvania, and New York. They include U.S. cities such as Chicago, Miami, Cincinnati, Cleveland, Seattle, Rochester, Lansing, and San Diego.[8] The sample includes 61 local districts from Michigan and Ohio. Considered together, these districts, on average, have demographic and achievement levels that are characteristic of the United States as a whole.[9]

## The Total Number of Topics Intended to Be Covered

As before, the first thing we looked at is the total number of mathematics topics that districts intended to cover over the first 8 years of schooling. The results for this collection of districts mirror those for states. The number of mathematics topics ranged from 18 to 44 topics. For states, this range was from 24 to 42 topics. Only one district intended to cover 18 topics. If this outlier is removed, the range for the other 100 districts is from 26 to 44 topics.

More than 50 districts intended to cover 36 topics or more. This means that children in the district that intended to cover only 18 topics would receive exposure to only half the number of topics that the children in those 50 districts received. Three-fourths of the districts varied by 10 topics or fewer. To the extent that the topics not covered in some districts are crucial to developing mathematical skill and literacy, it does not matter whether the number of topics not covered was three, four, or even fewer. If any important topics are omitted, then there will be deficiencies in the mathematics learning opportunities provided.

As was the case for states, districts in the sample did not all intend to cover the same mathematics topics in 1st through 8th grades. Virtually all districts intended to cover the standard arithmetic topics of addition, subtraction, multiplication, division, fractions, decimals, and percents at some grade or grades. However, topics such as the properties of fractions and decimals, geometric constructions, and the idea of the slope of a line were most likely to be left out by at least some districts. For example, only about 60% of the districts intended to cover geometric constructions.

## The Grade at Which Various Topics Are Covered

Figure 2.7 illustrates the variability of the districts for the 352 topic-grade combinations. For most topic-grade combinations, between 10% and 80% of the districts intended to provide coverage. The typical (median) value over all topic-grade combinations indicated that about 50% of the districts intended to cover each combination. As was pointed out earlier, this represents the largest variation possible. The variation among districts is thus even larger than it was among states. In short, when it comes to the learning opportunities children receive, it doesn't just matter which state they live in but, even more so, in which particular school district they live.

Figure 2.8 represents the variation among districts in intended coverage of coherence combinations. The results were similar to what was presented for states, but with some notable differences. First, there were no coherence combinations that *all* districts intended to cover. Nor were there any

**Figure 2.7. Distribution of the percentage of districts that intended coverage of 352 topic-grade combinations.**

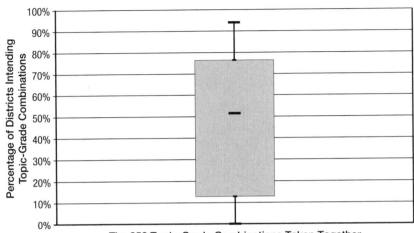

The 352 Topic-Grade Combinations Taken Together

*Note.* For an explanation of how to interpret box and whisker plots, see Figure 2.1.

coherence combinations that *no* districts intended to cover. The typical (median) percentage of districts that intended to cover the topic-grade combinations from the coherence benchmark was 83%. Seventy-three percent to 89% of the districts intended to cover half of these 99 key topic-grade combinations. This tells a story similar to what we saw for the states. However, the districts are slightly more variable and they show slightly greater deviation from the international benchmark than states. All of this suggests not just inequalities among districts in mathematics learning opportunities but also important deviations from the coherence model in some districts.

Key topics that are necessary for understanding the basic ideas of number are the same ones for which there was the greatest variability across districts. These include the properties of whole number operations, properties and relationships of fractions and decimals, prime numbers, and orders of magnitude in numbers. On average, only 68% of the districts intended to cover these key topics at the critical grades, leaving about one-third of districts that did not intend to cover them at the appropriate time. There was also substantial variation among districts when it came to geometry, where the average percentage of districts that intended coverage was only 69%. This was especially true for the key areas of geometric relationships and the Cartesian coordinate system. There were also considerable differences among districts in the number of topics intended to be covered in 1st through 8th grade, as shown in Figure 2.9.

**Figure 2.8. Distribution of the percentage of districts that intended coverage of the 99 topic-grade combinations.**

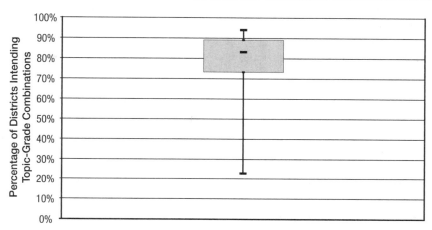

Topic-Grade Combinations (99) in Coherence Model

*Note.* For an explanation of how to interpret box and whisker plots, see Figure 2.1.

**Figure 2.9. Number of mathematics topics districts intended to cover.**

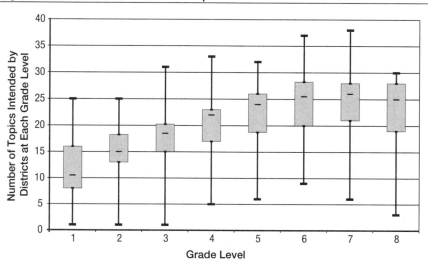

*Note.* For an explanation of how to interpret box and whisker plots, see Figure 2.1.

## District Variations Within a State

We have demonstrated that a large amount of variation existed across the pool of 101 districts sampled, a pool that crossed state lines. What we have not shown is whether there would be similar variation among the districts within a single state, which is necessary to make the claim that where one lives, even within a state, matters in terms of educational opportunities.

This issue can be examined for the three states in which we have sampled a sizable number of districts. These include Michigan (30 districts), Ohio (30 districts), and California (25 districts). In Michigan and Ohio, the districts do not necessarily constitute a representative sample for the whole state involved. In California, however, the districts were selected to represent the whole state. The results are at least highly suggestive for Michigan and Ohio, more so for California and, by implication, suggestive for other states as well.[10]

Since the year 2000 and the advent of the No Child Left Behind Act, there has been a greater push on the part of states to influence the curriculum in their districts, especially in key areas for NCLB (which includes mathematics). The results of state assessments are publicly reported. The determination of how districts are progressing with respect to NCLB is based on such state assessments that are themselves based on state standards. The question we explore here is whether this state-level involvement has made the districts within the state more like each other in what they expect to cover.[11]

Figure 2.10 shows the distribution of the percentage of districts within each of the three states examined in their coverage of the 99 topic-grade combinations from the benchmark model of coherence. In Michigan and Ohio, we can see that most of the districts intended to cover most of these topic-grade combinations. In Michigan, the percentages ranged from around 35% to 95% of the districts, with a typical (median) value of around 80% of the districts. In Ohio, the percentages range from 3% to 97% of the districts. In spite of this wide range, the median is very high (about 97%), implying that, for a typical topic-grade combination among these key coherence combinations, 97% of the districts intended to cover the topic at the critical grade. These medians indicated that the variability for the topic-grade combinations essential to coherence was relatively small. This was even more true in Ohio than in Michigan. In spite of this general pattern, both states have key topic-grade combinations in which there is greater variability. For example, in Michigan, only 43% of the sampled districts intended to cover proportionality in 5th grade. In Ohio, only 15% of the districts intend to cover proportionality problems, a related topic. These are only two examples among many.

So far, the data seem to support the conclusion that variability among districts within states is less than among districts across state lines. However,

**Figure 2.10. Distribution of the percentage of districts that intended coverage of the 99 topic-grade combinations in three states.**

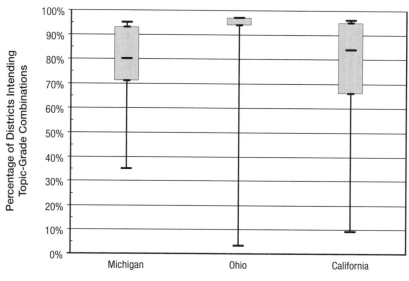

Topics (99) in Coherence Model

*Note.* For an explanation of how to interpret box and whisker plots, see Figure 2.1.

there is another part to this story related to focus. How much variability is there for topic-grade combination *outside* the coherence benchmark model? That is, to what extent do districts cover topics that place them at odds with the concept of coherence? This might come, for example, from intending to cover a topic before the prerequisite topics have been properly covered.

Figure 2.11 illustrates the variability for these *outside-the-benchmark* topic-grade combinations. Here, the variability is much greater. More extensive coverage of these outside-the-benchmark combinations indicates a diminishment of coherence. Since the time for instruction is limited, it would likely have a negative impact on intended coverage of the *inside-the-benchmark* combinations by causing them to receive less instructional time. This kind of coverage can lower focus. It also tends to confuse students about the logic of the mathematics being developed. The variability for these combinations in both Michigan and Ohio was substantial. Values ranged from 0% to 97% of the districts. The median was around 35% in Ohio and 46% in Michigan.

The conclusion is thus more complex than it might seem at first. In one way, districts within the same state are more similar in what they intend to cover among the topic-grade combinations consistent with the coherence

Figure 2.11. Distribution of the percentage of districts in three states that intended coverage of the outside-the-benchmark topic-grade combinations.

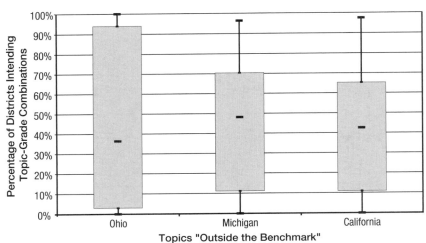

*Note.* For an explanation of how to interpret box and whisker plots, see Figure 2.1.

benchmark model. However, they also are as dissimilar as the pool of districts across state lines in the outside-the-benchmark combinations, thus varying in the amount of focus and in the clarity with which the coherence will emerge. Coherence is defined not just by consistency with the intended topic-grade combination of the top-achieving countries but also by what is not intended. Inequalities in content coverage can be created by large variations in either dimension.

California's case is quite different. The data are older, collected early in 2000 as California was beginning to operate under its 1997 standards, which resulted in a major controversy—one that has been dubbed the "math wars" (Jackson, 1997; Schoenfeld, 2004). Figure 2.10 shows that there were large variations among the California districts. The percentage of topics intended for coverage ranged from 9% to almost 100%. The typical (median) value was 84%. This is much more variable than in Michigan and Ohio. This greater variability is likely a consequence of the state standards being new. They had been in effect only a few years when the data were collected.

The percentage of local districts intending outside-the-benchmark coverage was extremely variable and similar to the results for both Michigan and Ohio (see Figure 2.11). The median value was 41%, implying that about 60% of the districts did not cover the outside-the-benchmark combinations and about 40% did. This has consequences for focus and clarity, as discussed earlier.

## A Special Look at Algebra and Geometry

For most of the world's countries that are our economic competitors, middle school mathematics curricula are about algebra and geometry (Schmidt et al., 2001). However, these topics do not just suddenly appear in 8th grade. This content is *ramped up*—introduced and gradually built upon—across the earlier grades. Especially in 6th and 7th grades, key topics for the development of algebra and geometry are typically covered.

Most of the topic-grade combinations characterizing algebra in the benchmark model are covered by over 90% of the 101 districts in our sample. Coordinate geometry is one of the few critical topics that are not as widely covered. How important is such an omission? This is not only an important topic for geometry but also for developing understanding in algebra. It is a key to understanding the idea of slope in linear functions. The equations of lines can be represented geometrically through the use of coordinate geometry and it thus becomes a key tool in understanding these essential concepts of algebra.

In the benchmark model of coherence, this topic was introduced in 5th grade, developed over 6th and 7th grades, and then used in 8th grade as it is linked to algebra. However, only about 40% of the sampled districts intended to cover this topic during 6th and 7th grades. Almost all introduced it in 5th grade and covered it in 8th grade. More than half of the districts lacked continued intended coverage of this topic in 6th and 7th grades.

The subject of geometry is typically not well covered in America's schools. TIMSS indicated that this area was among the United States' weakest in terms of student achievement. Around 80% to 85% of the districts intended to cover most of the seven topics for geometry in our framework and in the benchmark model. Still, given how central geometry is to modern mathematics and its uses, this is lower than desirable. About 20% of the districts did not intend to cover these topics. As a result, the students in the district would be unlikely to be taught these critical topics during their first 8 years of schooling. Tessellations and geometric constructions also have lower intended coverage, although they are less crucial to the development of mathematics thinking. Geometric constructions were to be covered by only around 30% of the districts. Although 20% does not sound like a large number, to the extent to which this sample is representative of the United States as a whole, this implies that children in some 3,000 districts would most likely not be exposed to important geometry topics during these critical grades.

## SCIENCE CONTENT VARIATION

The chapter has focused on mathematics—a fundamental topic for developing the quantitative literacy necessary as the language of science. However, mathematics is hardly the only area in which states and districts vary in their coverage. Science is another key area for which we have data and which we intend to examine from time to time in this book.

Looking at least at this one other subject-matter area helps strengthen our argument about inequalities as a systematic feature of American education rather than one that is particular to mathematics. Additionally, science is an area for which there are no Common Core State Standards. So, the portrait created here not only captures what has been and what is but what will likely continue to be the case for the foreseeable future. It provides still another example of why America needs common standards. We cannot deal with the sciences in the same depth as we do mathematics (otherwise, the book would be longer than it already is). We intend, therefore, to present only selections of the data by way of illustrating the lack of coherence and focus in other subjects. We begin with a consideration of intended coverage as indicated by state standards and their local district equivalents. We also look at classroom and school data for the sciences in Chapters 4 and 5, respectively.

### Content Variation in State Standards

Let us first look at the number of topics in the sciences that states intend to cover in the 1st through 8th grades, according to their own standards documents. The standards examined here were in effect in early 2000. The NCLB legislation demanding state-level expectations by grade only came into effect in the year 2007, just when we began work on this book. Thus, it is likely that many of these state standards have been or are in the process of being rewritten.

Since science standards were not mandated by the NCLB legislation, only 44 states had standards that we could analyze. One state (Iowa) did not have science standards at all. The other five states had standards, but they were so general in nature that specific content expectations could not be clearly identified.

The variation in the state standards was extremely large, even larger than for mathematics. Our science topic framework had 79 science topics (see Appendix C). One state indicated that it intended to cover only 16 of those 79 topics. At the other extreme, another state indicated that it intended to cover 73 of the 79 topics. The typical (median) number of topics that states intended to cover anytime between 1st and 8th grades was 54. The middle 50% of the states ranged from 49 to 59 topics that they intended to cover somewhere during these eight grades.

There were 79 topics in our science framework (developed in a way similar to our mathematics framework) and eight grades were considered. Thus, there were 632 possible topic-grade combinations for the sciences in 1st through 8th grades.

Figure 2.12 indicates the percentage of the 44 states examined that intended to cover each of the 632 topic-grade combinations. The states did not all agree on even one of the 632 combinations. However, they did agree on excluding 43 of the combinations. The range of combinations indicated for coverage was from 0% to 98% of the states, and the median was 48%.

As we noted earlier, there was no single topic-grade combination that all of the examined states indicated they intended to cover. Ninety percent or more of the states agreed that they should cover only about 10 of the combinations. This was about 2% of the possibilities.

As with mathematics, we used a benchmark model for coherence in the sciences based on the curricula of high-achieving countries (Schmidt et al., 2005).[12] Considering only those coherence benchmark topic-grade combinations, Figure 2.12 shows the variability to be less but still quite large. The coherence benchmark model for the sciences includes 63 of the 79 topics and, using these 63 topics, involves 136 topic-grade combinations. The percentage of the states that intended to cover these benchmark combinations ranged from 19% to 93%, with a median (typical) value of 69% (higher than for the total number of such combinations but still indicating considerable variation among states).

For the sake of comparison, the median for mathematics, as found in Figure 2.5, was 90% with a similar range, except that the upper value of the range was 100%. The median value for science was 69%, with a range from

**Figure 2.12. Distribution of the percentage of states that intended coverage of the 632 topic-grade combinations and the 136 coherence combinations in science.**

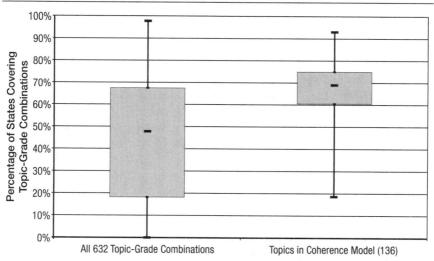

*Note.* For an explanation of how to interpret box and whisker plots, see Figure 2.1.

19% to 93%. This still represents a large amount of variation, especially given that it is for the benchmark model of coherence—where the goal of quality and equality should be that all topic-grade combinations are covered by 100% of the states. Thus, few differences were seen in the percentage of states that intended to cover the inner core of coherence topics. Even for topic-grade combinations that are important to ensure coherence, typically around 30% of the states did not intend coverage. For mathematics, the comparable figure was 10%. Even this smaller figure seemed large for such important benchmark areas. For science, that number is three times greater, implying serious geographically based inequalities.

The issue of inequality seems to loom even more prominently in the sciences, the area many consider to be essential for the United States to maintain its position of leadership in innovation. It is an area that Bill Gates and other business leaders see as critical if the United States is to maintain its economy and standard of living (Zuckerbrod, 2007).

Let us illustrate this issue with the specifics for two topics that are central to the development of understanding in biology, especially given the advances in understanding DNA and the human genome. These are the topic of atoms, ions, and molecules and the topic of chemical changes. The benchmark model of coherence in the sciences suggests that these topics should be covered in 7th and 8th grades. However, only three-fourths of the states indicated that they intended to cover atoms, ions, and molecules in the 7th or 8th grade. Only 61% indicated that they intended to cover chemical changes in the 7th grade and 71% in 8th grade.

Consider also the topic of human nutrition. Certainly, this is central to understanding the pandemic of overweight children that threatens to become even worse (Ogden, Lamb, Carroll, & Flegal, 2010; U.S. Surgeon General, 2001). In the benchmark model of coherence for the sciences, this topic is intended for coverage in 7th and 8th grades, after topics in chemistry have been covered. However, only about one-third of U.S. states intended to cover this topic in 7th and 8th grades.

On the other hand, almost half of the states intended to cover human nutrition in 1st and 2nd grades. Although there may be nothing wrong with such an early introduction to the topic, what would be covered in those grades is almost certainly at a lower level of sophistication than coverage in 7th and 8th grades would be after some exposure to chemistry topics, as is done in other countries. Even in 1st and 2nd grades, only about half of the states were covering this content, which suggests the maximum variability possible among the states. The absence of more coverage at a more sophisticated level at 7th and 8th grades by two-thirds of the states not only suggests variability among the states but wide deviation from the benchmark model.

Turning to another aspect of state science standards, we look briefly at the focus of the intended content coverage. The typical (median) number was around 30 topics in each of 1st and 2nd grades, and around 40 in 6th, 7th, and 8th grades. The typical number of topics was between 30 and 40 for 3rd, 4th, and 5th grades. The number of topics intended for coverage ranged from around 10 to 50 in the earliest grades and from 20 to 60 in the middle grades. Such a varied picture seems hard to defend as sensible, reasonable, or desirable.

## What District Standards Say About the Sciences

Looking within states, how do local school-district science standards vary in their expectations? Our examination of this area involves only the 60 Michigan and Ohio districts used earlier for mathematics.

One fact is quite surprising. The greatest agreement for the coherence combinations found in the benchmark model is to intend *not* to cover certain combinations. While coverage equality could be achieved by either all districts intending or all districts not intending to cover combinations, not covering them is very undesirable, given that they are part of the coherence model. Unfortunately, in the sciences this is not the case. The median for coherence combinations in the sciences is 39% of the districts. This means that about half of the coherence combinations have fewer than 40% of the districts intending coverage and 60% or more agreeing not to cover those topics at the appropriate grade or grades. One-fourth of the combinations have 28% or fewer of the districts intending coverage, so 70% or more intend not to cover them. By contrast, in mathematics, 24 coherence combinations were intended by virtually all (95% or more) of the districts in four different states. This was not true for any of the districts in the two states examined for science.

What about focus? How many topics did districts intend to cover at each grade? Typically, about 20 topics were intended at each grade through 4th grade, increasing from 25 to 28 for 5th through 8th grades. The variability was substantial. Some districts did not intend to cover *any* science topic in 1st grade. Some intended to cover five topics or fewer at each grade all the way through 6th grade. On the other hand, some districts intended to cover 60 or more science topics at each grade.

The extremes are so disparate with respect to equality of content opportunity that, among these 61 districts, some pay almost no attention whatsoever to science through the first six grades, while others try to cover almost everything at every grade during those same six grades. The latter extreme is unlikely to lead to focused or coherent instruction in the sciences and is the epitome of "a mile wide and an inch deep" approach.

There was even more variability in the sciences at the district level than there was at the state level. This is particularly remarkable since the districts all came from two states, while the variability at the state level was over 44 states. Probably the most striking finding is not the substantial variation among districts but the variation among topics at appropriate grades (as set out by the benchmark model of coherence). In mathematics, more than three-fourths of the districts covered these topics at their appropriate grades. In science, only a minority of districts covered these topics at the appropriate grade. Equality in content coverage seems even more illusive in the sciences than in mathematics.

## THE CONSEQUENCES OF STATE AND LOCAL CONTROL OF THE CURRICULUM

The goal of this book is to investigate inequalities in content coverage across U.S. schools. This chapter examined the inequalities in intentions deriving from the structure of the American educational system—that is, the way schooling in America is organized. Given that the American system is not one system but an amalgam of 50 state systems, each with its own set of districts, results in around 15,000 different systems, and hence, many versions of what mathematics U.S. children should learn, as reflected in the state and district standards. The question posed in this chapter is, are American schools, as organized, the great equalizers that we wish them to be (Hanushek & Rivkin, 2006)? The data examined here indicate a clear answer: No. For mathematics specifically, this answer may change, at least at the state level, depending on the implementation of the Common Core State Standards. Given such a large variation in content coverage in an area like mathematics, it is hard to believe that such inequalities do not exist in other subject areas as well.

The fact that such large differences also exist at the district level, even within the same state, is even more disturbing. Given that the geographical distance between two districts within a state may be very small, this variation in content coverage gives new meaning to the phrase "born on the wrong side of the tracks." This might better be recast as "born on the wrong side of the street," if that street is the boundary between two school districts.

For mathematics, the district variation within states also foreshadows the difficulty that lies ahead in the implementation of the Common Core State Standards. The variation among districts reported here existed even in the presence of state standards measured with state assessments. Why, then, would one expect there to be less variation among these same districts just because their states have adopted the Common Core State Standards?

The clash of the two American ideals described earlier in the chapter is clear from the data presented. The tradition of state and local control of the curriculum results in multiple versions of what topics students are expected to learn. The resulting variation in content coverage creates inequalities in opportunities to learn, thus inhibiting the role of schools as the great equalizers in society. But what are the possible consequences of those inequalities? Economically, we increasingly live in what Tom Friedman describes as a "flat world" (Friedman, 2005). In this flat world, U.S. children will have to compete economically with children from other countries. One of the advantages of a highly developed country such as the United States might well be the rigorous educational opportunities it can provide its children that other, less developed countries cannot provide. However, it turns out that this is true for only some of our children, due to our fragmented system for determining content expectations. As a result, the United States has fostered educational inequalities, and has also deviated from what the countries with the highest-achieving children offer to their children in school—both of which have the potential to impact our economic development (Hanushek & Woessmann, 2007).

Equality of educational opportunity is not just a matter of economics. It is also a matter of fairness. It is hard to defend the status quo either legally or philosophically. It would be difficult to justify our present system to American parents or the public at large. The only reason there has been so little outcry about these matters is probably that the public and parents have largely been unaware of them.

It can be psychologically difficult to walk in another person's shoes, to imagine what it is like to live a life very different from our own. Yet, differences in content coverage for American schoolchildren are very real. Educational inequality is not just a matter of race or income; it affects White, middle-class children simply on the basis of where they live. It shapes and limits their lives. This difficulty in imagining others' lives may make it difficult for us to understand the impact of different educational opportunities for children living in social and economic conditions very different from our own, even if we are opposed to such differences in principle. Perhaps that is why it seems so easy for us to lament the situation while also feeling that it is "just the way it is," and thinking that little can be done about it.

In this chapter, we have tried to help make it clear that inequalities in learning opportunities is "the way it is" for not only some but *all* of our nation's children. Opportunities for learning are influenced by such ordinary happenstance as where a child's parents happen to live—which state and even which community within the state. Geographic location should not play such a central role, especially when we possess the power to limit its effects; all that is lacking is the political will to act. The Common Core State Standards are an excellent starting point. They provide needed common standards, initially in mathematics and science, but likely in other subjects as well. Already, the same states that have adopted the Common Core State Standards for Mathematics have also adopted the Common Core State Standards for English Language Arts. The Common Core State Standards point toward what can be done, but the data presented in this chapter show how difficult the road will be to overcome what has been the status quo. The next chapter looks at how mathematics content coverage varies for different groups of students.

## CHAPTER 3

# Social Class, Race, and Equality of Opportunity

When we think about inequalities in educational opportunity, we usually think of certain children as being the most vulnerable to these inequalities: those in high poverty, those in rural settings, racial minorities, and ethnic minorities. As a result, when we want to examine lack of educational equality, it may be natural for many of us to think of race and social class as a basis for this inequality, since we believe that they will experience it if any students do. As we have seen in the last chapter, these are not the only bases for inequalities in content coverage. However, they certainly are worthy of more focused study.

Such inequalities have existed within the U.S. educational system for many decades, if not centuries. Awareness of them came to a head with the 1954 U.S. Supreme Court case *Brown v. Board of Education*.[1] There is a long history of attempts by the government and others to end school segregation and race-based inequities through busing and other means, by both legal rulings and community efforts. However, recent reports have indicated that there are many new and continuing threats to achieving equity in education.[2]

Of continuing relevance in debates about educational inequality are studies related to funding schools through property taxes and the quality of teachers providing instruction.[3] Both of these factors are relevant to the quality of opportunities to learn and thus to the issues of equality discussed in Chapter 1. However, we have argued that such factors affect equality (at least in part, if not mostly) indirectly through their impact on the quality of instructional activities that create learning opportunities and content exposure. In Chapter 2, we presented data that show large differences in opportunities to learn among districts even within the same state. In this chapter, we examine whether those differences are related to differences in social class and minority status.

## VARIABILITY IN LEARNING OPPORTUNITIES RELATED TO SOCIOECONOMIC STATUS

First, we look at the differences across districts in opportunities to learn. This is similar to the analyses we did in Chapter 2, but now we look at the data with respect to demographic differences among districts. We grouped 61 districts from Michigan and Ohio[4] into the following four categories according to students' socioeconomic status:

1. Low SES/high-poverty districts that are mostly urban with a high percentage of minority students
2. Low- to lower-middle-class districts with varying percentages of minority students, half of which are rural, mainly Caucasian districts, while the other half has sizable minority populations, ranging from 33% to 77%
3. Middle-class districts with a modest, more nationally representative percentage of minority students
4. High SES/wealthier districts that are mostly suburban and include a small percentage of minority students

The classifications described above are general characterizations used in the remainder of the book. They were formed primarily on the basis of the socioeconomic status (SES) of each district. Two indicators were used to define SES. The first is the percentage of students in a district who were eligible for the federal program of free and reduced-price lunches,[5] a measure of poverty. The second indicator is the percentage of parents in the districts who had a college or university degree involving 4 or more years of study. The two criteria were combined to define the four groups, as specified in Table 3.1. This grouping combined similar districts from both states.

On average, the four groups of districts were distinctly different. For example, the average percentage of students eligible for free or reduced-price lunches varied from 6% to 64% (see Table 3.2). The average percentage of students with college-educated parents also varied substantially, ranging from

**Table 3.1. Ranges of values for the two SES indicators for the four SES groups.**

| SES Group | Average Percentage Eligible for Free/ Reduced-Price Lunches | Average Percentage Whose Parents Are College Educated | Number of Districts |
|---|---|---|---|
| Low SES/High-Poverty (I) | 56–79 | 6–11 | 7 |
| Low- to Lower-Middle-Class (II) | 29–44 | 7–26 | 11 |
| Middle-Class (III) | 8–25 | 0–36 | 28 |
| High SES (IV) | 2–19* | 39–66 | 15 |

*Note. The range for all but one district was 2 to 9. That district was included in Group IV because it included a large number of children from parents who had attended a university.

over half to less than 10%. The four groups of districts were not directly based on the racial and ethnic identity of the students, but the percentage of African American students in the districts ranged on average from 60% to 5% (see Table 3.2).

## The Number of Mathematics Topics Covered

It may seem something of an anticlimax that, after defining the four distinct types of districts, no statistically significant differences were found among them in the typical (median) number of mathematics topics intended to be covered in the first eight grades. The median number for three of the groups was 36 and the median for the fourth was 37. Actually, this is quite consistent with the numbers reported for all 101 districts in Chapter 2.

There is one difference worth noting, however. The number of mathematics topics intended for Group IV, the highest SES group, was somewhat larger than was the intended number of topics for Group I, the lowest SES group. The difference, however, was only two topics, with the differences within each of the four groups ranging from six to nine topics. This variation within the groups of six to nine topics can have a meaningful effect, but is the same point we made in Chapter 2 concerning the variation among all 101 districts in our sample. What is new is the small difference in the number of topics *among* the four groups as opposed to the differences *within* each group.

These data, at least at the level of the number of mathematics topics intended to be covered in 1st through 8th grades, are in harmony with those who argue that the *Brown v. Board of Education* decision has gradually brought about a level playing field in matters of SES and race. The next question we must address will be whether this pattern will hold as we go beyond the simple number of topics intended to be covered to the more detailed and crucial issue of which topics are intended for which grades.

Table 3.2. Average demographics of the four SES groups.

| SES Group | Average Percentage Eligible for Free/Reduced Price Lunch | Average Percentage Whose Parents Are College Educated | Average Percentage Who Are African American | Average Percentage Who Are Caucasian |
|---|---|---|---|---|
| Low SES/ High-Poverty (I) | 64 | 9 | 60 | 27 |
| Low- to Lower- Middle-Class (II) | 35 | 16 | 22 | 70 |
| Middle-Class (III) | 17 | 20 | 8 | 88 |
| High SES (IV) | 6 | 52 | 5 | 88 |

## The Grades at Which Topics Were Covered

In Chapter 2, we examined which mathematics topics were covered at each of the first eight grades, looking at topic-grade combinations. Then we considered how many of the districts in our sample intended to cover the various combinations. The question we turn to now is, are there significant differences in intended topics across the four types of districts? Given the well-documented differences in achievement test results among different types of districts, one might hypothesize that the answer would be yes. But that turns out not to be true.

In Chapter 2, we looked first at all 256 topic-grade combinations. We found few differences in intended coverage across the four types of districts. We hypothesized that districts with larger numbers of high-poverty children whose parents were less well educated might set lower expectations for their students, including not intending to cover certain advanced mathematics topics at the upper grades—all of which would be inconsistent with the coherence benchmark. From our results, this appears to not be true.

We found little difference in the percentage of districts for each of the four groups in their intended coverage of the 99 benchmark topic-grade combinations. If there were differences among the groups of districts of differing SES, then they were more subtle differences than simple coverage of key topics at key grades.

Why does this seem so surprising? Perhaps, in part, because these findings are inconsistent with the conventional wisdom that students from lower SES family backgrounds tend, on average, to achieve less well academically and in general not to perform as well in school. The achievement gap is well documented. Are there other differences in content coverage across the SES-based groups of districts that might help explain the achievement gap between children from different SES backgrounds? We look next at the patterns of coverage.

How does a pattern of optimal content coverage such as that represented by the coherence model fail to be optimal? It fails by leaving out key topics in the pattern. That was not the case here. The pattern also fails to match the optimal model if it includes too many extraneous topic-grade combinations. Because instructional time is a relatively fixed resource that must be distributed among topics in each grade, spending instructional time on extraneous topics takes away time from the desired topic-grade combinations that make up the optimal pattern. If it becomes too diluted, the pattern can lose its optimality.

There are two kinds of dilution. The first is when topics are covered prematurely—that is, covered in grades earlier than those suggested by the coherence model. The second type of dilution involves continuing to cover topics after the coherence model suggests that one should no longer be covering them. We might describe these as diminishing coherence by *premature coverage* and diminishing coherence by unduly *persistent coverage*.

The four types of districts in the study differed in both of these kinds of diminishing coherence. First, let us consider *premature coverage* of topics. The high SES districts (Group IV) intended more coverage of this type than the other three groups of districts. However, the difference was not large (44% versus 35% to 39% for Groups I, II, and III).[6] This may be a case of unduly high expectations among high SES districts that feel their students should cover advanced topics earlier than others.

The pattern is different for diminished coherence related to *persistent coverage*. In this case, the high-poverty/low SES districts (Group I) tended to continue covering topics longer than the other three groups of districts.[7] This was also not a large difference, but it was a clear one. The percentage of Group I districts that showed unduly persistent topic coverage was 73%. The other three groups varied from 64% to 67%. The high-poverty districts tended to keep repeating elementary arithmetic topics even at 6th through 8th grade—more than was the case for less poor districts, and certainly more than in higher-achieving countries. This may be taken as indirect evidence of students' failure to achieve the desired levels of mastery of these topics (or the belief that they cannot), along with the idea that persistent coverage of the same material will eventually produce greater mastery.

Taken together, these two findings form an interesting pattern with implications for differences in intended curriculum coverage in mathematics. High SES districts tend to introduce topics prematurely, perhaps from unduly high expectations coupled with the fallacy that to do so makes the curriculum more advanced. High-poverty/low SES districts, on the other hand, tend to hold on to topics and persist in their coverage, perhaps in the somewhat questionable idea that simple repetition will improve mastery of content. Both patterns—and the assumptions and practices that likely underlie them—are problematic. It is an empirical question (one that can only be settled by a different type of data) which is the greater problem. Both behaviors contribute to a lack of focus and dilute the coherence in mathematics instruction. Such differences could affect student achievement.

These findings suggest that there are two policies at work in two different kinds of districts. The actual form of the policies cannot be determined from the data, but the nature of the policies can be inferred. For high SES districts (often with lower minority enrollments), a policy of "earlier is better" seems to be in place. However, when such a policy leads to mathematics instruction that departs from a model of optimal curriculum coverage and is coupled with lower achievement compared with high-achieving countries, this clearly suggests that "earlier is not necessarily better." The second type of policy seems to be one of "keep trying" for students in urban, high-poverty/low SES districts. Again, the results suggest that the policy of persistent coverage of past topics is not helping these students.

## Inequalities Within the SES-Based Groups of Districts

The previous sections of this chapter showed that the inequalities in learning opportunities *among* districts that we observed in Chapter 2 were not systematically related to differences in the SES composition of the districts. There were few differences and few inequalities in learning opportunities among the four groups of districts other than the types of diminished coherence. This in no way implies that the quality of instruction was the same, or that the amounts of time spent were the same, and so on. There simply were few differences among the groups in which topics were specified by the districts to be covered and which topics were intended in key grades.

There is another issue, however. From Chapter 2, it is clear that there were differences (inequalities) in learning opportunities among the districts. But did that variation itself differ across the types of districts? If the answer is yes, then this implies that there would be different levels of heterogeneity for each of the groups. For example, are the high SES districts more similar to each other than the higher-poverty districts?

The data showed that the group of high-poverty/low SES districts (Group I) had a much greater degree of internal homogeneity (see Table 3.3). The middle-class districts (Group III) were much less homogeneous as a group. Of the 352 possible topic-grade combinations, the four groups had 184, 112, 49, and 101 topic-grade combinations in which all districts within Groups

Table 3.3. Number and percentage of the two topic-grade combinations within each of the four SES district types that reflect different degrees of within-group consistency.

| SES Group | Number of the 352 topic-grade combinations that all districts within the group agreed to cover or not cover | Percentage of the 352 topic-grade combinations that all districts within the group agreed to cover or not cover | Number of the 99 topic-grade combinations that all or all but one district within the group agreed to cover | Percentage of the 99 topic-grade combinations that all or all but one district within the group agreed to cover |
|---|---|---|---|---|
| Low SES/ High-Poverty (I) | 184 | 52% | 88 | 89% |
| Low- to Lower-Middle-Class (II) | 112 | 32% | 58 | 59% |
| Middle-Class (III) | 49 | 14% | 17 | 17% |
| High SES (IV) | 101 | 29% | 63 | 64% |

I, II, III, and IV, respectively, intended to cover that combination (or none of the districts within the group intended to cover that combination). A larger number here indicates more similarity (homogeneity) within the group. The data suggest that districts within Group III had greater inequalities and differences in content coverage.

To further illustrate the point, suppose we set a criterion that all or nearly all of the districts in a group intended to cover key topic-grade combinations from the coherence model. We examined 99 key topic-grade combinations using this criterion. The highest-poverty districts had a greater degree of consistency among themselves for the key topic-grade combinations. Only 11 of the 99 benchmark topics did not meet the criterion. This means that almost 90% (88 of 99) of the key topic-grade combinations had nearly unanimous planned coverage among districts in Group I. The highest SES group of districts had over one-third that did not meet the criterion, while middle-class districts had the greatest degree of heterogeneity in intending to cover key topic-grade combinations from the coherence model, 83% of which did not meet the criterion.

However, the criterion used is very strict. It would not be met for a particular topic-grade combination if as few as two districts in a particular SES district group did not intend to cover that combination. The group of districts representing the middle class (Group III) was the largest, with more districts as members. This makes it more likely to find two districts in the group that did not have the same intentions as the others.[8]

We must use caution about generalizing from these results. The districts for which we had data were not random samples of the districts within each of the four SES-based groups across the whole of the United States. Without a random sample, care must always be taken in assuming that the patterns will hold more generally. However, if these results can be generalized, the implication is that the high-poverty/low SES districts are more alike in what they intend to cover and when they intend to cover it than they are different. They would seem to have more equality in their intended content coverage of mathematics.

What might explain why low SES districts varied the least in their intentions? One possibility is that the high-poverty/low SES districts are under closer scrutiny, given their poorer academic achievement and the fact that they receive more federal assistance than districts in the other groups. These districts have about 65% of their students eligible for free or reduced-price lunches, compared with about 15% in Group III. The big, urban districts (Group I) also have an organization that facilitates dialogue among the districts.[9]

## State-Based Versus SES-Based District Groupings

When the 61 districts were grouped by state rather than by SES (Michigan versus Ohio), the number of agreements in intentions (either to cover or not) for the 352 topic-grade combinations were 44 for the Michigan districts and 60 for the Ohio districts. Agreement for SES-based groups ranged from 101 (for the high SES districts in Group IV) to 184 (for the high-poverty/low SES districts in Group I) combinations for which all districts agreed on whether they intended to cover or not cover the topic-grade combinations. Only the middle-class districts (Group III) mirrored the state groups in their intentions for topic-grade combinations (49 for Group III, compared with 44 for Michigan and 60 for Ohio). This is not surprising, since Group III represents the majority of districts in Michigan and Ohio. It also represents the majority of districts in the United States.

These results suggest that the SES composition of a school district is of greater importance than the state in which the district is located as a basis for achieving within-group similarity. This is true even though the SES-based groups have no authority structure to guarantee this level of homogeneity and, unlike states, no mechanism by which equality in learning opportunities is endorsed or mandated. This means that the SES-based similarities are more a matter of common culture and that socioeconomic commonality may be more powerful than formal governmental structures, at least under current policies.

The variation in learning opportunities is very large among districts generally (as we found in Chapter 2). However, we found in this chapter that, on average, this variation does not seem to be systematically related to the SES composition of districts. The grouping does show that three of the four types of districts (all but the middle-class district) are more similar in their intended coverage than a grouping of districts based on the state in which they are located.

Suppose that we randomly select one district from Michigan and one from Ohio with the same SES composition. Suppose also that we randomly select two districts from Michigan with different SES compositions. Suppose further that we randomly select two districts from Ohio with two different SES compositions. The two districts with the same SES composition from different states are likely to have more similar intended content coverage than would be the case if two districts from the same state with different SES compositions were chosen.

The same pattern across the SES-based groups held up when we looked only at the 99 topic-grade combinations of the benchmark model of coherence. For Group I (the poorer districts), II and III (the middle-class districts), and IV (the wealthier districts) there were 62, 31, 0, and 43 *unanimously* agreed-upon topic-grade combinations, respectively (different from the data presented in Table 3.3, which allowed one district exception per group). This again contrasts remarkably with the state groupings for these 99 combinations. There were no unanimously intended topic-grade combinations in either Michigan or Ohio. The only SES-based group that had a pattern similar to that of the states-based group was Group III, the middle-class group (with no unanimously intended combinations).

## CONTENT OPPORTUNITIES IN URBAN DISTRICTS

To get at urban versus non-urban differences, we looked in detail at the planned (intended) learning opportunities for 11 large urban districts, compared with the general pattern across all districts and with the international benchmarks. Part of what makes these districts unique and worth further study is that SES varies among schools within cities, often quite markedly. However, major urban areas usually have large numbers of minority students. They also have the schooling complexities introduced by extreme poverty.

The analyses to this point have involved only two major cities—Cleveland and Cincinnati, which were in Group I. Additional cities included in the analyses of the current section are Chicago; Miami; Seattle; Oakland; Louisville; San Diego; Rochester, New York; and Jersey City.

The urban districts did not differ greatly from other types of districts in terms of curricular structure, just as there were few differences among district types with various SES compositions. Of the 10 urban districts examined, 81% of them intended to cover the typical topics in the coherence model at key grades. For all 101 school districts examined in Chapter 2, 79% intended to cover the typical topics at key grades. Considering all 352 possible topic-grade combinations (44 mathematics topics and 8 grades), on average, 47% of the city districts intended to cover the typical topic-grade combination. When looking at all 101 school districts from Chapter 2, the median was 47%. All of the other indicators that we examined led to the same conclusion—urban districts intended learning opportunities that were not very different from those of all districts more generally.

This pattern is also consistent with the results by SES discussed earlier. Urban districts tended to be more homogeneous in what they intended to cover. For example, of the 352 topic-grade combinations, the urban districts agreed on 86 of these combinations (they agreed to cover 26 of them and agreed not to cover 60 of them). For the 101 districts, the corresponding agreement was for only five of the topic-grade combinations.

In short, urban districts differed from other districts only in being more homogeneous than other districts in their intentions. We found the same result for low SES districts (Group I).

## INEQUALITY IN 8TH-GRADE MATHEMATICS AMONG DISTRICTS

In this section, we focus on the percentage of students in a district who covered algebra and geometry in their 8th-grade class. Students in the United States typically are tracked into different mathematics courses at the 8th grade. This practice is discussed further in Chapter 5. Districts can vary in how this tracking policy is carried out, or even in whether they have such a policy. Limiting the percentage of 8th-grade students in a district who take the courses focused on algebra and geometry is an example of a policy that can impact content coverage and, as a result, foster inequalities in content coverage within the district.

Figure 3.1 plots, for 13 school districts, the relationship between the percentage of students in the district whose parents have a 4-year university degree and the percentage of students who are taking a challenging 8th-grade mathematics course focused mainly on algebra and geometry. The data came from a 1999 repeat of the TIMSS study that was done for several countries and U.S. school districts and states.[10] The 13 districts included large cities such as Chicago and Miami as well as smaller urban areas such as Rochester, New York. They also included suburban and rural areas. All were included in the analyses of Chapter 2. The urban districts mentioned here were among the districts discussed in this chapter.

It is clear that in those districts with a higher socioeconomic level (a larger percentage of university-educated parents), a larger percentage of 8th-grade students took a more challenging 8th-grade mathematics course. A more challenging 8th-grade mathematics course is defined here as one that includes substantial coverage of algebra and geometry. Chapter 2 and the

**Figure 3.1. Relationship between parents' education and percentage of district students taking more challenging 8th-grade mathematics (involving algebra and geometry).**

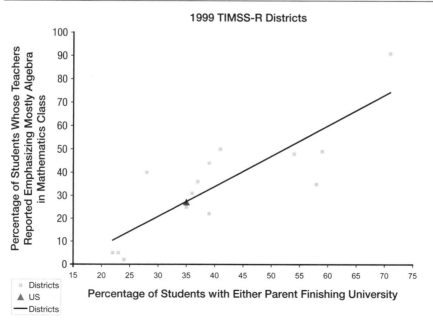

benchmark model of coherence for mathematics make it evident that this type of mathematics curriculum is more consistent with what is covered in most TIMSS countries, especially high-performing countries. Using the percentage of students in a district who are eligible for free or reduced-price lunches as another measure of social class produces the same result.

The regression line found in Figure 3.1 portrays a strong relationship that is linear in nature.[11] The SES indicator of university-educated parents accounted for a large percentage of the variance (75%). The nature of the relationship (as indicated by the regression line) predicts that a district with 20% more university-educated parents than another district would have an additional 25% of its students taking a more challenging 8th-grade mathematics curriculum.

The district with the largest percentage of university-educated parents (about 70%) has almost all (about 90%) of its students in a more challenging 8th-grade mathematics curriculum. By contrast, in the three districts that have 20% to 25% university-educated parents, virtually no students study algebra and geometry in 8th grade. Educational opportunity varied by district. Important mathematics content (measured by international benchmarks) was missing for most students in lower SES districts.

Given that mathematics is hierarchical—later topics depend on earlier topics—what is covered in the 8th-grade mathematics curriculum reflects the level of rigor and demand in the mathematics curriculum in earlier grades. Hence, weaker 8th-grade mathematics follows from weaker mathematics in the earlier grades. A comparatively undemanding 8th-grade mathematics curriculum also limits the mathematics that students can take successfully in high school. A similar analysis involving the 60 Michigan and Ohio school districts leads to much the same conclusion. These data indicate that the educational background of a child's parents and where they live make a marked difference in the opportunities that child has to learn mathematics.

## EXPECTATIONS VERSUS IMPLEMENTATION

At first glance, the results presented in this chapter seem contradictory. The earlier sections indicated that how intentions varied across districts was not systematically related to the SES or racial composition of those districts. The content standards held by the 11 cities we investigated and the Group I (high-poverty/low SES, urban) districts in Michigan and Ohio were essentially the same as those of other districts (even Group IV's high SES, suburban districts). On the other hand, the previous section indicated that, although the *intentions* were similar, the policies *implemented* (at least for 8th-grade mathematics) produced very different learning opportunities in the high-poverty/low SES districts than in the high SES districts. That is, we saw significant differences in what was actually offered to 8th-grade mathematics students. Children in high SES districts were more often in classes that focused on algebra and geometry, while children in lower SES districts took more basic mathematics.

The first set of results related to intentions is inconsistent with common expectations for high-poverty/low SES districts versus high SES districts, especially as they relate to achievement test results, which consistently show that children in high-poverty/low SES districts perform less well. If these children had the same learning opportunities as those in other districts, why did they not perform as well on achievement tests? Does this indicate that those who argue that children of lower SES backgrounds cannot in general succeed in school are right (as the book *The Bell Curve* argues)?

The last analyses above looked at how children were placed in 8th-grade mathematics courses compared with the international standard, the benchmark for 8th-grade mathematics, which focuses on algebra and geometry. In the United States, no matter what the official intentions were (or even in spite of them), this standard was not met for the majority of students, especially those in high-poverty/low SES districts. The first set of analyses examined intentions; the last examined what was actually done. Although there is no gap in official intentions, there is a tremendous gap between high-poverty/low SES districts and high SES districts in what was actually implemented in real classrooms.

Intentions are ultimately only words on paper. Implementation is a matter of practice—of real actions in real classrooms. Analyses of intentions can be important, but they must be weighed against the policy actually put into place. Our analysis suggests that the goals expressed by current district policy are simply not being met. We need to move beyond intentions of content coverage, since these do not seem to be enough to ensure good results and equitable opportunities for high-poverty/low SES and urban students. The devil appears to be in the details of implementation. We turn to this in the next chapter.

## CHAPTER 4

# Into the Classroom:
# The Content Opportunities
# Children Actually Experience

Decision making in American education has been described as shared (Elmore, 2000). This is certainly a reasonable description of decisions about curriculum. States define what they believe children should know at each grade level. Even in the upcoming Common Core era, where 40-plus states have agreed to adopt a common set of standards, each individual state had the choice of whether to make the Common Core State Standards its own state standards. In most states, such standards mainly serve to advise school districts. Only in some states are they mandatory. Local districts share in the final decision of what is intended for children to learn in one or both of two ways. Local districts share *directly* in the curriculum decision by specifying their own standards that modify state standards. In addition (or instead), they may share authority over the curriculum *indirectly* through their choice of a particular textbook series. Textbooks have strong effects on what is actually covered in classrooms, regardless of local districts' official positions or the state standards involved.

Shared curriculum decision making also involves schools and their teachers. When combined with the practice of local school control of the curriculum and a tradition of teacher autonomy unique to the United States, this makes what happens in the local classroom the final arbiter of the content children are actually taught.

To be clear, when we use the phrase *teacher autonomy*, we are referring only to the latitude teachers have to make decisions about content coverage in their classrooms. It is here, in the classroom, where the tension between external control and autonomy plays out (Shulman, 1983). State, district, and school policies and mandates, together with textbooks and assessments, attempt to constrain or at least influence teachers' content decisions, but such factors seem to have little power (Elmore, 1983; Floden et al., 1988; Freeman & Porter, 1989; Schwille et al., 1983). The results presented throughout this book, but especially in Chapter 6, confirm the strong role that classrooms, through teachers, play in such content decisions. That is, intended learning opportunities are ultimately shaped into real opportunities by what goes on in the classroom. It is in the classrooms that issues of equality in content coverage finally play out.

Every fall, children are assigned to classrooms with particular teachers. The process by which this occurs is often opaque to parents and the public. It is one of those decisions that the public and the parents have turned over to the professionals. For the most part, parents assume that the process is being conducted fairly and well. Parents sometimes judge how good a teacher is or how nice he or she is, but what is often hidden from them is the impact that teacher assignments can have on their children's content coverage.

Because of teacher and school-level decision making, inequalities may exist among schools within the same district, and even among classrooms within the same school. State and district attempts to ensure educational equality have only a limited effect, in spite of the mechanisms of state and district standards and associated assessments. Data from TIMSS indicated that this is a comparatively unique situation in comparison to other countries. In most TIMSS countries, teachers do not typically determine the actual content of classroom instruction (Schmidt et al., 2001). The United States is virtually alone among the countries in permitting teachers to have such a strong influence on what is actually taught. The U.S. approach places teachers in the role of content brokers (Porter, Floden, Freeman, Schmidt, & Schwille, 1988). Even apart from formal systems of shared decision making, the United States has a long tradition of teachers choosing what to teach once the classroom door is closed (Schwille et al., 1983).

In the U.S. educational system, the traditions of local authority and individualism come into conflict. Local authorities (school boards) and teachers shape content learning opportunities. These decisions may limit individual students' chances to achieve to the best of their abilities. Shared curriculum decisions set two American traditions against each other.

Such variation within individual schools and classrooms can occur in terms of what topics are or are not covered. It can also occur in the time allocated to cover various topics. It is at the classroom level—at the most local and personal level affecting every child –where content inequalities with lifelong consequences arise. In a truly equitable system in which the playing field is level for all students, there would be no variation in basic content coverage (whether a topic is taught or not) across classrooms, especially for the 1st through 8th grades. We would expect that the time devoted to teaching a topic might vary slightly across classrooms, but those differences should not be substantial. This chapter examines such classroom variation.

We are advocating for a level playing field in terms of content coverage. No educational system can guarantee equal outcomes, but policy can do more to encourage equal learning opportunities. In a system with basic fairness, all students would have similar opportunities and the chance to compete on an even basis. Different abilities, different motivations, and different efforts would still combine to produce winners and losers—or, at least, differences in achievement, to abandon the sports metaphor—but at least all children would have a fair chance to achieve.

An additional consideration might be, should the playing field be level? Should those with more ability be given more advanced and demanding content coverage than those less able? We will address this question in Chapter 5.

## CONTENT COVERAGE IN ELEMENTARY CLASSROOMS

We first look at elementary classrooms—that is, classrooms for 1st through 5th grades. Teachers in 61 districts were asked to fill out a form indicating the number of class periods over the course of the school year in which they taught each of 29 topics in mathematics. The 29 topics were those most common to 1st through 5th grades. We and others have found the procedure to be both reliable and valid (Porter, 1993). This information was gathered from 2,625 teachers, about 525 teachers in each of 1st through 5th grades. The teachers who supplied this information were from classrooms in Michigan, Ohio, and Seattle, Washington.[1]

### The Mathematics Topics Taught in 1st Through 5th Grades

Using the data collected, we characterized the percentage of teachers in each grade who taught each of the 29 topics that we surveyed. We do not mean to imply that teaching all of the 29 topics in each of the five grades is desirable. Each topic-grade combination represents a potential learning opportunity, as described in Chapter 2, and we use these combinations only to see the percentage of possible learning opportunities that became real learning opportunities as a result of what went on in the classrooms.

For those combinations consistent with the benchmark model, we would hope to see 100% of the teachers at the specified grade level reporting that they had taught the topic involved. In addition, we ought to have 100% of the teachers reporting that they did not teach those combinations that are not in the model. This is desirable for the sake of equality, since it implies that all the children in all the classrooms experienced only coverage of the important topics at their appropriate grade levels, at least in some form. From here on, we simplify our language; we talk about teachers having taught topics although, more correctly, we should say that they *reported* having taught topics.

Unfortunately, teachers taught some off-benchmark topics at the indicated grade and not every teacher in the indicated grades taught the on-benchmark topics. There was not a single topic for which all of the teachers reported teaching the topic at the grade levels specified by the benchmark model. For each topic that the benchmark model indicated should not be taught at a particular grade level, at least one teacher reported having taught it.

There were several topics taught by virtually all (90% or more) of the teachers in each of 1st through 5th grades (see Table 4.1). They included topics such as the meaning of whole numbers and arithmetic operations with whole numbers. In contrast, there was only one topic—slope—that nearly all teachers reported not teaching in the five grades.

On average, only 58% of the teachers taught a specific topic at a specific grade level, indicating substantial variation among what was taught in the 1st- through 5th-grade classrooms. This goes to the heart of the argument we are making. Differences in content coverage do not just happen at the level of what is intended by states and districts. They also exist in what is actually taught in classrooms.

The range describing the variation in content coverage was substantial for the middle 90% of teachers (we use the middle 90% to eliminate the few who might have been unusually high or low in what they said they covered). For different topic-grade combinations, the percentage of teachers teaching them varied from around 10% to 95%. In 1st and 2nd grades alone, we might have expected greater similarity in what was covered, since this represents students' first encounters with the formal study of arithmetic. However, the percentages ranged from 3% to 98% for different topics. Three percent taught slope in the two grades (probably in a very simple form), while 98% taught place value.

As another example, geometric shapes (triangles, squares, and so forth) were taught by around 60% to 65% of the teachers in each of the two grades. This implies that in these 60-plus districts, many children would not have had an opportunity to learn this basic topic, leaving them at a disadvantage. In other words, while 60% of the 449 1st-grade classrooms and two-thirds of the 547 2nd-grade classrooms covered geometric shapes, the rest—from one-third to two-fifths—did not. Assuming that there are roughly 25 children per classroom, around 5,000 to 6,000 children in those districts did not have the same opportunities to learn about geometric shapes that other children had. If these percentages held at the national level, this would imply a tremendous difference in content coverage related to this particular arithmetic topic, with more than a million students lacking such coverage. And this is just an example of *one* topic.

Parents are probably unaware of such differences in learning opportunities and do not know whether topics such as geometric shapes are being covered in their own child's classroom. Not many would know to look for such things or even how to look for them if they tried. Since this kind of difference is not very visible, parents are likely to assume that their children are getting "what they need," even though that might not be true. As the data demonstrated, by 4th and 5th grades, not all children had opportunities to

**Table 4.1. Teacher coverage of mathematics topics in grades 1–5.**

| Mathematics Content Categories | Percentage of Teachers Covering Content | | | | |
|---|---|---|---|---|---|
| | Grade 1 | Grade 2 | Grade 3 | Grade 4 | Grade 5 |
| Whole Number Meaning | 98 | 98 | 98 | 98 | 97 |
| Properties of Whole Number Operations | 91 | 94 | 96 | 96 | 93 |
| Fractions | 65 | 71 | 86 | 91 | 95 |
| Decimals | 11 | 22 | 64 | 81 | 90 |
| Relation of Fractions & Decimals | 8 | 19 | 52 | 72 | 91 |
| Percentages | 13 | 20 | 48 | 69 | 89 |
| Properties of Fractions & Decimals | 18 | 26 | 49 | 63 | 74 |
| Number Sets & Concepts | 28 | 28 | 37 | 49 | 64 |
| Other Number Topics | 7 | 9 | 17 | 32 | 60 |
| Number Theory | 19 | 24 | 49 | 75 | 83 |
| Estimation & Number Sense | 87 | 94 | 96 | 96 | 96 |
| Measurement Units | 93 | 95 | 96 | 96 | 95 |
| Perimeter, Area, & Volume | 43 | 78 | 87 | 92 | 92 |
| Measurement Estimation & Errors | 41 | 54 | 62 | 70 | 73 |
| Geometry Basics | 63 | 76 | 89 | 95 | 92 |
| Polygons & Circles | 62 | 66 | 73 | 81 | 84 |
| 3-D Geometry | 51 | 53 | 54 | 62 | 67 |
| Geometric Transformations | 72 | 79 | 80 | 87 | 83 |
| Congruence and Similarity | 48 | 77 | 80 | 87 | 86 |
| Proportionality Concepts | 7 | 8 | 20 | 35 | 64 |
| Proportionality Problems | 26 | 33 | 44 | 46 | 55 |
| Slope | 3 | 3 | 5 | 7 | 10 |
| Patterns, Relations, & Functions | 76 | 75 | 66 | 69 | 70 |
| Linear Equations | 17 | 22 | 26 | 32 | 41 |
| Other Equations & Inequalities | 18 | 31 | 33 | 45 | 50 |
| Representing & Interpreting Data | 87 | 87 | 91 | 94 | 94 |
| Probability & Uncertainty | 61 | 63 | 69 | 77 | 68 |
| Sets & Logic | 9 | 8 | 16 | 24 | 26 |
| Other Topics | 23 | 32 | 29 | 35 | 35 |
| **Number of Sampled Classrooms** | 460 | 556 | 631 | 550 | 438 |

learn about geometric shapes. Around 20% did not have that opportunity at either 4th or 5th grade. These could, of course, be the same children who also were not afforded such opportunities in the earlier grades.

Consider the important arithmetic topic of fractions. A majority of the top-achieving countries provided instruction in fractions in 3rd through 6th grades. All of those countries provided such instruction in 4th and 5th grades. The actual percentage of the Michigan-, Ohio-, and Seattle-sampled class-rooms for this topic went from 86% in 3rd grade to 91% in 4th grade and 95% in 5th grade. The percentage of students who did not get the oppor-tunity to study fractions in these classrooms was comparatively small. The study of fractions is one of the most important topics in early mathematics, a topic that creates a bridge to later mathematics. It is also a topic that is difficult for students to learn.

Let us push this illustration further by assuming that these percentages are representative of the U.S. school population as a whole. For fractions in 3rd through 5th grades, we estimated how many children would be denied learning opportunities if the topic of fractions was not covered: approxi-mately 600,000 3rd-graders, 400,000 4th-graders, and 200,000 5th-graders. Small percentages can represent large numbers of real children affected by missed opportunities.

A different picture emerges when we turn to just those topic-grade com-binations that are part of the benchmark model of coherent mathematics instruction. As explained in Chapter 2, it is not enough for a classroom to cover a topic. The topic must be covered in a particular grade or grades in order to allow for an orderly, coherent building up of mathematics under-standing. Cover a topic too early and it is likely that it will not be covered at the needed depth. This would happen because not all of the topics pre-requisite to learning the given topic at a desirable depth would have been covered. On the other hand, delaying coverage of a topic could eliminate or forestall other topics for which the topic serves as prerequisite knowledge. Therefore, the actual grade or grades in which a topic is covered is critical to building up mathematics learning, as evidenced by what happens in high-achieving countries.

For the topic-grade combinations in the benchmark model in 1st through 5th grades, on average, 83% of teachers in our sample taught the topics involved at the appropriate grades, with percentages ranging from 26% to 98%. There is clearly less variation among the 2,625 classrooms in our sample for the benchmark topics, but again, given their importance, leav-ing nearly 20% of the students without such content coverage is a serious problem, both in terms of public policy and especially in terms of its impact on the lives of those children.

Many topic-grade combinations do not come close to being covered by all or virtually all of the classrooms. Since school mathematics is cumulative, with one topic building on others, such gaps can be fatal to the development of essential understandings in mathematics. (Gaps at critical junctions put students in a hole that only gets deeper over their school years.) Students who may not have started behind, fall behind, and those who are already behind fall even further back.

Key topics that were not covered in all of the classrooms at the grades appropriate for coherent development included decimals, the relationship of decimals to fractions, and properties of decimals and fractions. These topics are essential to a child's understanding of the number system and its properties. These are particularly strong examples of serious inequalities in content coverage that occurred in about 20% to 35% of the classrooms in our sample. Nationally, this suggests that there are serious omissions for as many as a one to one-and-a-half million children in 5th grade alone.

## The Length of Time Allocated to Topics Taught in 1st Through 5th Grades

Learning opportunities are determined not simply by whether a topic is taught but also by how much time is allocated for instruction on that topic at a particular grade. This is a measure of the depth of coverage. Of course, other factors affect the quality of instruction, and thus, the quality of learning opportunities. However, no matter what the quality of instruction, a learning opportunity will be limited if too little time is made available for the instruction of a particular topic. Too much time can also be a problem, but this has different consequences that we will discuss later.

Within bounds, more time spent on teaching a topic is generally better, since it allows the teacher to give the topic greater focus and approach it in more detail. The meaning of *more time* is, of course, relative to the breadth of the topic. The opposite of this focused coverage is to devote little time to it, which inevitably makes for a shallow level of instruction. Even the highest-quality teaching cannot overcome time constraints. Limited-time instruction often results in the failure of students to adequately absorb the material and the need to cover the same topic again at a later grade. Since the total amount of teaching time for mathematics is limited, this kind of repetition becomes a major factor that undermines the effectiveness of later-grade instruction.

The typical time needed to adequately cover a topic at a given grade is not well known. Certainly, it varies for different children and those with different experiences in earlier grades. However, schools and even classrooms are *aggregates*—that is, collective learning environments. Most teaching is based on the needs of an entire class, and not on the needs of each individual. Teaching decisions on how much time to give to a topic are largely based on what it takes for an average child, or the plurality of children, in the class to satisfactorily learn that topic. In the United States, these decisions are usually left to individual teachers.

There are caveats to the general principle that more time is better. Spending too much time on one topic reduces the time available for other topics. Too much time may also result in student boredom and inattention and could thus be counterproductive.

In this section, we look at time allocations for mathematics topics. Unfortunately, there is no well-accepted consensus on how much teaching time should be allocated to each topic at each grade. This means that there is no clear sense of what would be an acceptable amount of variation in time for a topic that would not result in inequalities in educational opportunity. Recognizing this, we present the variation in the number of days (class periods) each topic was covered, as indicated by the teachers.

Answering questions about differences in time allocated is best addressed topic by topic. However, this can result in too much detail, especially for those whose interest is not in the specific details of mathematics. We try to overcome this problem the same way we did in Chapters 2 and 3, by providing a summary over all 29 topics.

The nature of the summary here is somewhat different from that in Chapter 2, due to the nature of the data. In Chapters 2 and 3, the data measured whether a topic was covered or not. Here, the data measure a set of times for each topic.[2] For example, for 1st grade and for each topic, we have the teacher's estimate of time spent teaching that topic for more than 400 1st-grade classrooms. The issue is not the average amount of time for each topic, but the variations and differences in those times among the classrooms. If children in one 1st-grade classroom get more time than children in another 1st-grade classroom, this is potentially evidence of differences in opportunity, especially if those differences are large.

To estimate variation in allocated time, we first estimated the range of time allocations for each topic across all sampled classrooms. Since there might be unusually high or low time allocations for a few atypical teachers, we eliminated the most extreme 10% of the values (the highest and lowest 5%). We did this by taking the time allocation that 95% or fewer of the teachers used (the 95th percentile) and subtracting the time allocation that 5% or fewer of the teachers used (the 5th percentile). We will call this the *90%-range* for each topic, since this is the difference in time allocations for a topic for 90% of the classrooms.

We then summarized these values (the 90%-ranges) over the 29 individual mathematics topics. The median of these values indicates the variation—as measured by the 90%-range—of a typical mathematics topic. A topic with a larger average value will have greater variation in time allocations than one with a smaller mean. This greater variation implies that it is more probable that there are inequalities in content coverage for that topic.

We also looked at the variability across the estimated 90%-ranges for the 29 individual topics. If the value measuring that variability is small, it indicates that the typical variation (as represented by the average 90%-range) is representative of most topics. If the value is larger, it implies that, for some topics, the 90%-range would be considerably larger or smaller than the average.[3]

Figure 4.1 shows the box and whisker plots of the 90%-ranges for 1st through 5th grades. The median value suggesting the typical variability for a topic ranges from 15 days at 1st grade to about 10 days in 4th grade. This result suggests that a typical mathematics topic taught in elementary school varies in 3rd- and 4th-grade classrooms by about 2 weeks, and by almost 3 weeks at the other grades.

It could be argued that such variation is desirable, since some of these classrooms have children who need more time on a topic. Certainly, this argument has some merit, but it is an open question how much more time is needed in those cases, especially in the elementary grades. Does there really need to be a difference of 2 weeks or more in teaching time for a typical topic? Remember, there are typically only 36 weeks in a school year. As a result, such large differences imply that other topics may receive little teaching time or may not be covered at all, since total mathematics teaching time for each classroom is a "scarce resource" that requires careful allocation. Such a phenomenon might explain the results in the previous section, where certain topics were not covered in some 20% to 35% of classrooms.

**Figure 4.1. Distributions of the 90%-ranges of teachers' instructional days of coverage for the 29 mathematics topics (grades 1–5).**

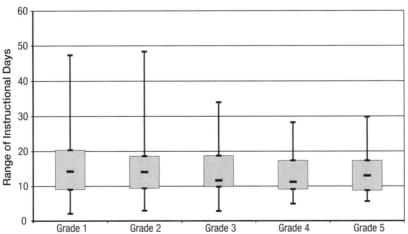

*Note.* For an explanation of how to interpret box and whisker plots, see Figure 2.1.

Given that limits on learning opportunities in mathematics are cumulative, gaps multiply over time and profoundly influence what is learned. A closer examination of the distributions found in Figure 4.1 shows that for some topics the differences in teaching time are only around 1 or 2 days (class periods), but the differences for other topics can be as great as 25 to 50 days. It is important to note that the largest variations occur in the primary grades (1st through 3rd grades), where the foundation of arithmetic is established. It is here that such differences could have the most profound effects, given the cumulative nature of mathematics learning.

However, the data must be interpreted carefully. Some topics take longer to cover than others. For example, arithmetic operations with whole numbers (adding, subtracting, and so on) takes longer to cover in the early grades than a topic such as geometric shapes. We should expect more variation among classrooms for a topic that receives a large amount of teaching time, compared with one that typically receives less teaching time. For example, a difference of 5 days for a topic that is typically covered in 30 days might not be particularly large, since it represents only a variation of about 15% in teaching time.

At 1st grade, the three topics with the largest variation in teaching time are those that have the most time allocated for teaching them. They include place value and whole number operations—two of the three topics included in the benchmark model for coherence to be taught in 1st and 2nd grades. In our sample, each of these two topics was allocated, on average, about 26 days of teaching time across the 460 1st-grade classrooms in our sample. Some 1st-grade classrooms spent 50 to 60 days for each of these two topics (not necessarily the same classrooms for both), while other classrooms covered each of these topics only for about 5 to 10 days.

Even for each of these essential 1st-grade topics, the differences are enormous. It is difficult to imagine that differences of more than 2 months of instruction time can be anything other than a reflection of inequalities in learning experiences created by the arbitrary way in which teaching time is allocated in the United States. Put another way, in one 1st-grade classroom, the children spent around 6 months, or two-thirds of the school year's mathematics time, studying both place value and whole number operations (mostly addition and subtraction). The corresponding time was only around 1 month in another 1st-grade classroom. It seems hard to claim that such differences are unimportant and insignificant. Yet, these are not even the most extreme values in the study, since we have eliminated the 10% most outlying values.

Fractions illustrate a different type of situation. This topic is not part of the benchmark coherence model for 1st grade, yet it was covered by about two-thirds of the sampled classrooms. We would question the wisdom of that choice, both because of what is done in the high-achieving countries that provided the benchmark model and because it does not really make much sense mathematically to introduce this topic simultaneously with fundamental concepts of number such as place value. However, 76% of the states called for coverage of fractions in 1st grade. The average amount of teaching time for fractions was relatively small in 1st grade—about 8 days (class periods)—yet fractions had a 90%-range, indicating that some classrooms spent almost a month on that topic.[4]

Another way to look at these differences in teaching time without looking at each of the 29 topics separately is by grouping topics into broader categories that are more easily identified by people who are not involved in mathematics teaching. Figure 4.2 presents a box and whisker plot for basic arithmetic.

For basic arithmetic, 1st-grade classrooms typically spent around half of the year (we assume that 160 of the typical 180 school days in a year involve mathematics instruction—the other days being used for other school-related activities such as testing, field trips, and so on) studying the topics that made up that category, which is no surprise. What is a surprise is that some classrooms spent only about one-fourth of the year while others spent three-fourths of the year. This implies that the difference between two classrooms drawn randomly from our sample could be about half an instructional year—that is, 4 months of instruction. Similar results were found for 2nd-grade classrooms.

**Figure 4.2. The number of instructional days (class periods) allocated by teachers to arithmetic for grades 1–5.**

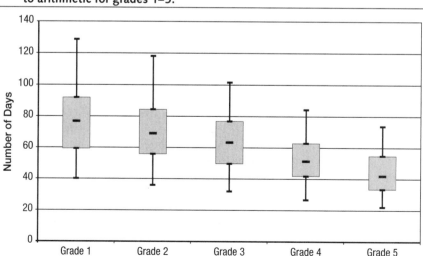

*Note.* For an explanation of how to interpret box and whisker plots, see Figure 2.1.

The variation among classrooms was smaller for data representation, where the typical amount of teaching time was only about 13 days, with a 90%-range of 28 days. Geometry is also an interesting case in which the variation is striking. The typical amount of teaching time spent on geometry was about 30 days for 1st- and 2nd-graders. However, some 1st- and 2nd-grade classrooms spent as much as 55 days on geometry while others spent only 3 to 6 days. The United States does particularly poorly in geometry in cross-national achievement comparisons. Even our high school Advanced Placement (AP) students did not do well in geometry compared to similar students in other countries (U.S. Department of Education, 1998).

The emphasis in topics covered shifts somewhat in 4th and 5th grades. A fair amount of arithmetic is still included (around 40 to 50 days), but now something we call "transition arithmetic" is also included. Transition arithmetic includes fractions, decimals, percents, ratios, and proportionality. Figure 4.3 shows a box and whisker plot for transition arithmetic.

Transition arithmetic is an important topic for 5th grade and is found in the benchmark coherence model for that grade. The average was about 11 weeks of instruction, but some classrooms spent almost 15 weeks, while others spent as few as half as many days.

The implications are clear whether one examines the variations for individual topics (Figure 4.1) or for global topic areas (Figures 4.2 and 4.3). There is great variation among classrooms in the allocation of instructional time to various topics.

**Figure 4.3. The number of instructional days (class periods) allocated by teachers to transition arithmetic for grades 1–5.**

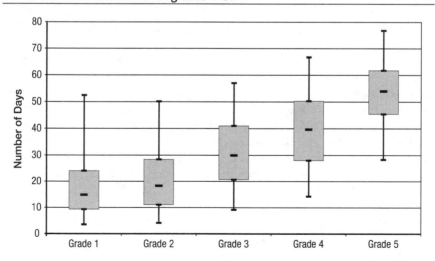

*Note.* For an explanation of how to interpret box and whisker plots, see Figure 2.1.

## CONTENT COVERAGE IN MIDDLE SCHOOL CLASSROOMS

We now turn our attention to middle school (6th through 8th grades). We gathered data from the same sample of districts that we used in examining 1st through 5th grades. There were 269 6th-grade classrooms, 252 7th-grade classrooms, and 256 8th-grade classrooms in the sample. We questioned teachers about the 30 mathematics topics that were considered most appropriate for middle school grades.

### The Topics Taught in Middle School

For each of the middle school grades, there were no topics that were taught or omitted by all of the teachers. The percentage of teachers in each of the three grades who covered a topic was about 70%. This was substantially higher than for the primary grades but similar to 4th- and 5th-grade classrooms. At 6th grade, 90% or more of the teachers covered whole number arithmetic, fractions, decimals, and percentages (see Table 4.2). By 8th grade, this had dropped to around 70% to 80% of the teachers. These topics appear to be core material covered by almost all teachers in 6th grade. However, there were a small number of classrooms in which the teacher reported that the topics were not covered. In general, however, there were few instances of serious inequalities for these basic arithmetic topics.

The story was different for geometry. The average percentage of teachers covering the geometry topics was 79%, somewhat lower than the 86% for arithmetic topics. That percentage for arithmetic was even higher at 6th and 7th grades (about 92%). There were large variations in the coverage of three-dimensional geometry—only about 65% of 6th- and 7th-grade teachers in the sample reported covering this topic, but less than half (47%) covered it at 8th grade. Geometric transformations and congruence and similarity—topics that deal with relationships in geometry—were covered by about 70% to 85% of the teachers in the three grades. Slope and functions—two topics central to the development of algebra—were covered by 78% to 79% of the 8th-grade classrooms. By contrast, data representation was covered by over 90% of the classrooms at each of the three grades. For most countries, middle school is the time of transition from arithmetic to algebra and geometry. However, in our U.S. sample, many classrooms (20% or more) did not cover key topics in algebra and geometry in each of 6th, 7th, and 8th grades.

### The Length of Time Allocated to Topics Taught in Middle School

Figure 4.4 shows the box and whisker plots displaying the variation in teaching time for the 30 middle school topics in 6th, 7th, and 8th grades. The

**Table 4.2. Teacher coverage of mathematics topics in grades 6–8.**

| Mathematics Content Categories | Teachers Covering Content (%) | | |
|---|---|---|---|
| | Grade 6 | Grade 7 | Grade 8 |
| Whole Numbers | 95 | 86 | 72 |
| Fractions | 97 | 92 | 78 |
| Decimals | 90 | 90 | 69 |
| Relation of Fractions & Decimals | 91 | 90 | 70 |
| Percentages | 95 | 94 | 79 |
| Properties of Fractions & Decimals | 80 | 79 | 74 |
| Negative, Rational, & Real Numbers | 76 | 90 | 92 |
| Other Number Topics | 91 | 83 | 91 |
| Estimation & Number Sense | 94 | 90 | 79 |
| Measurement Units | 95 | 91 | 84 |
| Perimeter, Area, & Volume | 97 | 92 | 86 |
| Measurement Estimation & Errors | 86 | 79 | 65 |
| Coordinates & Lines | 94 | 91 | 94 |
| Polygons & Circles | 90 | 82 | 79 |
| 3-D Geometry | 64 | 65 | 47 |
| Geometric Transformations | 81 | 73 | 68 |
| Congruence & Similarity | 80 | 87 | 77 |
| Proportionality Concepts | 81 | 89 | 88 |
| Proportionality Problems | 70 | 85 | 83 |
| Slope | 10 | 44 | 78 |
| Patterns & Relations | 81 | 88 | 87 |
| Functions | 48 | 63 | 79 |
| Expressions & Simple Equations | 81 | 88 | 93 |
| Linear Equations & Inequalities | 43 | 75 | 91 |
| Other Equations & Inequalities | 26 | 38 | 68 |
| Representing & Interpreting Data | 95 | 92 | 91 |
| Probability & Uncertainty | 77 | 73 | 71 |
| Elementary Analysis | 19 | 29 | 33 |
| Sets & Logic | 19 | 25 | 26 |
| Other Topics | 35 | 40 | 35 |
| **Number of Sampled Classrooms** | **460** | **556** | **631** |

**Figure 4.4. Distribution of the 90%-ranges of teachers' instructional days of coverage for the 30 mathematics topics (grades 6–8).**

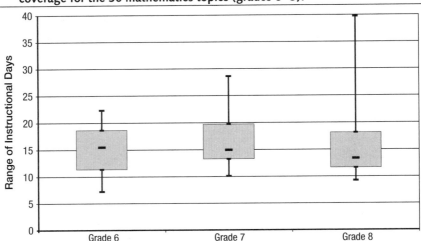

*Note.* For an explanation of how to interpret box and whisker plots, see Figure 2.1.

median number of days (class periods), which gives a typical value for the 90%-range, was around 13 to 15 days, which is similar to 1st through 5th grades. The typical variation represented about 2 1/2 to 3 weeks of teaching time. For some topics, the variation was as little as 10 or fewer days, while other topics had differences of 5 weeks or more.

There were several topics with large variations for 6th grade, including whole numbers, fractions, decimals, perimeter, area and volume, and data representation. All of these topics had a 90%-range of around 1 month. Some classrooms spent as little as 4 days on each of these topics, while others allocated as much as 5 weeks. A small number of classrooms actually spent no time at all on some of these topics in 6th grade.

Similar differences existed in 7th and 8th grades for whole number arithmetic, negative numbers, the coordinate system, and data representation. Several of these topics are part of the standard algebra curriculum. Internationally, algebra is the main topic at 8th grade, yet in our sample, we found differences in teaching time that in some cases approached 5 weeks. Such differences would signify that algebra is not as central in the United States.

As with grades 1 through 5, we looked at four broader areas that combine specific topics—algebra, geometry, data, and arithmetic. Sixth-grade mathematics is a transition year. Arithmetic is still prominent and takes up about half of the school year's teaching time (combining arithmetic and transition arithmetic). The variation across the 267 6th-grade classrooms we studied was quite large. The 90%-range was about 3 weeks of mathematics teaching time for basic arithmetic and 11 weeks for transition arithmetic.

The extreme case was one classroom that spent the entire year's mathematics instruction on basic arithmetic and nothing else.

Transition arithmetic involves fractions, decimals, percentages, ratios, and their interrelationships together with the idea of proportionality. The benchmark model of coherent mathematics makes transition arithmetic a major priority in 6th grade. In our sample, some classrooms spent around 7 weeks on these topics, while others spent about 19 weeks, and one classroom spent no time at all on transition arithmetic.

As discussed earlier in this chapter, we had expected some variations in teaching time for topics that do not reflect systematically different content coverage. Not all teachers spend exactly the same amount of time on a topic. It would be unreasonable to expect them to do so. It probably would not even be desirable for them to do so, since classrooms of children vary in ability, interest, and other factors that influence the amount of teaching time needed. At some point, however, variations can become so large that they represent different visions of what content should be covered at that grade. In our sample, transition arithmetic received on average around 5 weeks of instruction in 6th-grade classrooms. Unfortunately, we do not have an adequate theory or even empirical grounds to suggest the appropriate amount of variation around the average of 5 weeks.

Suppose we accept the wisdom of these 267 teachers across three states and assume that 5 weeks is a reasonable amount of time to teach transition arithmetic in 6th grade. How much variation around this average of 5 weeks would be considered tolerable rather than representing vastly different views of what mathematics content should be taught? Without a well-developed guideline to follow, we decided to examine what the variation was for these same topics in the top-achieving country in TIMSS, Singapore, and used this as an empirical model of what natural variability should look like.[5] The estimated variation in teaching time across Singapore classrooms for transition arithmetic was about half (56%) of that for the U.S. classrooms.[6]

Singapore was chosen not only because it was the highest-achieving country. It was also chosen because it has a strong national ministry that regulates that nation's content coverage. The national curriculum for Singapore was also used to help define the benchmark model for coherent mathematics instruction. Having a national curriculum and the means to enforce the way it is implemented by teachers removes content coverage as a variable among the country's classrooms. Using such a country to estimate natural variation among classrooms assumes that there should be no systematic difference in learning opportunities, but only small variations "around the same shared vision." In the United States, the variations seemed too large to be simply natural variations.

Removing variation in the intended curriculum or standards—as in Singapore's case—provides a reasonable estimate of the variation in teaching time for transition arithmetic in 6th grade if there are no systematic differences in vision for what should be accomplished. The variation in Singapore was only about half of what was observed in the United States. So, under these general assumptions, one-half of the variation in the United States could be estimated to be natural, random variations in teaching time among classrooms. The other half seems likely to be attributable to different views of what content should be covered among the teachers in the different classrooms.[7]

What does all this mean in practical terms? If we assume variation like that of Singapore for transition arithmetic in the 267 6th-grade classrooms in our sample, we would estimate variation of around 1 week to a week and a half from the typical value of 5 weeks. What we found was much more.

The other topic areas at 6th grade and all of the topic areas at 7th and 8th grades show large variation in the time teachers reported covering the related topics. In 8th-grade algebra, using the 90%-range, some classrooms spent as little as two-and-a-half weeks on algebra topics, while other classrooms spent over 4 months on the same area. The average amount of time allocated to the teaching of algebra was two-and-a-half months. Much of this difference is related to the practice of tracking, which will be discussed in the next chapter. One class allocated 6 months of the school year to algebra. Other classrooms did not cover algebra topics at all. Given the critical nature of algebra in developing quantitatively literate citizens, these inequalities take on great importance.

## A Further Examination of Differences in Time Allocations Related to Content Coverage

We leave aside the question of whether there is an ideal amount of instructional time for each topic to be adequately covered for a class. As stated earlier, there is little theory available to answer that question. In the previous section, we approached the issue in a normative way, using Singapore as the basis for the comparison. The approach taken in this section looks at the practical consequences of such variation. Clearly, total instructional time for any teacher or any class is limited within 1 school year. As a result, large variations in instructional time for any one topic will demand compensatory variation in instructional time for other topics.

We determined the average time allocated by teachers in our sample of 263 8th-grade mathematics classes to five broad categories of mathematics. As estimated from the sample, the "reasonable" allocations of time at 8th grade included 12 weeks for arithmetic, 1 week for data exploration, about 9 weeks for algebra, 7 weeks for geometry, and the remaining 3 weeks for other topics. We again assume that 32 weeks (160 days) are actually available for mathematics instruction. We are not suggesting that these time allocations are ideal or theoretically justified. They are only an example based on real teacher data that we can use to explore differences in time allocations for mathematics instruction.

For example, consider arithmetic. Our sample suggests an average of about 12 weeks allocated for arithmetic instruction. Now imagine that one particular classroom gives about 17 weeks to arithmetic instruction—an actual value from the data and one that is not an extreme case, since it is within the range for the middle 50% of all classrooms in the sample. Let us assume that this 17-week allocation is somewhat justified for this particular class. The dilemma that arises is that 5 weeks must now be made up at the cost of other topics. The topic of data could be dropped completely. Algebra or geometry coverage might be dropped or shortened; time for geometry could be reduced to only 2 weeks of instruction, and algebra could be cut down to only 4 weeks. Alternatively, both topics could be whittled down without dropping anything completely.

The point here is that time allocations matter because there is a fixed amount of time with which to work. One set of choices has an impact on choices for other topics—on whether they are even covered as well as the amount of time spent on them if they are covered. These issues are discussed further in a later chapter. There, we will see that the more advanced topics are the ones that are typically left out or receive greatly reduced amounts of instructional time.

## An Alternative Way of Characterizing Variability

It might seem that the point has been made: Middle school does not provide the same content coverage for all children. However, there is another way to demonstrate this conclusion that has powerful implications. One of the advantages of using international data to frame a discussion of the United States is that it not only provides a frame of reference but also allows us to develop criteria that are neither arbitrary nor ideological.

One example is provided by an index that we have developed from the TIMSS data: *international grade placement (IGP)*.[8] One of the questions that U.S. policymakers must consider is the level of rigor or demand of the U.S. curriculum. It is difficult to accurately judge one's own case. The international context provides an external benchmark for judging how demanding our mathematics curriculum is.

Although the position of the United States among its global peers is not the central question of this book, it is still of interest to know whether the average U.S. student is being prepared to face the competition of a global economy. The short answer is that they are not (Schmidt, Houang, McKnight, Cogan, & Jakwerth, 1999; Schmidt et al., 2001). Even if all students in the United States received the same basic learning opportunities and content coverage, they would still be behind their peers around most of the world and especially the top-achieving countries, who also happen to be the United States' chief economic competitors.

How far behind are we? How comparatively less demanding is our curriculum? Using this IGP index, we have estimated that by the end of 8th grade, U.S. students are *1 and a half to 2 years* behind their counterparts in TIMSS countries. This is an important context to understand as we look at learning opportunities in the United States. Not only are there inequalities in content coverage across the United States, but, on average, those opportunities are lacking in comparison to those that students receive in other countries—another fundamental kind of inequality.

Returning to the theme of the present work, however, we now use the IGP to further address the question of inequalities across classrooms. This statistic gives an indication of the grade level of the topic coverage in a classroom averaged over all the topics covered in the school year and taking into account how much time was spent on each topic. Since different topics have different IGP grade levels associated with them, how much time a teacher spends on each topic has an impact on the overall grade level of a classroom's mathematics content coverage.

Consider first the 438 5th-grade classrooms in our study. The typical U.S. 5th-grade classroom was covering topics at the grade level considered most appropriate from the international data. However, using the 90%-range, some classrooms were a grade level behind (4th grade), some were a grade level ahead (6th grade), and one outlier classroom covered a curriculum at the 7th-grade level. Yet, all of these were 5th-grade classrooms.

Median IGPs for all three middle school grades were the same, implying that by the end of 8th grade, students in a typical U.S. classroom had continued to study a mathematics curriculum that is at the 6th-grade level internationally—and have done so since 6th grade. That is, during 3 years of instruction, the content offered was essentially unchanged—there was no progress in mathematics knowledge. It is hardly a surprise, then, that we so often hear that many children are bored by mathematics at this point in their schooling, nor is it a mystery that they fail to compete with other countries at the 8th-grade level.

Yet this situation did not hold true for all classrooms. At each of the three grades, the middle 90% of classrooms showed a range of one and a half to two grades in what they covered. Some classrooms at the 8th-grade level have not even had the opportunity to study what would be considered a 6th-grade curriculum internationally. Although it was rare, some 8th-grade classrooms were studying what would be 3rd-grade material internationally. Others studied what would be an 8th-grade curriculum. It was very rare to find a U.S. classroom that actually met international benchmarks for content coverage. By contrast, some of the top-achieving countries are studying a 9th-grade curriculum in 8th grade (compared with the full range of countries studied).

## SOCIAL CLASS DIFFERENCES IN LEARNING OPPORTUNITIES

The question addressed in this section asks if the inequalities in OTL across classrooms are systematically related to socioeconomic status (SES). The classroom data were divided into the same four SES groups discussed in Chapter 3 using the district classification of where the classroom was located.

### Differences in Topic Coverage Across Types of Districts

For the elementary grades, there were no appreciable differences in OTL across the four SES groups. Teacher content coverage was very similar regardless of the SES of the district in which they taught. (This says nothing about the equality of the learning environment of the classrooms such as funding levels, resources, or the quality of instruction—only content coverage.) For example, at 5th grade, the typical student in a classroom in each of the four SES groups had a chance of covering the topic of fractions that was 94%, 100%, 94%, and 96%, respectively, for the four groups.

By middle school (6th through 8th grades), the situation had changed. According to the international benchmark model, 6th-grade mathematics should move from the more computational aspects of number to understanding the number system, in particular the rational number system. This includes factoring numbers; negative numbers; and the properties of fractions, decimals, and their interrelations. For these important topics, differences related to social class were clearly evident.

For students attending school in districts with a large percentage of low SES children and a large percentage of African American students (Group I), about 92% of the classrooms covered these topics. This is comparable to the wealthier districts (Group IV), where 95% of the teachers covered these topics. However, for those classrooms in the middle two SES categories, the percentage covering these topics were only about 80%. The district with one-third of the students in poverty and 22% African American students (Group II) had the lowest percentage of classrooms that covered these topics (only 78%). Students in these districts had only slightly larger than a three-in-four chance of encountering coverage of these fundamental topics, while students in the wealthiest districts had a 95% chance of encountering them.[9] Another way to look at this is to say that around 20% of the classrooms in the lower-middle-class districts did not study these topics, while almost all of the classrooms in the wealthiest districts did.

By 7th and 8th grades, the inequalities across the types of districts became even more pronounced. These grades began to prepare students for high school and the type of mathematics that the students would ultimately need either to enter college or to obtain a good job in today's economy. Differences at these grade levels represent crucial variations in learning opportunities. The first six grades are mostly about computational arithmetic, with the transition to more abstract notions of number being the exception in 6th grade (see above). In 7th and 8th grades, instruction moves on (or should do so, by international standards) to generalize those operations, treat them more abstractly, and begin the study of equations and functions.

An important change is noticeable at 7th grade. The higher the SES of the district, the more likely it was that transitional arithmetic topics (fractions, decimals, percentages, and so on) were covered in the classroom. At the same time, the higher the SES of the district, the less likely that basic computational arithmetic involving whole numbers was still being covered at that grade level. Percentages are given in Table 4.3.

Although the differences across district types in covering arithmetic were relatively small, the differences in transition arithmetic were more significant. Around 15% of the classrooms in the poorest districts did not cover transition arithmetic topics. Virtually all of the classrooms in the wealthier districts did.

Inequalities in algebra were even more pronounced. About one-third of the classrooms in the low SES districts did not cover typical algebra topics, while only about half as many (18%) failed to do so in high SES districts. This is a difference of almost 16% between the two types of districts. The other two district types fall in the middle, although the two lower SES district types (Groups I and II) are very similar. A similar pattern of inequalities exists for geometry topics, but at a lesser level.

By 8th grade, the differences generally decreased. Since transition arithmetic and geometry were so heavily covered in the 7th grade in the high SES districts, more classrooms in these districts no longer covered some of these topics. For example, at the 7th grade, almost 90% of the classrooms covered a typical geometry topic, but at the 8th grade, this fell to just over 75%. If lower SES districts covered these topics less often, it is not because they had been covered in 7th grade but rather because the topics were simply not covered.

The same general trend of inequalities among the different types of districts holds for algebra topics in the 8th grade. Around 20% of the classrooms in the two low SES district types (Groups I and II) did not cover algebra

Table 4.3. Average percentage of 7th-grade teachers covering broad categories of mathematics topics by SES.

| Mathematics Content Categories | Type of District | | | |
|---|---|---|---|---|
| | Group I | Group II | Group III | Group IV |
| Arithmetic | 94 | 92 | 88 | 88 |
| Transition Arithmetic | 86 | 93 | 88 | 96 |
| Geometry | 79 | 78 | 85 | 90 |
| Algebra | 66 | 69 | 72 | 82 |

topics. Only about 12% did not do so in the high SES group of districts. For the lower-middle-class districts (Group II), twice as many classrooms did not cover algebra topics as did classrooms in the high SES group of districts. An 8th-grade student randomly assigned to a classroom in a lower-middle-class district with 22% African American students would be almost half as likely to study many algebra topics as a student who was randomly assigned to a classroom in the high SES group of districts.

The differences in algebra and geometry between the low SES districts and the high SES districts lessen from 7th to 8th grades. There is increased coverage of algebra and geometry in 8th grade in the low SES districts. However, in these districts, fewer classrooms had begun coverage of those topics in 7th grade than in the high SES districts. For more classrooms in the high SES districts, this was the 2nd year in which this material was covered. For more classrooms in the low SES districts, this was the 1st year in which this material was covered.

## Time Allocation Differences Across Types of Districts

Time was allocated for studying arithmetic, including whole numbers, fractions, decimals, and percentages, in all of the elementary grades (1st through 5th) across all SES groups. Summarized cumulatively over the first five grades, the difference in the total amount of instructional time for arithmetic for the first five grades differed by only about 10 more days for the two lower SES types of districts (Groups I and II) than for the two higher SES types of districts (Groups III and IV).[10] However, for data, geometry, and introductory algebra, wealthier districts (Group IV) studied these topics on average for about 8 more days over the five grades.

There is a small trade-off between topics. Time spent on basic computation in the elementary grades was larger in the two poorer district types; on the other hand, time spent on geometry and algebra was larger in the two wealthier district types. This difference foreshadows what happens in the middle grades. Seventy percent of the differences in allocated arithmetic time were due to covering whole number arithmetic—addition, subtraction, multiplication, and division—in the lower SES districts, while only about one-fourth were due to covering fractions, decimals, and percentages in the lower SES districts.

One possibility is that the lower SES districts have devoted more time to building basic skills, especially with whole numbers. They were probably able to do so by leaving out some of the more conceptual aspects of arithmetic, such as how arithmetic ideas are generalized in algebra. The differences are not large, but they are the beginning of a significant pattern.

Realistically, the important question is whether the difference in time given to various topics, on balance, helps or hurts students from lower SES districts. Many of these students live in poverty, and school may represent their best chance for escaping that poverty. One effect of this small difference is that these students might well be less prepared for the middle-grades curriculum. If these students are not prepared for that move, or are less well prepared than students in higher SES districts, schools may compensate by weakening the middle school mathematics curriculum, leaving these students even further behind. This is less likely to happen in the two higher SES types of districts, where the parents themselves are already better educated. The result may be the poor getting poorer and the wealthy getting wealthier, both educationally and, in the long term, economically as well.

By the middle grades, the differences in time allocations continued to reflect the same trend, but the differences were larger. For the two lower SES types of districts, the small inequalities noted in earlier grades were exacerbated further. The middle-class districts (Group III) now looked more like the poorer districts (Groups I and II) in the time they gave to some topics.

High SES suburban districts spent much less time on whole number arithmetic than the other three types of districts did. This was especially true at 7th grade, where children received, on average, 3 weeks less instruction on whole number arithmetic, allowing these students 3 extra weeks to devote to more advanced topics. Addition, subtraction, multiplication, and division of whole numbers, along with basic measurement units and estimation, were still covered in these grades, even in the high SES districts. This did not even include fractions, decimals, and percents. These topics were no longer formally intended to be covered in middle school by a majority of the high-achieving countries.

In the low SES urban districts (Group I), the differences grew even larger, to more than 4 weeks on average during the year. A difference of even 3 weeks, let alone 4, is likely to be critical in 7th grade, because at this time instruction in algebra and geometry becomes more formal and constitutes a big part of the curriculum. Devoting more time to whole number arithmetic takes away from opportunities to learn higher-level mathematics.

Combining these 7th-grade variations with those at 6th and 8th grades, the difference in whole number arithmetic instruction for an average child in the suburban group of districts (Group IV) and an average child in one of the three other types of districts was about 5 weeks (25 days) of school time on average, out of a total of 32 instructional weeks—almost one-sixth of the year. For the two lower SES types of districts, cumulatively over the first eight grades, children received on average 37 days (over 7 weeks) more instruction in whole number arithmetic than children in high SES districts.

It might be argued that more instruction in the "basics" of arithmetic is a virtue, especially for children who have a more difficult time in school. To this, we reply: not when the cost is much less time to cover the other mathematics topics that prepare the way for more advanced study.[11]

It is surprising that the cumulative difference in time allocated to teaching transition arithmetic across the four district types was not as large as for whole number arithmetic, and in the opposite direction. The high SES/suburban districts allocated an average of around 2 weeks more instruction to transition arithmetic than did the other three district types.

The roughly 50 countries of TIMSS focused on algebra and geometry in the middle grades, not on arithmetic. How do the four U.S. district types vary in their coverage of these two areas (combined)? The two lower SES types were quite similar, so we compared them with the suburban districts. The middle-class districts were somewhere between the other three district types.

The suburban districts allocated on average almost 5 weeks (23 days) more time to algebra and geometry instruction in the three middle school grades than did the two lower SES districts. The comparison suggested a nearly perfect trade-off: The difference in whole number arithmetic was 5 weeks more in the two lower SES districts, while the difference in algebra and geometry was almost 5 weeks more in the high SES districts. The earlier comparison included the middle-class districts with the two low SES districts, but excluding them yields the same basic difference in arithmetic instruction. While children in the high SES districts studied algebra and geometry on average for over 46 weeks in the three middle school grades, students in the two lower SES district types studied those topics for only 41 weeks.

This significant difference among districts likely influences achievement. However, even the best U.S. districts should not be praised too highly. Across all four types of districts, only about 40% of total middle school mathematics instructional time was spent on algebra and geometry. This compares unfavorably with students in other countries, where the average was more than 60%. This suggests one possible reason why U.S. students perform comparatively poorly in international tests such as TIMSS.

The difference was quite large if we look only at 7th grade and compare time for algebra and geometry for students from the high SES districts with those in the two lower SES districts—more than 3 weeks (17 days). The cumulative difference over all three grades was 5 weeks, indicating that the majority of the difference was coming from the 7th grade. Seventh grade is a critical transition point between arithmetic and algebra. A difference here is very telling. Yet, at this critical transition point, these same lower SES districts allocated 3 weeks more to basic arithmetic than did the high SES districts. The trade-off is clear. Further, this trade-off, coming at a key grade, generates inequalities that are not easily remedied. The students from the two lower types of SES districts are handicapped before they enter 8th grade and high school, a handicap that is neither easy nor likely to be corrected.

The differences discussed here are sizable, important, and consequential. They exemplify why the so-called playing field is not level at all. If education is the gateway to a better life, who needs a demanding education more than children from the two lower types of SES districts? These students are the ones for whom such opportunities are critical. The gateway to a better life demands a level educational playing field for these children, for whom so much else is already far from level. Yet, the mathematics data suggest that the field is on an incline that is tilted to their disadvantage. What chances do these students have with such inequalities at earlier points in our education system, before high school and college? College is now viewed as essential for the better-paying and more rewarding careers of the 21st century and these students are all but precluded from following these careers, pushed instead toward much more remedial work by the time they reach 8th grade.

The inequalities demonstrated in this chapter suggest the hypothesis that inequalities exist across districts more generally. Two children from different districts have a very small chance that the mathematics content coverage they receive in their classrooms will be the same. There is a small chance that this instruction will cover the same topics in the same grades. There is a small chance that the amount of time allocated for instruction on those topics will be the same. Some differences are large, especially those dealing with algebra and geometry in the middle school grades. Four to five weeks less instruction on an important topic is meaningful and important. Some differences are crucial to building up a coherent understanding of school mathematics. We now see that some of these cross-district differences are related to the SES of the community in which the classroom is located.

We found that differences in the educational system existed not only in what was intended by the state or district but also in terms of what was actually taught in classrooms. The fact that these classroom experiences are related to SES brings to light another issue. The results in Chapter 3 indicated that there were no differences by SES across districts in terms of what districts intended to be taught. Low SES districts essentially had the same goals (planned opportunities) for mathematics instruction as did high SES districts. As we discussed in that chapter, this was not what one might expect, given the performance of the low SES districts' students on national and state tests.

The results of this chapter may offer a possible explanation. What was planned was not what was delivered. Differences emerged at the level of what topics were taught and how much time was given to them in various grades, even without considering differences in resources, quality of instruction, and motivational climate. These differences could be the bias of low expectations on the part of teachers when the official policy of the district did not reflect those low expectations. What role does the teacher play in this? We will return in Chapter 7 to teachers' backgrounds and characteristics as they relate to this issue.

## CONTENT COVERAGE IN HIGH SCHOOL CLASSROOMS

The point of the previous sections of this chapter is clear: The content covered and experienced by students before they enter high school is highly variable. Students do not enter high school on an equal footing. Are these differences remedied in high school? Do students graduate from high school with a more equal exposure to mathematics, or are the differences further widened? We address those questions in this section.

### The High School Mathematics Topics Taught

It should be no surprise that educational inequality grows greater in high school. In the United States, high school is not designed so that all students take the same courses. Because students will not all end up in the same careers, it is not necessary for them all to have the same exposure to all of the same mathematics topics. This is a reasonable policy for designing high school education. However, it also makes clear why high school does not remedy differences in learning opportunities that occurred earlier.

Here, we focus on the differences created by covering content differently for the same category of course—Algebra I, Geometry, Algebra II, Calculus, and so on—and put aside the issue of differences in course choices. (Chapter 5 addresses the issue of tracking, of deliberately placing students in different sequences of learning opportunities, either by policy or by their personal choice.)

Differences in exposure to mathematics content created by different course choices may or may not be considered as generating inequalities depending on which courses are considered optional. Opinions differ on which courses should be taken in common and which should be left up to choice,[12] a topic we will discuss in the next chapter. However, there should be no debate about whether Algebra I or Geometry should be similar courses for all students.

To study variation in content coverage in high school, we divided the courses taught by the teachers in the 61 districts into 12 categories. We used this many categories of courses in order to compare "apples to apples" rather than "apples to oranges." The course categories included Basic Mathematics; Pre-algebra; Algebra I; Geometry; Algebra II; Functions, Statistics, and Trigonometry; Integrated Mathematics I, II, III, and IV; Precalculus; and Calculus (including Advanced Placement [AP] Calculus).

Looking at topic coverage in each of the different course categories, we found for the most part what we expected. Virtually all Algebra I teachers covered the various equation topics. Virtually all Geometry teachers covered all the basic geometry topics, including geometric proofs. Most of the Algebra II teachers covered nonlinear functions and more-advanced-equation topics.

All Calculus teachers covered calculus. There was not much variability in the basic topics covered that defined a specific area of mathematics, be it in algebra, geometry, or calculus courses.

There were some variations worth noting. Trigonometry was covered by half of the Algebra II teachers, virtually all of the Precalculus teachers, and about one-third of the Algebra I classes. Surprisingly, almost all of the algebra classes covered some statistics.

General, remedial courses (Pre-algebra and Basic Mathematics) were the most variable. Three-fourths of these classes covered basic linear equations. Virtually all teachers in these courses covered the arithmetic topics of fractions, decimals, percentages, and whole numbers. Since the purpose of these types of courses was to prepare students who were already behind to be ready to take Algebra I, this variability was likely to exacerbate the previous inequalities. As a result, these differences also seem likely to carry over into the Algebra I course that the students in these courses eventually take. Because it is a remedy provided at such a late stage and is so variable, it is unlikely to compensate for earlier differences in learning opportunities.

Integrated Mathematics courses were the other type of course that showed substantial variation. There were four different types of such courses, designed for each of the four grades of high school. Geometry was the most variable area of mathematics covered in Integrated Mathematics courses. For each of the four courses (I, II, III, and IV), from 10% to 80% of the teachers covered key geometry topics. For example, three-dimensional geometry was covered in the four courses by 50%, 48%, 30%, and 0%, respectively, of the teachers. Only some of the teachers in the four courses covered geometry proofs—15%, 28%, 48%, and 60%, respectively.

One pattern that emerged for the integrated courses was that a particular topic might be covered in a specific year by almost all of the teachers, but with considerable variability occurring for that topic in the other 3 years of courses, with the topic covered only by some teachers. Trigonometry, an important topic, provides a good example. In Integrated Mathematics III (or whatever it was called locally), 99% of the teachers covered trigonometry. In Integrated Mathematics I, II, and IV, 5%, 32%, and 60% of the teachers, respectively, covered trigonometry. Apart from whether this belies the philosophy of integrated mathematics courses, such variability is likely to make a difference in terms of student learning. This is true even though almost all students would study trigonometry in the 3rd year of the course sequence (should they continue that far).

## Variations of Time for Topics in High School

The previous section relates only to which topics were covered or not covered. Let us now consider the second aspect of learning opportunities— the amount of time allocated to various topics. To do this, we categorized the 39 topics in the high school teacher questionnaire into nine broad areas. They included arithmetic, geometric objects, geometric relationships, introductory algebra including linear equations and inequalities (labeled beginning algebra), more advanced algebra topics including slope and functions (labeled intermediate algebra), advanced number topics related to algebra (labeled algebra foundations), data and statistics, measurement, and advanced mathematics (including calculus). For each of the different types of courses, we calculated the amount of time each teacher allocated to covering the relevant topics. The average for all of the teachers who taught a given course is shown in Figure 4.5.

First, consider the Pre-algebra course. Teachers in these courses allocated a substantial amount of time to covering basic arithmetic topics—about one-fourth of the school year's time. However, differences among teachers were considerable. By contrast, focusing on beginning algebra (ostensibly the purpose of the course), coverage varied. Some teachers allocated no time to it, while others allocated over one-fourth of their instructional time. Similar variations occurred for teachers of Basic Mathematics courses.

Algebra I teachers typically allocated about one-half of the school year (45%) to covering both introductory and more-advanced algebra topics. Including advanced number topics that were relevant to algebra (algebra foundations) raised the total to about 60% of the year. The other 40% seems largely to have been allocated to arithmetic, geometry, and statistics.

**Figure 4.5. Average percentage of teaching time for mathematics topics in high school courses.**

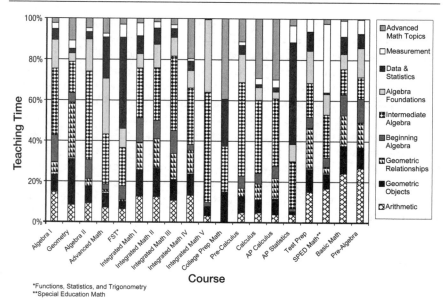

\*Functions, Statistics, and Trigonometry
\*\*Special Education Math

The enormous variability in the content coverage of algebra courses is best typified by the time spent on intermediate algebra topics. Teachers, on average, allocated about one-third of their class time to covering these topics. However, the range of time for these topics varied enormously, with one teacher spending only 12 instructional periods on these topics and another allocating more than 100 periods (20 weeks) to these same topics. These topics—which include slope, quadratic equations, systems of equations, and linear functions—define the internationally benchmarked core of a first algebra course, whether or not it is called algebra. Covering them in 12 periods amounts to not covering them at all, or at a minimum not covering them deeply enough to lead to student understanding. Eliminating these extreme cases, the differences in learning opportunities were still substantial. For example, the middle 50% of algebra teachers varied in covering these topics by as much as 1 month (20 periods).

Geometry courses focused both on geometric objects and on geometric relationships. Covering geometric relationships is perhaps the most distinguishing feature of high school geometry, compared with earlier work in geometry. High school geometry teachers, on average, allocated about 9 weeks (45 periods) to covering geometric relationships. However, some teachers allocated as few as 4 weeks to this area, while others taught these topics for as long as 13 weeks.

Algebra II is a course that is increasingly required for high school graduation in many states. However, it also demonstrated extremely large variation in the content coverage of more advanced topics such as nonlinear functions and complex equations. The middle 90% of teachers of this course varied by 55 periods (about 11 weeks) in the time they devoted to these topics. It seems unlikely that children in these different courses—courses that ostensibly cover the same material—could be considered to have had equivalent learning experiences, regardless of the quality of instruction.

Such large variations were also found in integrated mathematics courses. For example, in Integrated Mathematics II (or whatever it was called locally), the intermediate algebra topics showed a range of almost 75 periods in time given to them—that is, almost 4 months of the school year. Even to consider labeling these two versions of a course with the same title is misleading, if not unethical. A reasonable parent would expect the courses to be roughly the same. How could parents ever know that such enormous and important differences in learning opportunities existed in two different versions of the same course? Worst of all, how could they know which offering was their child's experience and opportunity?

Geometry courses also traditionally have focused on geometric proof, and they continue to do so internationally. But this is not so in today's U.S. geometry courses. The time allocated to geometric proof varied greatly, with some teachers giving no time to this critical topic and others covering this area for over 6 weeks of the geometry course. Even calculus courses have substantial variation.

## CONTENT COVERAGE IN SCIENCE

Consider science as it is taught in the 1st through 5th grades. We looked at the distribution of time across the classrooms in our sample for each of the five grades and for four big areas of science—earth science, biology, chemistry, and physics. There was substantial variation in content coverage at each of the five grades. Earth science coverage differed by over 8 weeks, as indicated by the 90%-range. Biology also differed by similar amounts. Chemistry and physics (which, obviously, are taught at very elementary levels) have smaller variations across classrooms, but these variations nonetheless have serious implications. For example, in chemistry, the difference across classrooms is about 6 weeks, but for some classrooms, there was no coverage of chemistry-type topics. This was also true for physics.

At the middle school level, the differences were more pronounced. We found numerous classrooms in which no biology was covered at all. This was true at each of the middle school grades.[13] This type of omission was much more prevalent than it was in mathematics, reflecting the often cited consequence of NCLB, under which mathematics is tested and science has only recently been added to the testing. (It was not being tested when these data were collected.)

Because science in the middle grades is covered in a layered fashion (with biology typically covered in 7th grade and physical or earth science in 8th grade), the zero coverage could be misleading. To eliminate this factor, we looked at the interquartile range, which included classrooms that covered the subject matter. The interquartile range for biology (the differences between the lowest fourth and the highest fourth of classrooms) was approximately 3 weeks at 6th grade and 4 weeks at both 7th and 8th grades. For physics, the differences were 2 weeks at 6th grade, 4 weeks at 7th grade, and 3 weeks at 8th grade. Finally, for chemistry, the interquartile ranges were smaller by comparison, around 2 weeks at each of the three grades. However, in general, the coverage was less overall. More classrooms did not cover any chemistry-related topics than did not cover any biology- or physics-related topics, and the maximum coverage for chemistry was only around 2 to 3 weeks for any classroom.

There were inequalities across classrooms in content coverage related to science similar to those found in mathematics; however, in some sense, these inequalities are more pronounced because so many classrooms include no coverage of any of the topics within the broad areas of biology, chemistry, and physics. Worldwide, chemistry and physics are typically the focus of 8th grade. For some children in the United States, there was no such coverage. For others, it was as much as half of their 8th-grade science class.

## CLASSROOM VARIATION

The introduction to this chapter suggested that it is at the classroom level that intentions are shaped into real opportunities. As a result, it is here that issues of equality in content coverage are played out. What the data from hundreds of classrooms told us is that this is, in fact, the reality in America's classrooms. We found substantial variation in which topics were covered, in how much time was allocated to them, and in the sequencing of the topics. The variation was large at all of the elementary and middle school grades and in both mathematics and science.

It is also a sad reality that high school mathematics experiences varied in content coverage—as much as in the earlier grades—even for what are ostensibly the same courses. This variability compounds the earlier variation rather than compensating for it. Students did not cover the same content even if they took the same courses.

## CHAPTER 5

# Tracking:
# Further Along the Road
# to Inequality

The data presented in Chapter 4 showed, among other findings about content, that content coverage varied greatly in 8th-grade mathematics classrooms. In fact, two 8th-grade classes in the same school did not necessarily cover the same topics and did not spend the same amount of time covering the topics that they did share. One policy that potentially influences such variation, especially in the 8th grade, is the policy of content *tracking*. Tracking is practiced most often in middle and high school, and particularly in mathematics. There is some evidence that such a practice also exists in other areas such as language arts, and in some schools, tracking even finds its way into the elementary grades. In this chapter, we use both 1995 Third International Mathematics and Science Study (TIMSS) and Promoting Rigorous Outcomes in Mathematics and Science (PROM/SE) data to explore tracking at both the middle and high school levels.

## TRACKING IN MIDDLE SCHOOL

We need to distinguish between tracking and *ability grouping*. Ability grouping involves grouping students during instruction in a particular subject according to a judgment of how able they are to learn that subject (often based on test results and teachers' evaluations). The defense of this practice is that it makes for a homogeneous learning environment, which is believed to be beneficial to the students involved. The content of instruction is the same across different ability groups, but the pace and the instructional techniques are likely to vary. In some cases, the depth with which a topic is covered may differ across groups even though the same topic is covered; a more advanced group may go more deeply into the same topic than a "slower" group. Such differences might have implications for topic coverage, depending on how much instruction differs for a topic among different ability groups. However, the goal of such a system still is to cover the essential topics for all students.

Tracking, on the other hand, has as its explicit goal the coverage of different topics for different groups of students. Students are grouped much as they are in ability grouping, but the topics covered are different across groups. Eighth-grade tracking in mathematics leads to different courses for different groups of students, most often "Regular Mathematics," Pre-algebra, or Algebra I. The rationale is again based on the notion of homogeneous learning environments. However, tracking goes further to ensure that some children—the "brightest"—are not held back by the "typical" students who cannot learn as quickly or as effectively. The underlying idea is apparently the belief that some students cannot learn high-level mathematics and need to be given a less demanding curriculum.

It is not clear whether parents understand tracking or its consequences. Nor is it clear how imperfect the system may be in determining who should be in which track. Many parents simply accept the professional advice of the school about what is best for their child. However, some parents challenge the placement of their child and demand that he or she be treated differently from how the school had planned. A recent study of urban parents gives some indication that they do not fully understand the implications of tracking or how to challenge it even if they wish to. This appears to be especially true of lower SES parents.[1]

Tracking in science is not as explicit or as pronounced as it is in mathematics. However, it does seem to occur in middle school, involving the nature of the biology course offered or a trade-off between biology and earth science. Tracking does not appear to be as widely practiced in elementary grades as in middle school, except in the area of reading. Ability grouping seems to be a more common practice at this level.

Tracking in kindergarten through 8th grade seems to be a uniquely American policy. It was not practiced in most countries studied as a part of TIMSS. There are countries that use ability grouping, but they teach the same core content across all groups. Even in Germany, where students destined for universities attend a different school from those who are not, the intended content coverage is the same.

## Course Proliferation: The Building Blocks of Tracking[2]

A unique characteristic of U.S. middle school mathematics is the large number of different courses that are available. Most TIMSS countries had only one mathematics course at each grade level. For example, in 8th grade, it was usually called something akin to "8th Grade Mathematics." The practice in the United States contrasts sharply with the international norm. A nationally representative sample of U.S. 8th-grade classrooms from TIMSS found many varieties of courses with such titles as Average Mathematics, Basic Mathematics, Advanced Mathematics, Gifted Mathematics, High Mathematics, LD

Mathematics, Remedial Mathematics, and Resource Mathematics. Other titles included Arithmetic, Pre-algebra, Algebra I, and Geometry. Obviously, not all these course titles were available in a single school, although quite often more than one was. The point is, judged by course names, not all U.S. children have the same mathematics learning opportunities at 8th grade, unlike children in many other countries.

To bring some order to these data, course titles were coded and assigned to one of six different curriculum types—remedial, regular, enriched, pre-algebra, algebra, and geometry. Not all of these different types existed in every school; the availability of these six types of courses was far from consistent from one school to the next. Students had access to a single type of 8th-grade mathematics in about one-fourth (27%) of the schools.[3] In most schools (81%), there was a regular mathematics course, consisting for the most part of arithmetic such as fractions, decimals, percents, ratios, proportionality, some introduction to algebra, and very little geometry.

About three-fourths of the schools offered at least two alternative mathematics course types in 8th grade. In some cases, schools offered up to five types of courses. Table 5.1 presents results for a nationally representative sample of 8th-grade students,[4] making it clear that some of the differences in 8th-grade mathematics learning opportunities discussed in Chapter 4 were a consequence of not having all schools offer the same type of mathematics at 8th grade. What is also clear is that not even all of the 8th-grade mathematics classes in the same school offered the same mathematics learning opportunities. Most U.S. 8th-grade mathematics classrooms are structured by design to deliver different content opportunities to different students. Even when a school chose to offer a single mathematics course type, it was not consistent across schools, further limiting students in some schools. Once again, this inequality was not necessarily by the choice of students or parents, but was effectively a planned inequality, whether by intention or by consequence.

Only those students who have access to an algebra course in 8th grade have content opportunities similar to those given in almost all schools in most other countries around the world. Between 70% and 80% of the students in the United States were not offered such algebra content.

Table 5.1 shows that there were nearly 30 different patterns of course offerings, a bewildering array of content opportunities for a typical 8th-grader. Even if students were given the freedom to choose which course type to take—and usually they are not—these choices would be restricted to what is offered in the particular school they attended.

Whether one believes that tracking of this sort is desirable or not, the system in place in U.S. middle schools creates differences in learning opportunities by design. Inequalities necessarily occur when a system allows a school to offer different courses and then determines which students are placed in which courses. In the United States, two structural sources of inequality in content

Table 5.1. 8th-grade mathematics course offering patterns for a representative sample of U.S. schools with 8th-grade classrooms and percentage of U.S. students in schools with each pattern.

| Number of Course Types | School Course Offering Pattern | Percentage of U.S. Students |
|:---:|:---|:---:|
| 1 | Regular Only | 21.4 |
| 1 | Algebra Only | 4.3 |
| 1 | Pre-algebra Only | 0.4 |
| 1 | Enriched Only | 0.4 |
| 2 | Regular & Algebra | 19.6 |
| 2 | Pre-algebra & Algebra | 9.0 |
| 2 | Regular & Enriched | 6.8 |
| 2 | Regular & Pre-algebra | 1.7 |
| 2 | Remedial & Enriched | 0.5 |
| 2 | Remedial & Regular | 0.3 |
| 3 | Regular, Pre-algebra, & Algebra | 15.9 |
| 3 | Remedial, Regular, & Algebra | 3.7 |
| 3 | Regular, Algebra, & Geometry | 1.9 |
| 3 | Regular, Enriched, & Algebra | 1.7 |
| 3 | Pre-algebra, Algebra, & Geometry | 1.5 |
| 3 | Remedial, Pre-algebra, & Algebra | 1.3 |
| 3 | Remedial, Regular, & Enriched | 1.1 |
| 3 | Remedial, Regular, & Pre-algebra | 0.9 |
| 3 | Enriched, Pre-algebra, & Algebra | 0.8 |
| 3 | Remedial, Enriched, & Algebra | 0.5 |
| 4 | Remedial, Regular, Pre-algebra, & Algebra | 2.5 |
| 4 | Regular, Pre-algebra, Algebra, & Geometry | 0.8 |
| 4 | Remedial, Enriched, Pre-algebra, & Algebra | 0.5 |
| 4 | Remedial, Regular, Enriched, & Algebra | 0.4 |
| 4 | Regular, Enriched, Pre-algebra, & Algebra | 0.4 |
| 5 | Remedial, Regular, Pre-algebra, Algebra, & Geometry | 0.9 |
| 5 | Regular, Enriched, Pre-algebra, Algebra, & Geometry | 0.5 |
| 5 | Remedial, Regular, Enriched, Algebra, & Geometry | 0.4 |

*Note.* Adapted from "Who Takes What Mathematics and in Which Track? Using TIMSS to Characterize U.S. Students' Eighth Grade Mathematics Learning Opportunities," by L. S. Cogan, W. H. Schmidt, & D. E. Wiley, 2001, *Educational Evaluation and Policy Analysis, 23*(4), p. 329.

coverage—differences among schools in what is offered and differences among classrooms within the same school—exacerbate the variation among different states, districts, and classrooms. This planned inequality occurs in part because at the time of the writing of this book, there were no nationally defined standards that applied to all students, as we await the implementation of the Common Core State Standards for Mathematics. A key indicator of the success of the Common Core State Standards' implementation will be the extent to which the practice of tracking is eliminated at the 8th grade.

The extent of differences among schools is made manifest by the fact that over one-third of U.S. 8th-graders attended schools in which two different 8th-grade mathematics courses were offered. A little less than another third were in schools where three different courses were offered. Six percent attended schools where four or five different 8th-grade mathematics courses were offered.

The different course patterns found in Table 5.1 can be summarized by the percentage of U.S. 8th-graders attending schools offering each of the six broad types of mathematics courses (Table 5.2). Most 8th-graders (81%) attended a school in which regular mathematics was offered. That does not mean that this same percentage took a regular mathematics course. It indicates only that the opportunity was available.

Some of the other findings are more surprising. Very few (13.1%) 8th-graders attended schools that offered a formal remedial course—other courses may have included remedial work, although they were not intended to be remedial courses. The TIMSS countries focused extensively on algebra in 8th grade. This means that providing a world-class mathematics

**Table 5.2. Percentage of U.S. 8th-grade students in schools offering each of the broad course types (by course type).**

| Course Type | Percentage of U.S. 8th-Graders Attending Schools Offering Course |
|---|:---:|
| Geometry | 6.0 |
| Algebra I | 66.5 |
| Pre-algebra | 37.1 |
| Enriched | 13.9 |
| Regular | 80.9 |
| Remedial | 13.1 |

*Note.* Adapted from "Who Takes What Mathematics and in Which Track? Using TIMSS to Characterize U.S. Students' Eighth Grade Mathematics Learning Opportunities," by L. S. Cogan, W. H. Schmidt, & D. E. Wiley, 2001, *Educational Evaluation and Policy Analysis, 23*(4), p. 328.

education for all students—a focus of many states and their governors— requires access to an algebra course in 8th grade. However, fully one-third of U.S. 8th-graders attended schools where an algebra course was not even an option. Shockingly, the majority (63%) of 8th-graders attended schools without even a pre-algebra course.[5]

In the United States, there is a widely held belief in the ideal of a level playing field and the desire for an educational system of the same high quality as that of the countries that are our economic competitors. Given this, what do we tell the more than 2 million 8th-grade students and their parents who did not even have an opportunity to study the mathematics that would put them on par with students from top-achieving countries?[6] Why should these students have been deprived of the opportunity that most, if not all, the children in the other 50 TIMSS countries had? The recent adoption of the internationally benchmarked Common Core State Standards by over 40 states not only provides the United States with a great opportunity to raise mathematics standards to those high levels but could also lead to the elimination of the practice of tracking. However, it is not clear that the adoption of these standards *will* eliminate this practice, which is engrained in the fabric of middle school mathematics instruction—only that their adoption *can* eliminate it.

## The Relationship of a School's Racial and Ethnic Composition to Course Offerings

In this section, we examine the relationship between school characteristics (such as size and student racial and ethnic composition) and course offerings. We investigated this matter by looking at the most challenging type of 8th-grade course offered by each school. We then related that most challenging type to the size and composition of each school.[7] We believe this represents a student's potential opportunity for the most challenging type of 8th-grade mathematics that he or she can take. Regular mathematics was taken as the baseline challenge, the minimum that should be available. We then looked at opportunities to take a more challenging 8th-grade mathematics course.

Opportunities for more challenging 8th-grade mathematics courses were related both to the percentage of minority enrollment and to a school's overall enrollment size. Smaller schools were less likely to offer the more challenging types of courses. Schools with larger percentages of minority enrollment were also less likely to offer the more challenging courses. We subdivided the sample into urban, suburban, and rural schools. School size was more important in urban and rural schools, while the percentage of minority enrollment was more important in suburban schools. The percentage of minority enrollment is closely related to socioeconomic status, for which it can be used as a proxy. The data clearly demonstrate that the level of challenge in 8th-grade mathematics courses offered was systematically related to the SES composition of a school.

This is consistent with and helps explain the results discussed in Chapter 4. In many low SES schools, students get less challenging content opportunities in 8th-grade mathematics than do students in the high SES schools (as noted in Chapter 4). By design, the courses that would provide the same opportunities as those for students in the high SES schools are not even offered.

### Who Takes Which Courses?

So far, we have discussed potential opportunities—what is offered in individual schools. The next step is to look at what courses students actually take. Table 5.3 shows enrollment results using the classification of course types used in the previous section. Considering the United States as a whole, each of the six course types can be thought of as a track. The percentages in Table 5.3 estimate how many 8th-grade students were in each track in 1995. The largest percentage—around 60%—of 8th-graders were enrolled in Regular Mathematics. Perhaps the most important point that can be seen in Table 5.3 is that not all students take the same course in 8th grade, a fact that is the result of an explicit policy of creating different middle school tracks. The same is true even as recently as 2011, where around 75% of the schools reported such tracking. However, the percentage of 8th-graders taking Algebra I, as indicated by NAEP results, has risen to around a third.

**Table 5.3. Percentage of U.S. 8th-grade students enrolled in each of the broad course types (by course type).**

| Course Type | Percentage of U.S. 8th-Graders Enrolled in This Course Type |
|---|---|
| Regular | 56.9 |
| Algebra I | 19.7 |
| Pre-algebra | 16.7 |
| Enriched | 3.1 |
| Remedial | 2.8 |
| Geometry | 0.7 |

*Note.* Adapted from "Who Takes What Mathematics and in Which Track? Using TIMSS to Characterize U.S. Students' Eighth Grade Mathematics Learning Opportunities," by L. S. Cogan, W. H. Schmidt, & D. E. Wiley, 2001, *Educational Evaluation and Policy Analysis, 23*(4), p. 327.

## Different Opportunities to Learn in Different Tracks

Table 5.3 shows a relatively small number of students in the enriched, remedial, and geometry tracks. For the next set of results, we reduced the number of tracks to three—regular mathematics, pre-algebra, and algebra. We now examine more directly the differences in content coverage that define these three tracks. Are the differences just in the labels of the tracks and courses? Alternatively, are there different types of topics covered, and do these topics receive different allocations in the relative amount of instructional time spent on them?

We estimated differences across the three tracks in the average amount of time that teachers allocated to the topics to be taught. Factors included differences for whole number arithmetic, fractions, decimals, ratios, and proportions. Teachers in the regular track spent almost a quarter of the year on these topics. Algebra teachers spent only about 10% of their time on them. On the other hand, teachers in the algebra track allocated almost one-third of their time (31%) to covering equations, functions, and slope. Teachers in the regular track spent less than a quarter of their time (21%) on these topics. Slope, functions, and equations are typical mainstays of an algebra course. These differences indicated that there were significant differences across the tracks in covering algebra-related content as a result of the practice of tracking.[8, 9]

Another way to characterize differences in how content is covered among the differing tracks is to use the average international grade level (IGP) associated with the topics that are covered in each track. This index was explained in Chapter 4. Recall from that chapter that the typical U.S. 8th-grade mathematics class has content coverage that centers around 6th or 7th grade on the international index. By contrast, the high-achieving countries' average centered around 9th grade.[10]

The estimated difference between algebra and the other two tracks was one grade level when using the IGP index on the U.S. sample from TIMSS.[11] What may be more surprising was that there was not a significant difference in the difficulty of the content covered (indicated by the IGP index) for regular and pre-algebra classes. The titles given by schools to these different course types suggest that there should be some difference in difficulty, but the difficulty of the content for the two types of courses was essentially the same. There may be ability differences among students that determined into which track they were placed when both courses were available in a school. Even so, students in pre-algebra courses faced mathematics content that was no more challenging than the content faced by those students placed in regular (general) mathematics courses at 8th grade.[12] This analysis of a U.S. national sample shows that there were real differences in learning opportunities afforded to 8th-grade students in different tracks—at least between algebra and the other two tracks.

## TRACKING IN HIGH SCHOOL

Tracking practices do not end with 8th grade, but continue into high school. The practical effect on learning opportunities for different mathematics content is the same. However, there is a difference in terms of the structure involved in high school tracking. Tracking in U.S. high schools has usually been defined by three groups related to future educational and/or vocational plans:

1. university or college preparation track
2. general track
3. vocational track

These three tracks are loosely and inconsistently defined. The first is designed primarily for those students who clearly plan to go on to college. The third track is designed primarily for those who do not plan to go on to college but, rather, intend to pursue vocational training. The general track is the most inconsistently defined. It is mainly for those students who have not made a clear choice for or against going to college or to vocational training.

How these tracks show up in U.S. high schools is not the same among schools, which is hardly surprising, given the extremely loose definitions of these three tracks. The courses included in each track are not necessarily the same for different schools. Even the courses that two students take in the same track in the same high school are not necessarily the same. For example, mathematics courses can and do vary considerably both between and within the tracks.

A more appropriate way to define tracks in high school is by the particular sequence of courses the students take. General labels (vocational, college preparatory) are not very descriptive or helpful, given the large variation within tracks. It seems better to define the tracks by the actual reality of who takes which specific courses and in what sequence. We can identify different groups of these and consider each of them a specific high school track.

As with middle school, high school tracking is possible because of the proliferation of different courses. Using course enrollment data from more than 14,000 seniors in 30 high schools across 18 U.S. school districts, all the different mathematics courses offered by these schools were recorded.[13] No further classification was done. Different course titles were not combined unless there were obvious misspellings or abbreviations that suggested that they were really the same course. Each course title was taken at face value and considered a potentially different course. For example, two course titles in which the word *geometry* appears were not considered the same unless the titles were identical. For instance, Geometry and Formal Geometry (actual course titles found in the data) were not considered the same course.[14]

Of course, it is possible that these two courses represent the same learning opportunities in mathematics. However, given the results discussed in Chapter 4, this was an assumption that we were unwilling to make. Our principle was simple. If schools chose to represent the general content they were teaching in a course (for example, geometry or algebra) by different course titles, then the most likely conclusion is that (at least to some extent) the content was different. If that were not so, then why would they not call the course by its usual designation—Geometry, Algebra I, and so on? The assumption that Geometry and Formal Geometry are the same seems an unduly risky assumption, even though it could be true. We erred on the side of caution and did not make such assumptions.

This examination of mathematics course titles in 30 high schools resulted in 286 different course titles, an unsurprising result given what we learned in Chapter 4. There were 43 course titles dealing with beginning algebra content, 31 dealing with geometry content, 10 dealing with advanced algebra content, and 7 dealing with precalculus content.[15] An array of courses with content considered below that of beginning algebra courses was also represented.[16] The most commonly listed courses were titled Algebra I, Geometry, Algebra II, Precalculus, Integrated Math 1, and Integrated Math 2. Each of the first three courses was taken by more than 6,000 of the students, which represents only about 40% each.[17] These were the courses most typically taken by those in the college preparatory track.

Given the obvious proliferation of courses, tracking in high school can result from two somewhat distinct sources. First, it occurs because there are many different types of courses available. Broadly speaking, there are algebra, geometry, advanced algebra, integrated mathematics, precalculus, calculus, statistics, and various kinds of basic mathematics courses. Which particular broad categories of courses a student takes roughly defines a track, but only at the level of course categories and not in terms of specific courses.

For example, most high school students take at least an algebra and a geometry course. Some add an advanced algebra course. Other tracks might begin with a general mathematics course followed by an algebra and a geometry course. Obviously, where a student starts and how many courses he or she takes would define a relatively small number of sequences or, as we are calling them, a small number of tracks. In this sense, some of the most common tracks would likely include the following:

- basic math, algebra, geometry
- algebra, geometry, advanced algebra
- algebra, geometry, advanced algebra, precalculus
- geometry, advanced algebra, precalculus
- geometry, advanced algebra, precalculus, calculus
- algebra, geometry

- algebra, advanced algebra, geometry
- two, three, or four courses of integrated mathematics

The second defining aspect of tracking derives from the fact that there are often multiple versions of courses in the same category within schools. As our discussion earlier made clear, at least in these 30 schools there were many versions of the same type of course—especially for the categories of algebra and general mathematics.

Although the two sources of differences combine in tracking, it is important to separate them in order to fully understand what is happening. They differ in terms of their policy implications. Each source could be defined, modified, or eliminated by different policy changes. One point remains clear: The combination of these two sources of variation generates a greater chance for differences in learning opportunity than would result from differences only in the categories of courses taken.

We turn now to the number and type of courses offered in each of the 18 districts that contain our 30 high schools to explore this issue further. We focus on the district rather than the school, since this is the level at which curriculum policy is determined and the level at which responsibility for the policies actually implemented lies. Within a district where there is more than one high school, there could be variations in the courses offered in each school as a product of district policy. We believe this source of variability is quite small, so we do not focus on it.

The earlier discussion showed a large variety of courses offered in the 30 high schools in the sample. This variety represented both variation among the 18 districts in which courses were offered and variation in what was offered within each district. Both of these sources contributed to the variability among classrooms discussed in Chapter 4. The variation within a district in courses offered provides the "building blocks" from which tracks are built. Generally, as the number of different course types within a district increases, the likelihood and scope of tracking (the number of distinct tracks) also increases. However, an equally important source of tracking derives from the proliferation of different courses within a general category such as algebra, geometry, and so on. As we discussed earlier, there were a large number of courses in each of these categories among the 30 high schools we studied. Now, we examine this in terms of the 18 districts by looking at the total number of mathematics courses offered in the district and at the number of alternative courses offered within each of the broad content categories.

Figure 5.1 indicates the number of mathematics courses offered in the high schools of each of the 18 districts studied. Since we wish to maintain the privacy of the school districts studied, each is labeled with a letter rather than its name. The number of courses ranges from 10 to 58. If districts were to have one course for each of the broad categories, then there would typically

**Figure 5.1. Number of high school mathematics courses offered by 18 districts studied (30 high schools).**

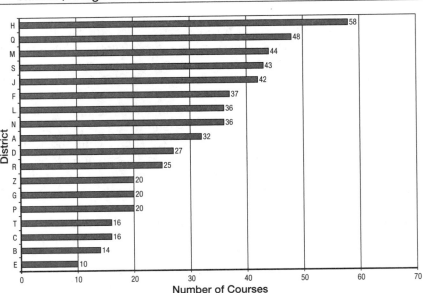

be fewer than 10 courses offered at the high school level. Only one district met that standard (District E, with 10 courses). Other districts had from two to six times as many courses.

Although the number of courses offered was very large for most districts, the notable item in Figure 5.1 is the large difference in the number of courses among the different districts. This variability among districts in the number and types of courses offered suggests large differences among high school seniors in the likely mathematics content they had a chance to learn by the time they finished high school. Students cannot take what is *not* offered. This can be especially limiting for more advanced courses. More than one course needs to be offered within a district to provide for a reasonably small number of tracks and to provide for student ability and interests. Representing the tracks by one course in each category—algebra, geometry, calculus, and so on—can do this. Including several alternative courses within a category only adds to the likely inequalities in learning opportunities. Including so many varieties of courses led to very large variations in content exposure for the 14,000 seniors studied.

## Number of Alternative Tracks

Course requirements for students who are preparing for college are generally more clearly defined and allow for less choice. Unfortunately, as was illustrated in the previous section of this chapter, those students not preparing for college are left with a large variety of courses to choose from. There are few requirements to guide them in course choices. As a result, students who are not in a college preparatory track define their own track by making their choices from the large array of mathematics courses available. In some cases, counselors guide the students' choices; but students do not always heed this guidance. Even the college preparatory track is not the same for all students, although the programs of study for students in this track do have much more in common. A further complication is that there are often several versions of the same type of course—for example, different versions of an Algebra I course—which exacerbates differences in tracks.

We recorded the particular selections of courses and the sequence in which they were taken for each of the 14,000 students. We considered this the track in which they were "placed" either by their own choice or as a result of the advice of their counselors and teachers. Defining tracks in this way would result in few tracks with many students in each in most of the countries taking part in TIMSS. However, since U.S. tracks are defined by wide variations in content coverage relatively unrestricted by district requirements, and a lack of uniformity in what students study, this more individualistic definition of tracks is needed to explore educational inequality in the United States.

One aspect of defining a track (as we are using the term here) is the number of courses taken over the 4 years of high school. Not all students take the same number of courses. This depends somewhat on state requirements for graduation. Some states designate the number of mathematics courses required for graduation; some do not. Figure 5.2 shows the percentage of students in each of 17 districts who take a particular number of courses.[18] One surprise is that in 2005, there was a sizable percentage of students in each of several districts who took only one mathematics course in high school. This percentage reached 25% in one district, but was zero (or virtually zero) in others.

In four of the 17 districts, almost all students took at least four mathematics courses. In the other districts, there was substantial variation in how many courses students took. Several districts had students who took from one to four or more mathematics courses. The number of courses taken varied within most districts.

Combining the different numbers of courses taken and the actual courses taken yielded a very large number of sequences (e.g., *content tracks*) for some districts (Figure 5.3[19]). There were more than 1,500 such sequences over all the districts, for approximately 10 students per track. Aside from the obvious differences among districts, there was tremendous variation within districts in the content coverage implied by these many different sequences.

Students may attend the same high school in the same school district. However, graduates will share little mathematics content. Although we do not suggest that all high school students should take the same mathematics courses, we do believe there ought to be a high degree of overlap across

Figure 5.2. Number of high school mathematics courses taken by high school students in 17 districts.

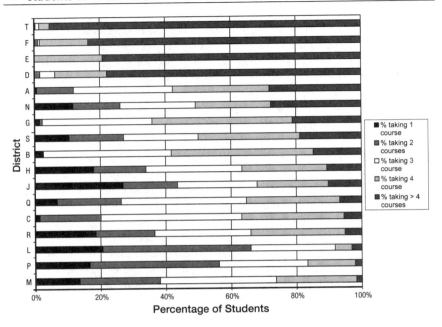

Figure 5.3. Number of mathematics course sequences actually taken by students in 19 districts.

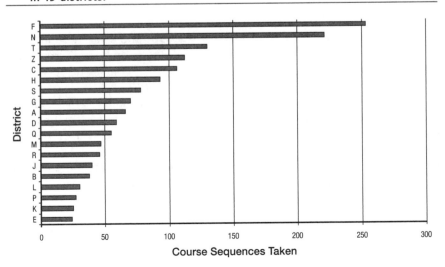

programs for most students and a relatively small number of mathematics tracks. Certainly, this number should be far less than 1,500.

Most students took one of a much smaller number of sequences (tracks). For example, only 14 patterns account for 51% of the students in one district with 253 different patterns among its students. Seventy-three sequences account for 75% of the students in that district. Although this is a large number, it is still less than 253. By contrast, the other 25% of the students in that district took one of 180 patterns. Overall, from 3 to 19 tracks account for 50% or more of the students in all of the districts, with one exception. In that district, 61 tracks or sequences account for 50% of the students. However, this implies that the other half of the students in most districts took a very large number of alternative sequences. Freedom of choice is a wonderful thing, but in this instance allowing too many choices can produce incoherent sequences in which each course does not build effectively on previous courses.

Figure 5.4 indicates that over half of the course-taking patterns were almost completely individualistic. Many sequences had only one student who took that sequence. The most commonly taken tracks among the districts were as follows:

1. Algebra I, Geometry, Algebra II (30%)
2. Algebra I, Geometry, Algebra II, Precalculus (32%)
3. Geometry, Algebra II, Precalculus, Calculus (24%)

**Figure 5.4. Course sequences taken by one or more students in 18 districts.**

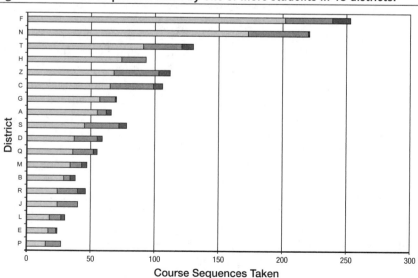

Sequences with 1 student ▪ Sequences with 2–9 students ▪ Sequences with ≥ 10 students

Using broad categories of courses helps reduce the overall number of tracks/sequences. We identified approximately 25 tracks using only the following broad categories—basic mathematics, Algebra I, other Algebra I titles, Geometry, other geometry titles, Algebra II, other Algebra II titles, Precalculus, Calculus, advanced mathematics beyond calculus, Statistics and Probability, and Integrated Mathematics I, II, and III. This simplifies the situation somewhat, although it may oversimplify the ways in which learning opportunities vary in the districts. Even with this simplification, the number of tracks (sequences) is extremely large.

## The Role of Algebra in Tracking

As stated often in this book, mathematics is hierarchical. New content builds on previous content. If earlier content is not learned well, then it is unlikely that later content will be learned satisfactorily. Within this hierarchy, algebra content is an abstraction and generalization of basic arithmetic. It is also an introduction to the more formal aspects of mathematics. As a consequence, the first algebra course plays a pivotal role in building up mathematics learning over the years of schooling and also plays an important role in tracking—in determining the sequence of mathematics studied by each student. When that first algebra course is taken becomes a defining point that shapes the high school track for each student. It will affect how likely it is that a student can effectively pursue various career opportunities. The choice of which first algebra course to take and when to take it conditions all future choices in mathematics through high school and even in college.

Certain courses become very unlikely options. For example, if a student takes Algebra I after 9th grade, it is very unlikely that he or she will take calculus in high school or even in college without extensive remedial work or precalculus courses. Many students have not had a calculus course in high school or are not ready to take the first calculus course immediately in college. There may be one or many courses that they must take in college before they can even begin the study of calculus. Faced with the prospect of additional mathematics study, many students opt for careers and majors that do not require calculus, cutting them off from many college majors and many of the most lucrative career possibilities.

The choice and taking of a first algebra course has a strong effect on the probable path of a student's career. Some students who are "late bloomers" may choose to take the harder and more time-consuming way to learn calculus and get to the major and career they desire. Even so, it will always take them more time, putting them behind many other students in the major and costing more money for additional college courses and semesters. Given the increasing importance of mathematics in many jobs and careers, this seemingly simple choice can have an enormous impact on the future lives of students (Mass Insight, 2004; Metz, 1990; National Academy of Sciences, 2002; The White House, 2004). The impact of this decision is so important that we must ask why such an important decision is left to choice rather than being a requirement for all children, as it is in many countries other than the United States.

It is at this point that tracking in middle schools influences high school course selection, to the detriment of students. In middle school, one of the first important content decisions is made, and it sets much of the rest of mathematics study in motion both before college and beyond. Policymakers and parents need to be aware that such choices, made when a child is only 12 or 13 years old (often under the schools' and counselors' familiar mantra of "doing what is best for your son or daughter"), have extensive consequences. This decision has ramifications for learning opportunities in high school and college. Naturally, it also influences career choices.

Numerous recent reports have indicated that higher-paying jobs demand greater preparation in mathematics. This is true for jobs that do not require a college degree as well as those that do. There is, of course, more to life than a large salary, but it is such an important factor that it should not be determined so early without the student realizing the consequences. In a recent issue of *Business Week*, an article entitled "Math Will Rock Your World" pointed out that jobs not normally thought of as mathematically oriented—such as marketing, design, consulting, food and beverage, police and intelligence, and media and advertising (Baker, 2006)—now require a reasonable understanding of mathematics, including statistics. These jobs do not necessarily require degrees in mathematics, but a familiarity with mathematics is essential to performing them.

Figure 5.5 indicates what students took as their first high school mathematics course for each of the 18 districts in our study. It is striking to note how much the first course varies across the districts. Over 60% of the students in one district took Algebra I at 7th or 8th grade and were taking high school courses beyond Algebra I as their first high school course. This contrasts markedly with another district, where about 60% of the students were taking Algebra I as their first high school course. Still another district had almost 50% of their students taking something below the level of Algebra I as their first course in high school.

In all 18 districts, the majority of students took a first course in algebra either as their first high school course or in middle school. Given this finding, 5% to 45% of the students in these districts will have been left behind in terms of the timelines of the opportunities to learn important mathematics content. This content gap at the beginning of high school makes worse the content gap in 8th grade. Districts often respond by expanding the definition of a first algebra course to include any algebra course, even those that turn out

Figure 5.5. Starting mathematics course level for high school students in 18 districts.

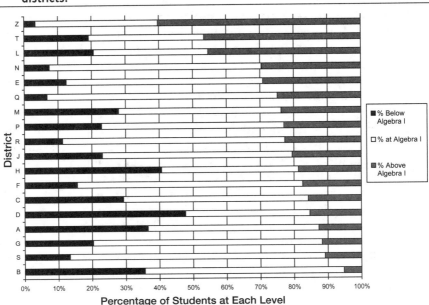

to be veritable phantoms as far as real algebra study goes. As a result, these districts halve the percentage of their students who start their high school course without having taken Algebra I (from almost 48% to 22%). This is a version of the old con artist's shell game. It may appear good on paper, but it will not serve students well in the long run. In this case, legislative pressure distorts the system rather than corrects it.

## The Cumulative Consequences of Content Tracking at 8th Grade

To study this issue, we used longitudinal data from the Longitudinal Study of American Youth (LSAY) that reported the content opportunities for each student as he or she progressed from middle school through high school. The students in this sample were followed from 7th grade through 12th grade.[20]

Figure 5.6 summarizes the cumulative content that was covered for each of five categories of students. The categories were based on when students took their first real algebra course (no further distinctions were available in the data). Eight categories of content were designated, including geometry, algebra (pre-, basic, and advanced), fractions, other arithmetic, data, and calculus.

Students who took their first algebra class earlier benefited by having a higher proportion of their 6-year total mathematics focusing on algebra, geometry, and precalculus. Overall, this proportion varied from over half

**Figure 5.6. Average percentage of each of eight categories of mathematics content taken by five groups of high school students over 6 years of schooling (LSAY data—7th through 12th grade).**

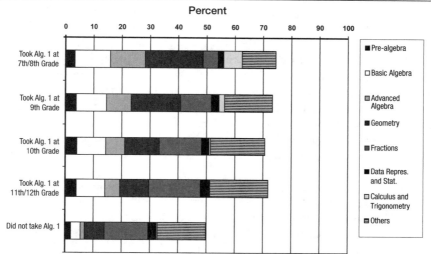

*Note.* The totals do not add up to 100% because, on average, students do not take 6 years of mathematics.

of the content covered being at this advanced level (for students who took algebra at 7th or 8th grade) to around 30% (for those who took algebra in 11th or 12th grade). Most students took algebra in 9th grade. Students who took algebra in the 9th grade had around 10% less coverage of more advanced mathematics than those who took it before 9th grade.

The average total percentage over the 6 years from 7th to 12th grades did not add up to 100% because, on average, students did not take 4 years of high school mathematics. This was true even for those students who took their first algebra course in 7th or 8th grade,[21] which is consistent with the results presented in Figure 5.2.

The dearth of mathematics course-taking by U.S. high school students is likely to change in the near future as many states introduce new requirements for high school graduation that require 3 or 4 years of mathematics. In some cases, the specific types of mathematics that must be taken (most commonly Algebra I, Geometry, and Algebra II) are stipulated, which should eliminate some of the most excessive tracking. Without further regulations, however, the second source of tracking (multiple courses within each of the three course types) will continue to exist and may even multiply as political pressures elevate. It is the intention of the new Common Core State Standards to minimize such variation in content coverage.

## SCIENCE TRACKING IN HIGH SCHOOL

The story for science is very similar to that for mathematics. There are many courses offered in many sequences and these courses and sequences vary greatly among the districts. The variety of courses offered included the standard science courses—Biology I and II, Chemistry, Physics, Geology, Earth Science, and Integrated Science. There were also typical more-advanced courses offered: Chemistry II, Introduction to Astronomy, and Advanced Biology. Among these advanced courses were also the various Advanced Placement (AP) courses, which were typically available in most districts. However, we also found courses with less common titles—Botany, Engineering, Ecology, Bioethics, Anatomy, Genetics, Vertebrate Zoology, and Aquatic Science, among others that are not as widely offered in the various districts.

Beyond these more traditional science courses, there were courses that seem to have been offered in the spirit of providing alternatives to the standard offerings. These included Food Science, General Science, Physical Science, Basic Biology, and BioScience. Both of these latter two biology courses were offered in a district that offered Biology I, Biology II, Advanced Human Biology, College Preparatory Biology, Environmental Biology, General Biology (A and B), Gardening I and II, as well as Advanced Gardening III and IV.

Figure 5.7 shows the number of courses offered in each of the districts. The range was from 7 to 55 different courses, a range similar to that for mathematics. It is hard to imagine how students attending these different districts could be considered to have had equal content exposure. In fact, two of the school districts in close physical proximity to each other offered 20 and 55 courses, respectively. That is, schools in one district offered more than twice as many different courses as the other district offered.

In some of the districts, the different numbers of courses came mainly from the number of advanced courses available. That kind of variation results in students having very different opportunities to advance their interests in science. Some districts offered only the basic courses, and thus, students in those districts were precluded from advanced study comparable to that of students in other districts.

In other cases, the differences came from having more lower-level courses available in addition to the standard ones (i.e., biology, chemistry, and physics). In this situation, the variety of courses offered allows some students to finish high school with courses that are typically middle school offerings, such as physical, life, or earth sciences, or to finish with courses that were scaled-down (one might even say, dumbed down) versions of the standard offerings. This is what is implied by having Biology A and Biology B courses in which the content of Biology I might be spread over 2 years, although

**Figure 5.7. Number of science courses taken by high school students in 16 districts.**

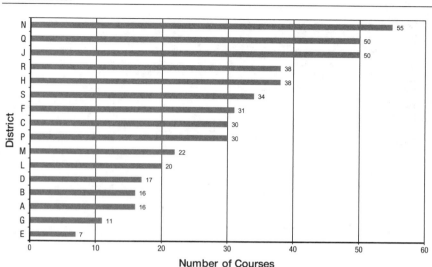

sometimes this represents two one-semester courses. The science area with the greatest number of alternative course offerings was biology. There were 20 different biology courses offered among the 16 districts.[22]

The great variety of science courses leads to many sequences (or tracks). Labeling sequences as tracks is especially relevant in science since, unlike mathematics, science is not so hierarchically organized. Different courses can more easily be put together in different ways to define a reasonable set of science learning opportunities. What we call "school science" is actually derived from at least five formal academic disciplines—biology, chemistry, physics, geology, and astronomy. Many different sequences of content can be organized, leading to very different learning experiences with science content. Each such sequence should really be labeled a different content track, since students who experience these different sequences would have opportunities to learn very different aspects of science.

There were as many as 367 different sequences in one district. Of these, only one student took each of 284 of the sequences (see Figure 5.8). Amazingly, the district with 367 sequences had only 719 students. To account for even 50% of these 719 students required using 47 different sequences. Only 10 of the 367 sequences involved 10 or more students. Surely, this district would be a strong candidate for being one of the "most tracked" schools in the United States. Even the "least tracked" district we examined had 13 different tracks. Figure 5.8 shows that a very small number of tracks (sequences) were needed to account for a majority (50%) of students—in most districts,

**Figure 5.8. Number of science course sequences taken by high school students in 16 districts.**

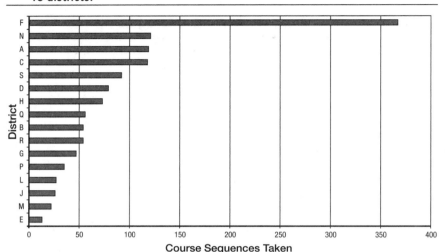

typically two to eight (11 of the 17 districts). For six districts, there were only five or fewer tracks needed to account for a majority of the students.

Biology I seemed to serve the same role for science that Algebra I did for mathematics. Figure 5.9 shows the percentage of students in each district who took Biology I as their first course in high school, varying from 2% to 86%. In one district, virtually all of the students started their high school science studies with courses below Biology I. In another district, almost three-fourths of the students took courses above Biology I as their first high school science course.

Unlike mathematics, there is no one canonical sequence in science dictated by the science content. However, in reality, science does have a dominant sequence that is canonical in practice. In most schools, that sequence is (and long has been) biology, chemistry, and finally physics. This structure is common practice rather than a product of the logic of the disciplines involved. Some scientists and science educators have suggested that, from a scientific point of view, it makes more sense to study physics first rather than last (Lederman, 1996). Figure 5.9 portrays the variability across the 16 districts.

The national data from LSAY show that those students who took Biology I in 9th grade were more likely to take chemistry than other students who took a lower-level course in 9th grade. Of those who took Biology I in 9th grade, 55% went on to take Chemistry. Far fewer of those who took physical, earth, or life sciences in 9th grade went on to take Chemistry. Those students who took Biology I in 9th grade were also more likely to take Physics (Reynolds, 1991; Reynolds & Walberg, 1992).

**Figure 5.9. First science course taken by high school students in 16 districts.**

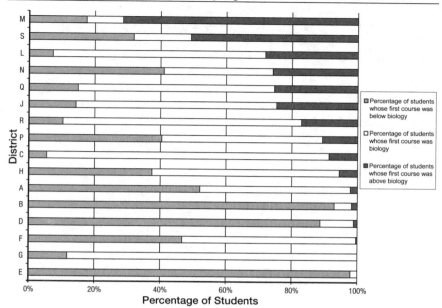

## TRACKING: WHAT WE MIGHT DO

Tracking at middle school clearly produces differences in content coverage, and thus in learning opportunities. This is a structural feature of U.S. schooling. It exacerbates differences in content coverage among students. In high school, inequalities in content coverage are created by a lack of specific course requirements, leading not just to the three tracks generally identified, but also to an excessively large number of content tracks, many of which make little sense from the point of view of the subject matter. The effect is the same whether content tracks are defined as a progression of course categories or by sequences of specific courses. The result is large variations in cumulative content coverage over the 4 years of high school.

Unlike the United States, most developed countries have clearly defined tracks in high school, which vary in number among countries. However, common to all are well-articulated requirements in terms of courses. This stands in marked contrast to the more laissez-faire U.S. approach. In other countries, a track defines a particular set of opportunities. In the United States, a content track only describes a broad category of loosely defined learning opportunities.

In the case of U.S. middle schools, the best means of improving outcomes may be to avoid tracking altogether, as is done in many other high-achieving countries. In many countries other than the United States, the pattern at the middle-school level is one course per grade for all students. Although the situation for high school is not so simple, it is clear that the United States needs a more sensible, limited number of tracks (sequences) that are less arbitrary and that reflect 21st-century economic realities. The United States has long held that children have a right to study what they wish to study in high school and that students have a "right to fail." It seems more reasonable to say that students ought to have a "right to succeed" as well, and to succeed at something that prepares them effectively for the real world they will face beyond school.

# Contributors to Inequality in Content Coverage: The Role of Organizational Structure

For several chapters now, we have explored how learning opportunities in mathematics vary in the U.S. educational system. There are large differences in opportunity to learn (OTL) due to state standards (a situation that will change as the Common Core State Standards are implemented in more than 40 states), district implementation of the standards, and what happens in individual classrooms. These differences in OTL hold true both for topics covered and for how much time is devoted to covering each topic. But as school choice has become more prevalent, including the options of charter and magnet schools, what amount of variation exists across schools? This question takes on added importance given the increasingly central role played by school choice. This chapter examines cross-school variation and places all four sources of variation in a common framework to make clear the relative contribution of each of the organizational structures (schools, districts, and states) to the total variation across all classrooms.

The probability of different learning opportunities across schools likely increases with class stratification. That is, the likelihood of such differences increases as one moves among social classes, especially from upper- and middle-class families to lower-social-class families. In fact, one of the most disturbing aspects of the data presented so far, especially in Chapter 4, is just how different content coverage was for students in high SES classrooms compared with students in low SES classrooms. The question in this chapter is, to what extent do such differences in content coverage reflect neighborhood composition?

## SCHOOL-LEVEL DIFFERENCES

In late 2008, the issue of cross-school variation became more salient for many parents living in Manhattan, in New York City, who had wanted to send their children to private schools and now faced a new reality due to the economic meltdown and the bursting of the real-estate bubble. Many of these parents would now have to send their children to public schools. At this point, parents were made aware that not all public schools are the same. They gathered information, gossip, facts—anything they could learn about the quality of public schools. If they could not send their children to private schools, then they wanted them to go to the public schools with the best reputations. This was often not the neighborhood school that their children had a right to attend.

Suddenly, the fact that public schools vary in nature and quality became a real problem for parents. Many found that the upsurge in enrollments in public schools suddenly meant that their neighborhood schools had waiting lists and were not able to enroll every student from their district even if the students had a legal right to go there. Many parents were furious (Gootman, 2009). After years of having little concern about public schools and their quality, these parents realized the danger of taking public education for granted. For them, the fact that neighborhood schools varied, quite suddenly, became a matter of acute concern.

Neighborhood schools inevitably reflect their neighborhoods. Although busing, magnet and charter schools, and social factors have had an impact on neighborhood schools, the schools are still principally shaped by the neighborhoods in which they are located and from which the majority of their students come. The demographics of the school largely reflect the demographics of the neighborhood. As such, the content covered in a neighborhood school may well be related to these demographics and contribute to cross-school variation. Most children throughout the United States still attend school in their own neighborhoods.

Even though neighborhood schools are part of the district in which they are located, they can also become a part of the fragmented decision-making process concerning curriculum and what content will be covered. A given school may have a principal who takes an active leadership role in setting school-level standards for curriculum and other matters. If the school is large enough to have subject-matter departments (e.g., for mathematics), those departments may be given the power to make decisions about curriculum content and instructional time. In other cases, teachers collectively may make a joint plan for what topics will be taught at which grade levels. They may take into consideration state and district standards but make their own decisions for their school.

Yet one more way in which school-based decisions can influence cross-school variation is that in many U.S. schools, content coverage is not coordinated among teachers but rather is an accumulation of unique decisions made by individual teachers (see the introduction in Chapter 4). Consequently, in many cases, there is really no curriculum for the individual school other than a common textbook. Instead, each teacher makes curriculum decisions for his or her own classes. Viewing all of these separate curriculum plans for all the teachers in a school, we have what serves as the *de facto* curriculum plan or set of standards for that school. Such a *de facto* curriculum often rests at least in part on the textbooks being used in the school, since teachers in the United States, like their counterparts around the world, typically build their curriculum plans around the textbooks they will be using.[1]

In middle and high school, school-level decisions are reflected in the courses that are offered. Middle school grades are typically covered by state standards, and how those state standards are operationalized by the school determines which courses are made available to students. The same principle operates for high schools, although more loosely. In addition, in many states, graduation standards are mandated for high schools. Many of these graduation standards are designated only in terms of course requirements or even just the number of courses required (Achieve, Inc., 2004).

In addition to school-based decisions and the demographics of the student population, another way the SES of a school can have an effect on content coverage is through the teacher hiring process. Schools in higher SES districts can pay teachers more money and, as a result, can hire teachers with deeper subject-matter knowledge. Such schools are also often more attractive places in which to teach. They can attract more-able teachers, although some teachers have such a particular concern for disadvantaged students that they will forego some of their own comfort and financial advantage in order to serve in a lower SES district. The result of all of this is almost sure to be variation among schools in what content is covered and how well. Each of these factors—school-level decision making, demographics, and hiring practices reflecting the SES of the school—introduce differences among schools in what content is covered.

We first explore how the rigor of the mathematics taught varied among the almost 400 elementary and middle schools we studied using the international grade placement (IGP) index used in earlier discussions of rigor in Chapter 4 (see Figure 6.1). These analyses were done with PROM/SE data, as were all analyses presented in this chapter.

The average IGP grade level centered around 5th grade for mathematics content taught in the first five grades and at 6th grade for grades 6 through 8. This is generally consistent with the results concerning classrooms discussed in Chapter 4. As before, this suggests that content may be incoherently presented (too early) in the elementary grades and may be too easy in the later grades of middle school.

What is most remarkable is how much the schools varied in rigor. The middle 90% of schools at most grades varied between 1.5 and 2.5 grade levels in the rigor and demand of the mathematics content presented. This represents a substantial difference in content coverage. For example, at 1st grade, there was over a two-grade difference among various schools. Such initial inequalities in content coverage in the early grades will likely follow

Figure 6.1. Variation among schools in the rigor of content coverage (IGP) in mathematics for grades 1–8.

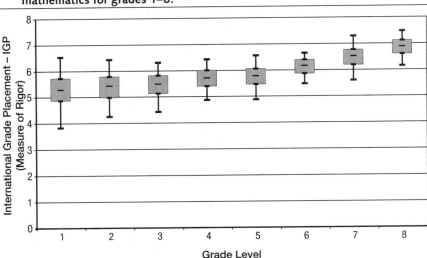

*Note.* For an explanation of how to interpret box and whisker plots, see Figure 2.1.

students into later grades. This could ultimately affect when a student takes algebra, with the aforementioned consequences on later mathematics course-taking (see Chapter 5).

The variation across schools in how much time is allocated to four broad areas of mathematics is presented in Figure 6.2, which shows the percentage of the school year typically allocated to arithmetic, transition arithmetic, algebra, and geometry. These results were created by averaging the time allocated to the topic areas over all the classes at a given grade level within a particular school. That is, the data for each teacher at each grade level in each school were averaged to get a value for the school for that grade level. As Figure 6.2 shows, there was substantial variation at each grade among the schools for each of the four broad topic areas.

Consider the coverage of basic arithmetic in 1st grade (see Figure 6.2), when children are first introduced to the number system. Exploring the idea of number begins at this point, with a focus on the base-ten number system (place value). This concept creates the foundation upon which further understanding and quantitative literacy is based.

The middle 50% of schools devoted from about 12 weeks to over half of their 1st-grade mathematics time to arithmetic, with an average (median) time of about 72 days, or 14 weeks. The middle 90% of schools covered basic arithmetic from between 8 weeks and 23 weeks. A similar pattern held in the 1st through 5th grades. It would be difficult to argue that 1st-grade coverage of basic arithmetic at these two ends of the spectrum could possibly be considered

**Figure 6.2. School-level mathematics content coverage of arithmetic, geometry, transition arithmetic, and algebra: Distributions of number of days of coverage for grades 1–8.**

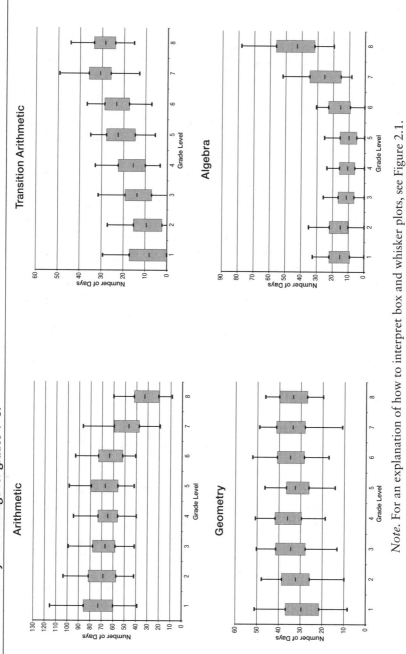

*Note.* For an explanation of how to interpret box and whisker plots, see Figure 2.1.

equal content coverage. The variation across schools in the amount of time allocated narrows in 3rd and 4th grades, with the middle 50% of schools reflecting a difference of about 4 weeks for basic arithmetic. Much like 1st grade, the middle 90% of schools has a very large range in 7th grade.

Primary grades do more than lay the foundation for the number system. They also set the foundation for the understanding of shape in two dimensions and forms in three-dimensional space. These are the beginnings of geometry. In geometry, the differences among schools are less pronounced (see Figure 6.2). For this topic area, the middle 90% differed by 6 weeks from the lowest amount to the highest in 1st grade. First-graders spent an average of about 30 days covering elementary geometry topics.

Instruction in transition arithmetic—including fractions, decimals, percentages, ratios, and proportions—reached its peak in 7th grade (see Figure 6.2). The time spent on this topic in 7th grade varied by almost 8 weeks (the 90%-range). This includes the study of the rational number system and its properties, which is fundamental for the study of algebra, in which fractions are generalized to make up many algebraic expressions. Differences in learning opportunities as large as what Figure 6.2 shows for 7th grade would likely have a major impact on how well prepared students would be for algebra.

Eighth-grade mathematics around the world is all about algebra and, with it, the transition from arithmetic to more formal mathematics such as that studied in high school. In Chapter 5, we discussed the impact of tracking on algebra study. The effects of tracking are not relevant when examining differences at the school level, since if the school is tracked, differences are averaged across the tracks.

Figure 6.2 shows that the variation was extremely large among schools at 8th grade. Some schools—considering together all courses offered—provided only 4 weeks of instruction in the area of algebra. Others spent around half of the year. For the middle 50% of schools, the difference was almost 5 weeks.

## THE ROLE OF STATES, DISTRICTS, SCHOOLS, AND CLASSROOMS RELATED TO INEQUALITIES IN CONTENT COVERAGE

The observed classroom variation as characterized in Chapter 4 (without regard to state, district, or school) estimates the total variation in OTL across all classrooms at a given grade level. This widespread variation makes educational policy issues extremely complex, since there are multiple sources from which such observed differences in content opportunities can arise, including differences between the following:

1. states
2. districts within a state

3. schools within the same district
4. tracks (different courses at the 8th grade or at high school) at the same grade within the same school
5. classrooms at the same grade within the same track and school

The focus of this section is on identifying the proportion of the total classroom variation in OTL that is related to three organizational features of the U.S. system: districts within states, schools within districts, and classrooms within schools. The PROM/SE data, discussed in Chapter 4, provide the most complete data set for examining this issue, but there were only two states from which data were collected and no data were available on tracks, so these features are examined separately—state differences in Chapter 2 and tracking at the end of this chapter using a different set of data.

The classroom—the site at which instruction occurs—is the place where potential inequalities become real inequalities. Why are we examining this variation again? The differences among the hundreds of classrooms studied at each grade level speak directly to differences in what is actually taught. However, these classrooms are in different schools and in different districts. Thus, the large differences among classrooms seen in Chapter 4 can come from different sources. Depending on the source of variation, the policy implications can be quite different.

Districts in each state can interpret state standards so differently in forming their own district standards that classroom differences can result. Further, even in the same district not all schools necessarily focus on topics at a given grade in the same way. Even different classrooms at the same grade in the same school could provide different content coverage (including not teaching them at all). This is the nature of the U.S. educational system as governed by distributed decision making. Differences in what is taught, and for how long, can arise at each of these levels: teacher (classroom), school, and district. This fragmentation will likely continue to be the case, even with the Common Core State Standards, and will be the greatest threat to their successful implementation. The danger is that the Common Core State Standards will simply become the new version of the state standards for those states that have adopted them. Whether they have more influence over districts, schools, and classrooms than has been the case under current NCLB legislation, both because of the national scale of the effort and the attendant support documents being developed, remains to be determined. However, before the impact of the Common Core State Standards can be studied, we can examine the costs of *not* having standards that ensure equality in content coverage.

In what follows, we partition the overall variation among classrooms into each of the parts that might contribute to it—districts within states, schools within districts, and classrooms within schools. Here, we used statistical variance as our measure of overall variation among classrooms. Chapter 4 showed that the basic variability in content coverage was considerable. What we will be doing here is determining what proportion of this variation can be attributed to each level of the educational system.[2]

The results of these analyses are important for educational policy in terms of how variation in opportunities affects American society and how this variability can be reduced. Different policies will be needed to reduce variation, depending on which level contributes more to content inequalities.

Before proceeding with the partitioning of the total classroom variation in IGP (an internationally derived index characterizing the curriculum, as defined in Chapter 4), we first characterize district variation. In Chapters 2 and 3, we described district variation in terms of *intended* coverage for the 60-plus PROM/SE districts. Here, we focus on the *implemented* content coverage, as measured by IGP at the district level. We did this for schools earlier in this chapter and now we do the same for districts. In doing so, we can complete the puzzle and see which of these structural features contributes most to observed classroom variation.

As with schools and classrooms, district coverage of content varied appreciably (Figure 6.3). At each grade, the middle 50% of districts varied roughly from about one-half to three-fourths of a grade level in what they implemented. The differences were even greater for the other half of the

**Figure 6.3. Variation among districts in the rigor of content coverage (IGP) in mathematics for grades 3–8.**

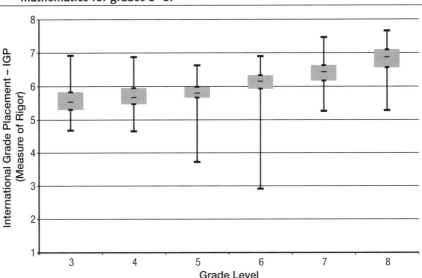

*Note.* For an explanation of how to interpret box and whisker plots, see Figure 2.1.

districts (the lowest fourth and the highest fourth); the differences ranged from two to four grade levels of difference in the content covered at each grade level. For example, 6th-graders in one district experienced a mathematics curriculum that had the rigor and demand of what, according to international standards, is a typical 3rd- or 4th-grade curriculum. In another nearby district located in the same state, 6th-graders experienced what was typical of a 7th-grade curriculum by international standards.

It is interesting to picture a district superintendent trying to explain such differences in content coverage to the parents of the children receiving the less demanding curriculum in mathematics, especially if the parents understood the implications of these differences in content coverage. Such a conversation does not arise very often because parents are usually not aware of such differences. In fact, the school officials themselves frequently do not realize the great differences among districts in terms of content coverage. Very often, they focus on buildings and resources, which have less direct effect on learning mathematics. In that case, the question of why such differences exist is not asked, and if it is asked, there is no reasonable explanation that could be given to parents.

Figure 6.4 shows similar results for science, with differences that are quite substantial, ranging from one to two grade levels. In both mathematics and science, the greatest variation was at 6th grade.

**Figure 6.4. Variation among districts in the rigor of content coverage (IGP) in science for grades 3–8.**

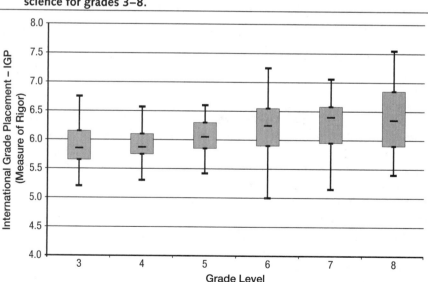

*Note.* For an explanation of how to interpret box and whisker plots, see Figure 2.1.

## VARIATIONS IN IGP DUE TO DIFFERENT ORGANIZATIONAL LEVELS
## OF THE EDUCATIONAL SYSTEM

So far, we have chosen to represent variation in topic coverage graphically through the use of box and whisker plots to represent the distribution of some aspect of content coverage. We did this when we examined differences among classrooms, among schools, among districts, and among states, but for the rest of this chapter we will use the statistical concept of variance. The larger the estimated value for variance, the greater the variability in the IGP index characterizing the rigor of classroom content coverage.

The results of partitioning the variances for IGP for mathematics for each of the first eight grades are summarized in Figure 6.5.[3] Each of the three levels contributed a portion of the total classroom-related variation in IGP. The amount for each level is called its *variance component* and was estimated using standard statistical procedures. The sum of the variance components is equal to the total classroom variance. As such, the estimated variance components can each be expressed as a percentage of the total. The size of the total variance itself, however, varied across grades, implying that at some grades, cross-classroom variability was greater.

### Variation in IGP Across the Elementary Grades

At the later elementary grades, teacher content coverage, as characterized by IGP, was more homogeneous (less variable) than it was for the earlier grades. The total classroom variance for 4th and 5th grades was essentially half of what it was for 1st grade. Remember that the IGP index (used in Chapters 4 and 5) indicates the rigor of content coverage by specifying in an international context the grade level at which most countries focused on the topic. In that sense, a greater value for variance at a particular grade level characterizes the grades at which the variation in this measure of rigor (or demand) is larger.

Why would there be a larger variance for IGP in the earlier grades? One hypothesis is that it could be related to variation in teachers' knowledge of mathematics. Teachers at the earlier grades, who have to teach all school subjects, have less mathematics preparation and, as a result, less mathematics knowledge, on average, but are likely to be more heterogeneous. This might result in differing notions across teachers of which topics are most important. Naturally, teachers would give more time to the topics they believe are important or for which they have had more specific preparation. Since this view would likely vary across mathematically naïve teachers, the result would be greater variation in the time given to different topics, leading to greater variation in IGP. On the other hand, the lower variation at the 5th-grade level might result from teacher specialization, where those with a better

**Figure 6.5. Variation in the rigor of content coverage (IGP) attributable to districts, schools, and teachers for grades 1–8.**

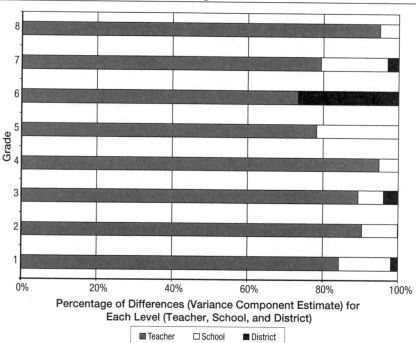

Percentage of Differences (Variance Component Estimate) for
Each Level (Teacher, School, and District)

■ Teacher    □ School    ■ District

background in mathematics teach all the mathematics classes, trading off with another teacher who covers other areas of the curriculum. This might bring about a more common vision of what to teach and, as a result, less variation in time for different mathematics topics. This is not something that can be determined from the data, but it seems to be a reasonable hypothesis to explain what we found.

In spite of the differences in the total amount of variation across the grades, the relative contribution (i.e., the percentage of the variance) for different levels of the system is somewhat consistent across the first five grades. Variation resulting from different time allocations on the part of individual teachers at the classroom level always accounted for the largest percentage of the variance—about 80% to 95%. The remaining, much smaller, percentages come from schools and districts.

After accounting for classroom variation, most of the remaining variation is among schools. The schools' percentage of variance accounted for 5% to 20% of the total. The largest proportion of variation due to differences among schools was at the 5th grade, where about 22% of the total variance was due to differences among schools. Why might there be greater differences in content coverage among schools at 5th grade? In many cases at this grade, schools are trying to prepare students for the transition from the elementary grades to the middle grades, where the nature of the mathematics that students study changes. It is possible that different schools have different visions of what students need as well as their own view of what constitutes greater rigor and a more demanding mathematics curriculum.

Finally, there appears to be little variation among districts that is unique and not the result of what is contributed by district differences in the teaching force, at least through 5th grade. The proportion of the variance attributed to districts is small. The only exception seems to be at 3rd grade, for reasons that are not clear.

## Variation in Instructional Time for Grades 1 Through 5 in Five Areas of Mathematics

Figure 6.6 shows the total variance and the relative contribution of the three levels for the time allocations associated with arithmetic, transition arithmetic, geometry, algebra, and data. The total variance was substantially larger for arithmetic than for the other areas of mathematics at each grade. The variance in instructional time for arithmetic at 1st grade was almost three times larger than it was for geometry, and eight to nine times larger than it was for data representation. By 5th grade, the total variance in arithmetic was less than half. Around 80% of the variance in instructional time was attributed to differences among teachers within schools, with just over 10% of the variance attributed to districts and a little less than another 10% (8%) accounted for by schools within districts. There was also significant variation from district to district in 5th grade. However, the vast majority of differences in instructional time for arithmetic at 5th grade were due to differences from teacher to teacher.

The large amount of variance in instructional time for arithmetic at the early grades is particularly problematic because instructional time allocated in these early grades lays the foundation for work in later grades. Put another way, this is where students are introduced to number and its basic properties, including an understanding of the base-ten system and the associated basic algorithms, which is the foundation for everything that follows. As a result, differences in content coverage related to number can only foster inequalities that are not only likely to grow in magnitude over time but which could be difficult to eliminate in the subsequent grades, even under the best of conditions. The decisions of individual teachers clearly dominate how time is allocated to instruction in the early grades, and as a result, the variation in those choices is a major source of the large inequalities characterized in Chapter 4.

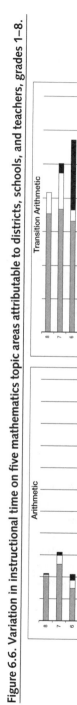

Figure 6.6. Variation in instructional time on five mathematics topic areas attributable to districts, schools, and teachers, grades 1–8.

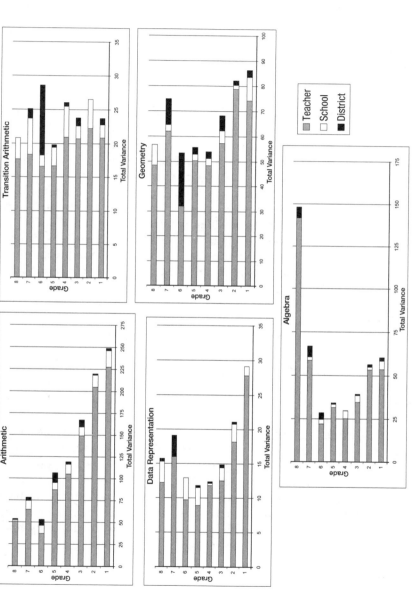

## Variation in IGP for the Middle Grades (6–8)

Figure 6.5 shows middle school results that are consistent with the results from the elementary grades. The total variation (in the IGP index) and the contribution of teachers to variation is about the same in middle school as it was for 4th and 5th grades. Differences due to teachers accounted for the largest percentage of the variation, representing about 75% to 90% of the total variance. At 8th grade, the relative contribution of differences due to teachers was among the highest, about 95%.

The largest proportion of variance in IGP that was attributed to differences across districts was just over one-fourth at 6th grade (27%). At 7th grade, the largest proportion of variation beyond the more than three-fourths (79%) attributed to teachers was that related to schools (within districts), whose proportion was almost a fifth of the variance (18%).

At 6th grade, students in many districts move from elementary school to middle school, where they encounter classes that are centered around particular subjects and taught by different instructors. In mathematics, these middle school classes were likely to be taught by teachers who are better prepared in mathematics (see Chapter 7). It was at this grade that the largest variation among districts took place. Further, 6th grade is the point in school mathematics in which the curriculum moves from arithmetic to the more formal aspects of mathematics. Study of whole number and fraction arithmetic merges with studies of the rational number system, a system that includes whole numbers, fractions, and negative numbers and views all of the numbers from a more mathematically sophisticated point of view. For the first time, the fundamental ideas of the various properties of the number system are studied. Basic algebra is also introduced. To put it another way, 6th grade is critical because it is there that school becomes more formal and is segregated into separate subject matters (often taught by specialist teachers) and, at the same time, the mathematics studied becomes more formal and begins to build the bridge to algebra and more abstract mathematics.

Yet, it is exactly in 6th grade that we find that a substantial proportion of the variance in the rigor of the mathematics is related to the district level. The implication is that district policies likely play an important role in creating such differences in content coverage. That variation is likely impacted by differences in district curriculum standards, textbook adoptions, and the subject-matter knowledge of the districts' 6th-grade teachers.

## Variation in Instructional Time for Five Areas of Mathematics

Examining the variation in each of the five broad areas—arithmetic, transition arithmetic, geometry, algebra, and data representation—suggests some important differences in topic coverage at the middle grades. For arithmetic, the total variance among all teachers in the time they allocated to covering arithmetic topics is smaller than it was in 1st through 5th grades. In fact, at 6th grade and 8th grade, the variance is only about half as large as it was in 5th grade.

The general pattern observed for elementary teachers continued into middle school. Most of the variation in time allocated was at the classroom level within schools, about 70% to 95% across the broad areas. That is, the differences in content coverage defined by the amount of instructional time came mainly from differences among teachers teaching at the same grade in the same school. These results suggest that 8th-grade children living in the same neighborhood (and thus, most likely of similar SES backgrounds) and attending the same school are likely to experience different amounts of instructional time allocated to the coverage of arithmetic.

As for 5th grade, a sizable part of the total variance in arithmetic (about 13%) was accounted for by differences among districts. This could reflect district standards, particular textbooks used, or general policies and practices. The district component of the variance was statistically significant at each of 1st through 6th grades.[4]

District differences also played a major role in variance at 6th grade for transition arithmetic. The overall variance in this topic was the largest of any grade. A large proportion of that variance, over one-third (36%), was attributed to differences among districts. We should recall that this is the mathematics topic with the heaviest focus during 6th grade. It includes fractions, decimals, proportions, ratios, negative numbers, and the rational number system, including more formally its properties. The variation in this area accounted for by differences among schools in the same districts was also comparatively large (almost 6%). The proportion of the variation due to schools within districts, together with the proportion due to differences among districts within states, accounted for over 40% (42%) of the variance in transition arithmetic. Apparently, at 6th grade, there are major school and district practices and policies that influence the allocation of instructional time to transition arithmetic. To create greater equality in content opportunity at 6th grade, it is critical to understand the practices and policies that create such differences. These results are consistent with those described for 6th grade based on the IGP index. The relative amount of variance related to differences among districts at 7th and 8th grades was much less. However, the proportion associated with schools within districts was larger (15% to 21%).

Similar to transition arithmetic, at 7th and 8th grades the variance for data that was attributed to teachers ranged from 75% to 84%. In general, more of the variance was due to school and district levels. The differences at 5th, 6th, and 8th grades for schools accounted for about 20% of the variance, while at 7th grade more could be attributed to differences among districts (over 16%).

In geometry, the largest overall amount of variance was found at 1st, 2nd, and 7th grades. As discussed earlier, the variation was dominated by differences due to classrooms within schools at 1st and 2nd grade. This could be related to differences in the knowledge of the teachers. In 7th grade, there were significant differences among districts.[5] Those district-level differences were largest at 6th grade, where just under 40% of the variance could be accounted for by differences among districts.[6]

Finally, we examined differences in time given to algebra topics. These differences are the focus of 7th- and 8th-grade mathematics around the world and increasingly in the United States. District-level differences were statistically significant at all three middle school grades. In fact, they failed to be significant at only one grade, the 5th grade. The relative contribution of district policies and practices ranged from around 5% to 15%, with the largest proportion at 6th grade (14%). At 8th grade, the dominant source of variation was classrooms within schools. This is most likely explained by tracking, which is discussed later in this chapter.

## VARIATION FOR SPECIFIC TOPICS

The previous sections looked at five broad categories of topics (such as algebra) for both the elementary and middle grades. In this section, we examine the specific topics that are essential at the elementary and middle school grades (e.g., fractions and linear equations). We also examine other topics that provide the deeper understanding of mathematics that goes beyond arithmetic and simple calculation to build a foundation for quantitative reasoning (properties of fractions and decimals, negative integers, and the rational number system).

Variation for fractions in the first five grades was very large. We have already noticed such large variation in the broader area of transition arithmetic, which includes fractions. Most of this variation for fractions came from differences among teachers. A significant proportion also came from differences among school districts (from 5% to 10% of the variance).[7] There were similar results for the topic of properties of fractions and decimals, with differences among districts ranging from 8% to 31% of the variance. That is, there were considerable differences among teachers and among districts for these topics that help to provide a deeper understanding in mathematics. As a result, depending on the teachers they had in 1st through 5th grades and the districts in which they attended school, children would receive very different preparation related to a deeper understanding of the mathematics they had studied.[8]

What about other specific topics? Most of the variance—80% to 90%—was related to differences among teachers in how they allocated their instructional time. Very little of the variance was related to differences among schools within districts or variation from district to district within a state. These results suggest that at the elementary grades, most of the variation among classrooms (discussed in Chapter 4) was due to differences in how individual teachers allocated their instructional time across topics—a regrettable outcome, since at these grades teachers are typically not well prepared in mathematics (see Chapter 7). More district or school guidance is badly needed to help these teachers, but it is generally not provided.

Not all variation in the first five grades was due to differences among teachers. For certain key topics—fractions and their properties—there was substantial variation due to districts and their policies. Most likely, this was due to district curriculum standards or the particular textbook series adopted by different districts. Fractions, which were central in these elementary grades, play a significant role in the development of the mathematics leading to algebra. That makes these differences for fractions among districts an especially significant source of different content coverage for students in the elementary grades.

This pattern continues after the first five grades and for the study of number systems including rational numbers, a topic that helps students understand the nature of much mathematics. Here again, there were significant differences among districts and schools—around 10% of the variance each at both 6th and 7th grades.[9] For the topic of fractions and decimals at the middle grades, differences due to districts and schools accounted for a significant proportion of the overall variation among classrooms in how much instructional time was allocated to this topic. Sixth grade is the place in the mathematics curriculum where this topic is typically a focus. At this grade, over 10% (11%) of the variance is attributable to differences among schools, and more than an additional 10% (13%) came from differences among districts.[10] By 8th grade, even more variance (17%) was due to differences among schools, while a smaller percentage was due to differences among districts. Similar results were found for the three topics of proportionality, functions, and linear equations. A substantial proportion of the total variance for each topic was related to differences among districts. This proportion was generally around 15% (ranging from 14% to 18% among the three topics).[11] Once again, the importance of district and school curriculum policies and practices at 6th grade surfaces for critical middle school mathematics topics, suggesting that districts are an important contributor when it comes to creating inequalities at a critical juncture in the educational experiences of U.S. children. This result holds true even after accounting for the differences related to classrooms and teachers.

## THE ROLE OF TRACKING

The results for 8th grade are particularly interesting. The greatest amount of variation was among classrooms at that grade, indicating that almost all of the total variance in how the mathematics curriculum was implemented at 8th grade was accounted for by differences among classrooms.

U.S. schools practice tracking at 8th grade, as discussed in Chapter 5. Tracking places children in the same school into different courses, which in the previous analyses would be part of the variance component related to classrooms within schools. Tracking contributes to differences among classrooms in the same school in terms of what mathematics content is covered. With tracking, different courses (and, thus, different classrooms in the same school) cover different content. This is especially true for Algebra I courses taught at 8th grade, compared with more general mathematics courses. Those differences would show up as variation due to classrooms in the analyses of this chapter.[12]

How can we tell how much of the variation in learning opportunities resulted from tracking rather than the more general variation among classrooms within schools? We used a different set of data—the U.S. TIMSS results—to disentangle these two factors.[13] These data were representative of U.S. 8th-grade classrooms. We used these data to derive components of the total variance for school, for track within school, and for classrooms within tracks and schools. That is, we identified differences for tracks in content rigor (using the IGP index) that were distinct from differences among classrooms within tracks purporting to teach the same course. The tracks were characterized either as Algebra I, Pre-algebra, or Regular Mathematics (regardless of the actual names of the courses in individual schools, which showed a variety of variations on these names—see Chapter 5) (Schmidt, Cogan, Houang, & Wiley, 2008).

One-fourth of the total variance was due to differences among schools. Another 40% was due to differences among tracks within those schools. The remainder (35%) was due to classes within tracks in those schools with tracking.[14] These results were based on a national sample without specifying the district level as a source of differences. They suggest that, among schools, about half of the class (teacher) variation could be attributed to differences in content coverage across the three tracks and almost the same proportion to differences among teachers. The variation among schools also included the variation among districts and thus represented both of these two sources of variation (about one-fourth of the variation taken together).[15]

Clearly, there was classroom or teacher variation in the middle school grades and, more specifically, in the 8th grade. Whatever the details of differences in how content was covered due to tracking, that single practice accounted for as much as half of the differences among classrooms in mathematics instruction at the 8th grade.

## IMPLICATIONS RELATED TO INEQUALITIES IN CONTENT COVERAGE

The findings about variation in content and instructional time discussed in this chapter involved statistical subtleties that are somewhat tricky to interpret. We try to summarize and simplify the results here. Figure 6.3 suggests that there were large differences among districts in the coverage of mathematics content. The results have real implications for students who attend school in the different districts. What is actually covered and for how much time varies among districts and produces very different learning opportunities for students.

However, the variance component analyses suggest that the large differences among districts are not primarily related to district curriculum policies. They result from the same type of classroom variation that exists within districts and schools, only now manifesting itself in classrooms across districts.[16] In other words, the district-level differences in content coverage were primarily related to differences among districts in the content coverage of the particular teachers they had on staff. The variation that can be attributed to differences among classrooms (teachers) within schools is so large that most of the variation among districts was largely due to differences created by teacher decisions about content coverage, rather than by district policy or practice. The same can be said about differences among schools. A significant contribution to differences among districts that could be attributed to district policies and practices (including the definitions of curriculum) were seen only at 3rd and 6th grades.

These findings, however, were only in terms of a general index for content coverage that characterized rigor (IGP). When we examined specific differences in content coverage for the five broad areas of mathematics or for individual topics, much more of the total variation occurred at other levels in the educational system such as schools and districts; however, the dominant source of variation remained at the classroom level, reflecting teacher content coverage decisions. These differences varied by the area of mathematics involved. For arithmetic, the overall variation in how instruction was implemented (e.g., instructional time) was largest in 1st through 5th grades while, relatively speaking, 5th and 6th grades had the largest proportion that was related to differences among districts. The greatest district-level impact on topic coverage by far—and consistent with the IGP results—was at 6th grade. This was true for all areas of mathematics other than data and statistics. For transition arithmetic and for geometry, that contribution was about one-third of the total variation.

Previous chapters have documented large differences in content coverage among classrooms, schools, and districts—differences that are so large that it makes it implausible to assert that all children receive equivalent learning opportunities in mathematics. If this is the inevitable consequence of maintaining the tradition of local (district) control of the curriculum as well as teacher autonomy with respect to what is taught, we as a nation are paying an exceptionally high price for the sake of preserving those traditions. More precisely, our children are the ones paying that high price. Parents and policymakers should be made aware that the cost of sustaining the tradition of local control of the curriculum is diminished prospects for an entire generation of American schoolchildren.

The analysis in this chapter implies that the greatest source of difference (variation) in what content is covered is due to teachers, which topics they choose, and how much instructional time they allocate to those topics. Classroom instructional time is the major resource that schools have for influencing student learning. How it is managed and allocated is perhaps the most critical decision made in schools. This important decision seems to have become the domain of individual teachers. Since these teachers vary greatly in mathematics knowledge, it is not surprising to find large variation in which topics are emphasized and for how long—that is, in how the mathematics curriculum is implemented in real classrooms regardless of the best intentions, policies, and plans that might have been stipulated at levels above individual teachers.

Can this practice be justified? Should such content decisions be left to individual teachers, especially in the early grades where (as will be discussed in the next chapter) the level of preparation in and comfort with mathematics is not high for most teachers? Should these decisions be made at the district level, the state level, or even the national level, in light of the Common Core State Standards, in order to reduce differences across classrooms and schools within each district? These are important policy questions for those responsible for U.S. schools. They are also important questions for which parents should be holding their children's school districts accountable. However, the average parent is unlikely to know how large and how random the differences that currently exist in U.S. schools are.

These practices fundamentally and arbitrarily compromise children's futures in significant ways. These practices seem impossible to defend as reasonable policy for how schools should be run. It also seems impossible to defend the practice of tracking, which accounts for about half of the variation among classrooms at the 8th grade. Are we as a nation so sure of placing children in appropriate tracks and courses by 8th grade that we can afford to limit their future opportunities as drastically as this practice does? Are we so sure that children by 8th grade have reached their full potential so clearly that they can be categorized and, as a result, have their future opportunities limited by what they take in 8th grade?

These same data indicate that the total variation among classrooms in the rigor of how mathematics content is covered nearly doubles in schools that practice tracking compared with those that do not. Tracking simply generates even more differences in content coverage. How can the nation even speak of No Child Left Behind in schools that practice tracking that produces such future-defining differences at such an early age? Teachers, principals, school superintendents, and school board members may see their policies with respect to tracking in practical, harmless terms. Yet the consequences of such policies are in no way harmless. Rather, what we are experiencing is the hidden destruction of the hopes of millions of children, destruction that is no less real or acceptable for being hidden.[17]

# Part II

# FACTORS THAT SHAPE CONTENT COVERAGE AND INCREASE INEQUALITY

## CHAPTER 7

# The Influence of Teachers on Opportunities to Learn

One thing that most of us remember best about school is our teachers. Thus, when solutions are proposed for reforming American schools in response to critical reports or disappointing test results, teachers are always among the first to be singled out. Proposals often turn first to improving the teaching force by focusing on higher quality. For example, in the NCLB era, considerable emphasis has been placed on a "highly qualified" teaching force. Districts must certify what percentage of their teachers is highly qualified. However, the states and school districts define what they consider "highly qualified," resulting in a great deal of ambiguity.

What does it mean to be a highly qualified teacher? The definition of a high-quality mathematics teacher has never been standardized. Therefore, although improving the quality of teachers and teaching is a common cry when we seek to improve schools, there is little agreement and scant empirical evidence that indicates what characteristics define a high-quality mathematics teacher. Even an obvious definition, such as a knowledge of mathematics, is problematic, since there is generally no agreement as to what specific mathematics knowledge is needed.

Some scholars have focused on creating content standards for teacher quality (Leithwood, Edge, & Jantzi, 1999); others have introduced the concept of teacher competence, defined in terms of the professional tasks, such as selecting and sequencing the content of instruction, that teachers are expected to be able to carry out (Blömeke, 2005; Bromme, 1992; Weinert, 1999, 2001). This approach suggests that teachers need professional knowledge and beliefs in order to accomplish such tasks. The literature identifies two types of knowledge that are clearly related to providing opportunities to learn: mathematics content knowledge and pedagogical content knowledge (Baumert & Kunter, 2006; Blömeke, 2002, 2005; Shulman, 1985).

For mathematics, recent empirical work has advanced our understanding of what mathematics knowledge is necessary for teaching mathematics (Ball & Bass, 2000; Ball, Hill, & Bass, 2005; Hill & Ball, 2004; Hill, Rowan, & Ball, 2005). The rest of this chapter lays out how this knowledge—in particular, mathematics content knowledge—is related to inequalities in content coverage, and provides data related to teacher content knowledge for a sample of teachers. Teacher content knowledge influences the quality of content coverage in two ways: first, in teachers' decisions regarding coverage of particular mathematics topics in the proper sequence and the proper depth; and second, in their ability to explain those topics to students.

Teachers are critical to the quality of instruction and schooling in general, and a great deal could be (and has been) written about this topic. In this chapter, we have a more modest goal. Our chief concern is with learning opportunities and the factors that help shape them, especially those factors that contribute to inequalities in content coverage. As a result, we limit our consideration of this important issue to the ways in which teachers have an influence on content coverage.

As discussed in Chapter 4, under the U.S. shared decision-making approach to determining what is to be taught in classrooms, and the practice of teacher autonomy, it is the teacher who becomes the *de facto* broker of content coverage. It is in the classroom that what content is actually covered is finally realized through the decisions teachers make about *which* topics to cover, *how long* to spend on each topic, and in *what sequence* to cover topics.

The result of this teacher content decision making—virtually unique to the U.S. educational system in its magnitude—was discussed in Chapter 4 when we considered variation in content coverage. In addition, besides the way they influence the coverage of content, teachers also influence the nature or quality of students' learning opportunities through their own content and pedagogical knowledge. High-quality teachers must have many different sorts of knowledge, including their knowledge of the pedagogical strategies related to the teaching of particular topics, their understanding of the cultural context in which their students find themselves, and their understanding of classroom management and how to motivate students.

In the case of mathematics, teacher quality also involves teachers' knowledge of mathematics as an academic or formal discipline and of the mathematics unique to the curriculum at the grade levels they teach. In combination, these types of knowledge define a teacher's professional competencies. Such knowledge is influenced by university preparation and teaching experience (Darling-Hammond, 1999; Rice, 2003; Whitehurst, 2002). As a result, it varies greatly among teachers.

A recent international study of teacher preparation (Teacher Education and Development Study [TEDS]) found substantial variation among U.S. graduating future teachers in their level of the relevant mathematics and pedagogical knowledge. The study suggests possible hypotheses as to why such large variation exists (Center for Research in Mathematics and Science

Education, 2010; Schmidt, Cogan, & Houang, 2011; Schmidt, Houang, & Cogan, 2011; for a related study see Schmidt, Blömeke et al., 2011).

Consequently, the variation in students' opportunities to learn may be greater because of differences in what their teachers understand about mathematics and differences in how they teach it. These differences may exacerbate the OTL variation we have already identified. We propose that there are two ways that teachers influence OTL. First, under the shared decision-making model by which schools operate in the United States, teacher choices influence content coverage. In general, teachers choose which topics they will teach, in what order, and for how long—regardless of state or district standards, as the results of Chapter 6 clearly indicate (as do the results of a series of studies we referred to in Chapter 4). The quality of those choices is one key aspect of teacher quality.

Second, teachers influence OTL by the quality, clarity, and depth of the learning experiences they create for the content being covered. The same content presented by two different teachers is not necessarily offered with the same clarity and depth. Consequently, the impact of the opportunity on student learning might well differ in the two situations. In that sense, the depth of knowledge and understandings that influence the quality of OTL also become a defining aspect of teacher quality.

Teacher quality, as related to OTL, can therefore be different for different subject matters (e.g., mathematics versus science) and, more specifically, different depending on the particular topic taught within mathematics. Teachers' depth and breadth of knowledge about mathematics as a discipline influences the choices they make when it comes to which topics to teach, in what sequence, and to what depth. For particular topics in school mathematics, teachers exert influence through their depth of knowledge of advanced mathematics specific to the conceptual underpinnings of those school-based topics (for example, fractions as a part of the rational number system).

Due to restrictions on the data we were able to collect, we address mathematics content knowledge in the second sense—as it relates to specific topics.[1] However, we believe that the broader, more general knowledge of mathematics may actually have a greater influence on OTL in the United States, since content decision making in the United States often falls to the individual teacher. In other educational systems, the content to be taught is typically well defined by the system itself through standards and course syllabi, and not by individual teachers (Schmidt et al., 2001). In those few places in the United States where curriculum is more centralized, specific knowledge may be the dominant influence on OTL through its influence on the quality of the instructional experience. We can only offer this as a hypothesis. It will also be important to see what impact the Common Core State Standards have in this regard.

## THE MATHEMATICS CONTENT KNOWLEDGE THAT
## TEACHERS SHOULD HAVE

Recently, considerable emphasis has been placed by the educational community on the knowledge that teachers should possess both in terms of the formal discipline of mathematics and in terms of the types of advanced mathematics related to the specific topics in a school's curriculum (Parker & Baldridge, 2004, 2008; Wu, 2011). The research suggests important differences in the knowledge expected of primary and secondary school teachers.

### Primary School Teachers

Data from the international TEDS study suggest that there are no common standards among U.S. teacher preparation institutions as to the types of mathematics knowledge necessary for primary school teachers (Center for Research in Mathematics and Science Education, 2010; Schmidt, Cogan, Houang, & McKnight, 2011; Schmidt, Cogan, & Houang, 2011; Schmidt, Houang, & Cogan, 2011; Schmidt, Houang, & Cogan, in press). This lack of standards resulted in substantial variation in the type and amount of coursework required by U.S. teacher preparation institutions. On average, about one-third of the teacher preparation coursework was in mathematics content. The general wisdom in the profession is that this typically should include content up through college algebra and introductory statistics and usually some geometry (often no more than what is provided by a high school geometry course). However, data from TEDS indicated that across all sampled U.S. elementary teachers, about half took a precalculus course, but only about one-fourth went on to take the regular calculus courses. Around half also took a linear algebra course (Schmidt, Houang, & Cogan, in press).

In many countries, the secondary school mathematics requirements for students who want to enter the university to become primary school teachers includes 4 years of mathematics, often including calculus topics. It has also been estimated from data collected in TIMSS that U.S. students graduate from high school 2 or more years behind students from other countries in the mathematics they have studied (Schmidt et al., 1999). As a result, U.S. students who graduate from high school and go on to become primary school teachers will likely have had a weaker pre-college preparation in comparison with those in other countries. Further, even with the type of strong secondary school preparation in mathematics just described, the students from other countries take additional mathematics courses at the university—around one-third of their teacher preparation coursework, as was the case in the United States.[2]

## Middle School Teachers

The general wisdom for middle school teachers is that their mathematics knowledge should be more extensive and have more depth than that of primary school teachers. It is often considered desirable for middle school mathematics teachers to have a college major in mathematics. As was the case with elementary teachers, TEDS results portrayed considerable variation in the preparation of teachers at this level in the United States. Some institutions required preparation leading to a mathematics major, some leading to a mathematics minor, and for others preparation similar to that of primary teachers. TEDS, as well as a small but more intensive study of teacher preparation—Mathematics Teaching in the 21st century (Schmidt, Blömeke et al., 2011), suggested that middle school teacher preparation in many of the countries studied includes what in the United States would be considered a mathematics major, including calculus and advanced topics such as abstract algebra and analysis (Schmidt, Houang, & Cogan, 2011). In the top-achieving countries in TEDS, half of the teacher preparation coursework was taken in mathematics, but not so in the United States (Schmidt, Houang, & Cogan, 2011). High school mathematics teacher preparation typically requires a major in mathematics, which is the case in virtually all countries, including the United States.

In this chapter, we examine the knowledge and background of teachers in mathematics and how it varies. Research indicates that, whatever teacher quality is in general, it is not evenly distributed among schools or school districts. U.S. teachers have choices as to where to work. The data indicate that these choices lead more capable teachers to choose to teach in districts with higher-income parents and higher-achieving students (Imazeki, 2005; Ingersoll & May, 2010; Lankford, Loeb, & Wyckoff, 2002; Peske & Haycock, 2006; Scafidi, Sjoquist, & Stinebrickner, 2007). In effect, students from low-income families tend to be less likely to have a higher-quality teacher, which likely influences content coverage.

## WHAT TEACHERS TELL US ABOUT THEIR
## KNOWLEDGE OF MATHEMATICS

We approached the question of teacher knowledge of specific mathematics content indirectly, by asking a sample of more than 4,000 teachers from the PROM/SE project to respond to the question, "How well prepared academically do you feel you are—that is, you feel you have the necessary disciplinary coursework and understanding—to teach each of the following?" We asked this question for multiple mathematics topics. The list of topics varied for teachers in primary and teachers in middle and secondary school combined

(PROM/SE, 2006). By relying on teachers' reports of their own feelings of adequate preparation, we only get at their knowledge indirectly. Fortunately, this approach is sufficient to demonstrate how much variation there is in teachers' content-specific knowledge, or at least in their feelings of adequate preparation. Furthermore, the candor of the results suggests a degree of face validity and, hence, integrity in the responses. The overall tenor of the responses is very consistent with other data on the issue, some of which suggest that the pattern reported here might be a best-case scenario (PROM/SE, 2006).[3] All results reported in this chapter are based on the PROM/SE data.

## Primary Teachers (1st Through 3rd Grades)

Primary teachers felt academically prepared to teach only the topics they taught to their students. Even for those topics, about one-fourth to one-half of the teachers surveyed reported that they did not feel well prepared. The teachers we surveyed were from the 60 PROM/SE districts located in Michigan and Ohio whose data were reported in other chapters.

Is it reasonable for teachers to focus only on the topics that they will teach? However reasonable such a position may appear, many of the more advanced topics for which teachers did not feel well prepared provide the mathematics background necessary to be truly well prepared to teach the more elementary topics at their grade level. To define a qualified teaching force, we adopted a criterion of 75% of teachers feeling well prepared to teach a given topic. We found that, over all sampled teachers, only *two* mathematics topics met this criterion: the meaning of whole numbers, including place value and operations with whole numbers.

Ideally, 100% of the teachers should feel well qualified to teach a topic. There were no topics that met this criterion. We used the 75% criterion in hopes that it would be large enough so that, within a school district, there would be a sufficient base of teachers to serve as a resource for all teachers. In particular, this would include the teachers who felt themselves less well prepared. Reaching this critical mass in a district might provide a strong message to all teachers that would have the effect of setting the norm for what is expected of them.

What happens if we lower the criterion to at least 50% of the teachers reporting that they are well prepared to teach a particular mathematics topic? In this case, eight additional topics met this standard. These topics are fractions, decimals, the relationship of fractions and decimals to each other, estimation, measurement units, geometry, handling data, and perimeter, area, and volume. Table 7.1 presents the percentages of teachers at various grade levels who felt well prepared to teach each of 28 mathematics topics. This table allows us to judge how much the criterion would have to be lowered to include all desired mathematics topics.

**Table 7.1. Percentage of teachers who indicated that they are academically "very well" prepared to teach each topic.**

| Elementary Topics | Grades 1–3 | Grades 4–5 |
|---|---|---|
| Whole Number Meaning | 83 | 84 |
| Operations & Properties | 77 | 78 |
| Fractions | 63 | 75 |
| Decimals | 44 | 64 |
| Relation of Fractions & Decimals | 41 | 62 |
| Percentages | 37 | 55 |
| Properties of Fractions & Decimals | 31 | 45 |
| Number Sets & Concepts | 35 | 38 |
| Other Number Topics | 16 | 17 |
| Number Theory | 19 | 29 |
| Estimation & Number Sense | 54 | 63 |
| Measurement Units | 60 | 59 |
| Perimeter, Area, & Volume | 51 | 69 |
| Estimation & Measurement Errors | 33 | 38 |
| Geometry Basics | 49 | 62 |
| 2-D Figures | 34 | 44 |
| 3-D Geometry | 19 | 22 |
| Geometric Transformations | 20 | 27 |
| Congruence & Similarity | 39 | 55 |
| Proportionality Concepts | 13 | 22 |
| Proportionality Problems | 26 | 31 |
| Slope | 7 | 5 |
| Patterns, Relations, & Functions | 34 | 30 |
| Linear Equations | 15 | 15 |
| Other Equations & Inequalities | 13 | 12 |
| Representing & Interpreting Data | 45 | 57 |
| Probability & Uncertainty | 27 | 32 |
| Sets & Logic | 11 | 9 |

| Middle & High School Topics | Grades 6–8 | Grades 9–12 |
|---|---|---|
| Negative, Rational, & Real Numbers | 65 | 94 |
| Number Bases | 27 | 62 |
| Exponents, Roots, & Radicals | 54 | 91 |
| Complex Numbers | 20 | 73 |
| Number Theory | 54 | 65 |
| Coordinates & Lines | 73 | 95 |
| Polygons & Circles | 58 | 82 |
| 3-D Geometry | 30 | 50 |
| Geometric Transformations | 44 | 52 |
| Congruence & Similarity | 61 | 84 |
| Proportionality Concepts | 41 | 82 |
| Porportionality Problems | 57 | 87 |
| Slope | 38 | 92 |
| Trigonometry | 24 | 83 |
| Patterns & Relations | 53 | 76 |
| Functions | 39 | 85 |
| Expressions & Simple Equations | 55 | 93 |
| Linear Equations & Inequalities | 51 | 94 |
| Quadratic & Polynomial Equations & Inequalities | 34 | 90 |
| Logarithmic & Trigonometric Equations | 10 | 56 |
| Systems of Equations & Inequalities | 22 | 75 |
| Representing & Interpreting Data | 69 | 82 |
| Probability & Uncertainty | 30 | 43 |
| Infinite Processes | 11 | 43 |
| Elementary Analysis/Change | 10 | 48 |
| Validation & Justification | 6 | 26 |
| Structuring & Abstracting | — | 18 |

If we reason that being well prepared in more advanced topics is necessary for primary school teachers to teach elementary mathematics, then we must conclude that there were important omissions from the list of topics that teachers felt well prepared to teach. Important exclusions from this list include topics in number theory, such as integers (positive and negative whole numbers), the rational number system, properties of common and decimal fractions, prime numbers, factors, exponents, and roots. These topics provide a base of mathematical understanding for teaching more elementary number topics.

Virtually all of the geometry topics (aside from the basics) are excluded by the 75% criterion. So are all of the proportionality topics and all of the algebra topics. These results imply that the quality of learning opportunities surrounding many of the mathematics topics taught in 1st through 3rd grades was not likely to be high. They also suggest that there is large variability in self-reported content-specific knowledge. For many of these topics, only a bare majority of 50% to 60% of teachers felt well prepared. As the percentage of teachers who feel well prepared moves from 100% to 50%, the variability in teacher knowledge increases. In fact, anything under an 80% versus 20% split of well prepared versus not well prepared implies a substantial variation among teachers in their mathematics knowledge. The more topics for which this was the case, the greater the likelihood for large variability in the quality of OTL across classrooms, even if the same topics were covered.

We now examine the extent to which the 75% criterion was met in each of the 60 districts. Unfortunately, no mathematics topic in 1st through 3rd grades reached the 75% criterion in all districts. Even for the meaning of whole numbers and operations with whole numbers, in some districts less than 75% of their primary teachers felt well prepared to teach even these most basic of all mathematics topics. This was true of less than 25% of the districts for the meaning of whole numbers. It was true for slightly more than 25% of the districts for operations with whole numbers.

Figure 7.1 presents the distribution of the percentages of teachers in each district who considered themselves academically very well prepared to teach each mathematics topic for each of the 28 mathematics topics in the 60 districts. Each district would be one data point for each topic. Each box and whisker plot (see Figure 2.1) is for one topic.

Notice that the median value for districts was below 50% for most of the topics in Figure 7.1. For any topic for which this median was below 50%, at least half of the districts had fewer than half of their primary teachers feeling well prepared to teach most of the topics listed in Table 7.1. For example, fractions was a topic expected to be taught in 2nd and 3rd grades in Michigan and Ohio, yet only about 25% of the districts met the criterion of having at least 75% of their primary teachers feeling very

Figure 7.1. Distribution of districts indicating the percentage of lower elementary teachers (grades 1–3) who indicated they were academically "very well prepared" to teach specific mathematics topics.

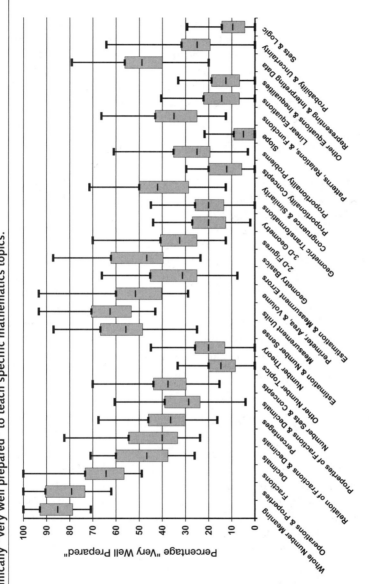

*Note.* For an explanation of how to interpret box and whisker plots, see Figure 2.1.

well prepared to teach fractions. No district met this criterion for decimals. Only a small number of districts met the criterion for other elementary mathematics areas (such as percentage, estimation, measurement units, and the basics of geometry).

The other striking feature of the results portrayed in Figure 7.1 is the large variability across districts. For example, for fractions, in some districts all of the primary teachers felt very well prepared, while in other districts only about half of the teachers felt very well prepared. For geometry basics (lines, angles, and so on), the results ranged from one district with only about one-fourth of its teachers feeling well prepared to another district in which about 90% of the teachers felt well prepared.

### Upper Elementary Teachers (4th Through 5th Grades)

The results for districts for 4th- and 5th-grade teachers were quite different. They are displayed in Figure 7.2 (in a way similar to what is done in Figure 7.1). For example, for eight different topics, all of the teachers in at least one district felt very well prepared academically for each of those topics. At the district level, the results for whole number meaning and operations were similar to those for 1st- through 3rd-grade teachers. Further, fractions also had a median value around 75%.

However, the variability across districts remains a striking feature for 4th- and 5th-grade teachers, particularly for decimals, percentages, and geometry basics. These are all topics that were supposed to be introduced in these grades in Michigan and Ohio. For example, for decimals, in one district only one-fourth of the teachers felt well prepared, while in another district virtually all teachers indicated that they felt well prepared to teach decimals.

### Middle School Teachers (6th Through 8th Grades)

We examined the pool of teachers from all of the districts taken together (see Table 7.1). From this perspective, there were no topics that at least 75% of the teachers felt very well prepared to teach. Only two topics came close. Among the whole pool of teachers, 73% indicated that they felt well prepared to teach the topic of coordinates and lines. Sixty-nine percent of the teachers indicated that they felt well prepared to teach the topic of data.

Eleven topics qualify if we relax the criterion to topics in which at least 50% of the teachers felt well prepared. This included the two topics just mentioned as well as nine others—negative, rational, and real numbers; exponents, roots, and radicals; number theory; polygons and circles; congruence and similarity; proportionality problems; patterns and relations; expressions and simple equations; and linear equalities and inequalities. The Michigan

Figure 7.2. Distribution of districts indicating the percentage of upper elementary teachers (grades 4–5) who indicated they were academically "very well prepared" to teach specific mathematics topics.

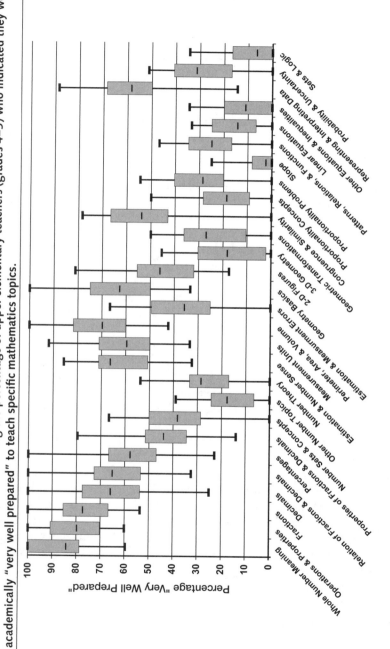

*Note.* For an explanation of how to interpret box and whisker plots, see Figure 2.1.

and Ohio standards call for including many of these topics at the middle grades. The fact that only about 50% to 60% of the teachers felt very well prepared to teach these topics suggested something of the magnitude of the problem that school districts face.

For example, there has been a strong national movement to include elementary algebra topics in the middle school, particularly in 8th grade. The Michigan and Ohio standards reflect this, as do the Common Core State Standards, which are in the process of becoming the new Michigan and Ohio state standards. Adoption of the Common Core State Standards brings states more into alignment with international benchmarks of what is expected in the equivalent of middle school.

The severity of the problems faced by these districts and, by inference, by the United States as a whole, was indicated by the fact that only about half of the teachers felt academically very well prepared to teach expressions and simple equations, as well as linear equalities and inequalities. Even fewer teachers (only around 25% to 40%) felt they had adequate content knowledge to teach other important algebraic concepts, including proportionality (41% of teachers), slope (38%), and functions (39%).

These results were for the group of teachers in the 60 districts as a whole. Now, we examine the issue at the district level, using the same criterion (75% of teachers indicating that they feel well prepared to teach a topic). The data are presented in Figure 7.3.

Figure 7.3 shows that there were only two topics for which the median district (and thus at least one-half of the districts) had 75% or more of teachers at the middle grades who feel that their academic background has prepared them very well to teach those topics. Those two topics were coordinates and lines, and data (PROM/SE, 2006).[4]

The results in Figure 7.3 for middle school teachers are even more striking than the results for primary teachers. The degree to which middle school teachers felt well prepared academically to teach most of the topics varied tremendously across districts. For example, consider the topic of linear equations and inequalities. One of the 60 districts had no teachers at all who felt well prepared to teach this topic. Another district had all of its teachers report that they were well prepared to teach it. Similarly large variations existed for other fundamental middle school topics (for example, exponents, roots and radicals, number theory, polygons, circles, congruence, similarity, proportionality, slope, and data).

These topics are at the heart of the more challenging middle school curriculum advocated by the Common Core State Standards. The tremendous variation is profoundly significant and likely shapes the opportunities to learn that are provided to students and, as a result, contributes to significant inequalities in learning experiences. These results also foreshadow the difficulty as states and districts implement the Common Core State Standards.

Figure 7.3. Distribution of districts indicating the percentage of middle school teachers (grades 6–8) who indicated they were academically "very well prepared" to teach specific mathematics topics.

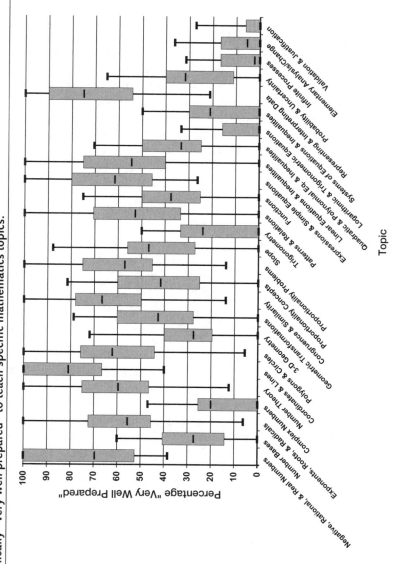

Note. For an explanation of how to interpret box and whisker plots, see Figure 2.1.

## High School Teachers

The story for high school teachers is rather different, which is not unexpected given their typically greater preparation in mathematics. Almost 60% of the topics met the criterion of having at least 75% of the pool of PROM/SE teachers from the 60 districts indicating that they were well prepared academically. The areas in which high school teachers indicated that they felt less well prepared were number bases, three-dimensional geometry, geometric transformations, logarithmic and trigonometric functions, probability, and calculus. These findings are, however, still cause for concern. For example, there is an increasingly strong push for the inclusion of probability and statistics in high school, as is found in the Common Core State Standards, yet less than half of the surveyed mathematics teachers felt well prepared to teach it. Teachers' self-perceptions of their preparedness seem likely, if anything, to overestimate what they know and how well prepared they are rather than to underestimate it.

Moving from the pool of all 60 districts to the district-by-district results (Figure 7.4), for a large number of topics (16), at least 25% of the districts had all of their high school teachers indicating that they felt well prepared to teach those topics. However, there was still great variation across the districts, especially for geometry topics including transformations, three-dimensional geometry, polygons, and circles. There was similarly great variability in the percentage of teachers who felt that they had the coursework to make them well prepared to deal with calculus, probability, number theory, and logarithmic and trigonometric functions.

## WHY TEACHERS FEEL SO POORLY PREPARED

We have surveyed how well prepared in terms of disciplinary course work teachers at various levels felt for teaching various mathematics topics in what is a fairly representative sample of 60 districts. In general, we would summarize the findings by stating that many teachers felt ill prepared to teach mathematics topics that are in state standards and in the new Common Core State Standards for mathematics. Why did these teachers feel so ill prepared?

There is perhaps a simple answer for the elementary and middle school teachers: They felt ill prepared because if we examine the coursework they studied during their teacher preparation, they *were* ill prepared. The new TEDS study results suggested this to be the case more generally, which clearly does not bode well for equality of learning experiences for students in these districts.

Figure 7.4. Distribution of districts indicating the percentage of high school teachers who indicated they were academically "very well prepared" to teach specific mathematics topics.

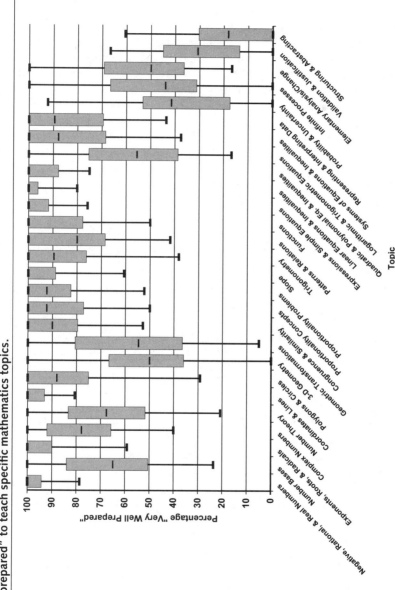

Note. For an explanation of how to interpret box and whisker plots, see Figure 2.1.

## College-Level Preparation

In this section, we summarize what teachers have told us about their preparation in mathematics at the college level and as graduate students. Table 7.2 indicates the percentage of teachers at each grade level in the 60 districts who have a major or minor in mathematics. In 1st through 4th grades, less than 10% have either a major or a minor in mathematics. Teachers at this level are typically generalists—they must be prepared to teach many different subject-matter areas. They do not have adequate time in their preparation to get a major or a minor in each of those subject matters.

At 4th grade, the international data paint a different picture. Unfortunately, the definitions are not precisely the same, but the data do provide us with a benchmark of sorts. Including those primary teachers with either a mathematics major or a minor in mathematics or science, around one-third of 4th-grade students on average had such a teacher in the countries that took part in TIMSS.[5]

Taking this estimate from the TIMSS data as an indicator of the percentage of teachers who had majored or minored in mathematics or science, this proportion was considerably higher than for the PROM/SE 4th-grade

**Table 7.2. Percentage of teachers at each grade level in the 60 districts reporting college preparation in mathematics.**

| Grade | Math Major Reported | Math Minor Reported | No Math Specialization Reported |
|---|---|---|---|
| 1 | 0.6 | 2 | 97 |
| 2 | 0.6 | 2 | 98 |
| 3 | 0.4 | 2 | 98 |
| 4 | 0.5 | 4 | 95 |
| 5 | 1 | 9 | 90 |
| 6 | 1 | 8 | 91 |
| 7 | 16 | 22 | 62 |
| 8 | 18 | 19 | 63 |
| 9 | 36 | 27 | 38 |
| 10 | 51 | 23 | 26 |
| 11 | 37 | 37 | 37 |
| 12 | 53 | 27 | 20 |
| *Aggregated Across Grades* | | | |
| Grades 1–3 | 0.5 | 2 | 97 |
| Grades 4–5 | 0.8 | 6 | 93 |
| Grades 6–8 | 10 | 15 | 75 |
| Grades 9–12 | 50 | 28 | 23 |

teachers, where the comparable percentage was 5%. The percentage was over 50% in Singapore and Russia. This suggests that, from an international perspective, other countries typically have around six times as many primary teachers who have a specialization in mathematics or in a related field of science.

The result is even more disturbing when we turn to the middle school mathematics curriculum and the higher level of mathematics offered there. Three out of four middle school teachers in the PROM/SE sample did not have a specialization in mathematics. At 6th grade, the percentage was much like that for primary teachers—only around 10% had a major or minor in mathematics. In 7th and 8th grade, this percentage increased to around 35% to 40%.

These numbers indicate that a very large percentage of middle school students were being taught increasingly more complex mathematics, as called for in the Michigan and Ohio state standards, by teachers who lacked a strong background in mathematics. These results offer one explanation for why so many middle school teachers did not feel very well prepared to teach many of the middle school topics discussed in the previous section. This also foreshadows problems of implementation, at least as the newly adopted Common Core State Standards are put in place, in Michigan and Ohio.

What about high school mathematics teachers? We would expect that all high school mathematics teachers would have at least a minor in mathematics, if not a major. But the actual results for high school are quite surprising. Less than half of all high school mathematics teachers surveyed had a major in mathematics. Almost one-third did not have either a major or a minor in mathematics. These numbers varied across the four grades of high school taught by the surveyed teachers. Almost one-half of the teachers whose major teaching responsibilities were at 9th or 10th grade did not have any specialization in mathematics. In 11th and 12th grades, over 71% of the teachers who taught primarily at those grades had some kind of specialization in mathematics.

Lest it seem too heartening that those teaching the most advanced courses (usually taken in the 11th and 12th grades) are better prepared in mathematics, we need to consider several caveats. It may be even more important to have well prepared teachers in entry-level courses usually taught in 9th and 10th grades. These courses serve as the foundation for more-advanced courses, may be even more difficult to teach, and are just as important in terms of preparing students for further study. But for these foundational courses, teacher content knowledge was not nearly as strong.

It is worth noting that on some of the more advanced mathematics topics (number theory, geometric transformations, logarithmic and trigonometric functions, and calculus) up to half of the teachers did not feel very well prepared to teach them. Perhaps these same 50% were those who did not have a major in mathematics.

## Mathematics Knowledge

One key part of the PROM/SE project was planning and carrying out content-based capacity building for teachers. As a part of this component, we administered a test of mathematics knowledge to a sample of teachers.

Table 7.3 shows the results. When viewed in light of Table 7.2, it strongly suggests that elementary and middle school teachers perceived their weaknesses accurately and reported them honestly. They appeared to be reporting that they were not well prepared academically to teach the mathematics content that they were being asked to teach.

Table 7.2 shows that, across grades, the percentage of teachers who did not have a major or minor in mathematics ranged from nearly all of the teachers at 1st grade to around one-half of them at 8th grade. Table 7.3 demonstrates that these same teachers were able to answer correctly only about half of the items, as compared with teachers with mathematics majors who were teaching at the corresponding grades. The teachers with mathematics majors were able to correctly answer about 70% of the same items. This gap of almost 20% is sizable and very important. It confirms what the teachers told us when they said that they were not well prepared. The problem at high school is more a problem of variability. The data indicated that most of the teachers had mathematics majors and that their mathematics knowledge was reasonably good. However, about one-third still did not have strong academic preparation.

## THE EFFECTS OF TEACHERS' MATHEMATICS KNOWLEDGE ON OPPORTUNITIES TO LEARN

Given these results about teachers' mathematics knowledge, it is tempting to blame elementary and middle school teachers for not being prepared, but we believe blaming teachers is a mistake.[6] Why? Because teachers prepare themselves according to the standards and guidelines established by the states that certify them and the teacher preparation programs that train them. Our point here is that such variation in academic content knowledge

**Table 7.3. The percentage of correct answers on a mathematics test for teachers at various grade levels and with varying credentials in mathematics.**

| Grade Level Taught | Math Major | Math Minor | No Math Specialization |
|---|---|---|---|
| K–4 | 67 | 61 | 49 |
| 5–6 | 70 | 74 | 55 |
| 6–8 | 74 | 69 | 47 |
| 9–12 | 74 | 70 | 64 |

is likely to affect the quality of content coverage. Since the content coverage described previously varied appreciably, these data indicate one possible reason for such variation as it is very likely that this lack of knowledge influences not only the quality of the coverage of particular topics but also the bigger picture as to how the teacher makes choices about which topics to cover, for how long (to what depth), and in what sequence. Such lack of knowledge further exacerbates the variation in content coverage in mathematics across classrooms, schools, and districts, resulting in further inequalities in OTL.

## CHAPTER 8

# The Role of Textbooks and Tests

Just as teachers have an impact on content coverage (see Chapter 7), so do instructional and assessment materials. Teachers of mathematics are prone to be influenced by the textbook, both in terms of topic coverage and emphasis (Barr, 1988; Davis, 2009; Fan & Kaeley, 2000; Freeman & Porter, 1989; Schmidt, 2011; Schmidt et al., 2001). In the TIMSS study, the relationship between instructional time as reported by U.S. teachers and the number of pages found in textbooks was marginally significant (Schmidt et al., 2001). To a lesser degree, the content covered by test items also influences which topics teachers cover in their instruction (Floden, Porter, Schmidt, Freeman, & Schwille, 1981; Hamilton et al., 2007; Shepard & Dougherty, 1991). This influence has been strengthened by the concern for failing schools as defined by performance on state assessments. NCLB and the current Race to the Top legislation have only increased the impact of test content on teacher content coverage and emphasis.

Is the fact that textbooks and tests influence content coverage inconsistent with the notion of teacher autonomy with respect to content coverage discussed in both Chapters 4 and 7? On the surface, it appears so. The positive, although weak, relationship of textbook and teacher content coverage found in TIMSS and the common belief that teachers teach to their state assessments all point in this direction. But the logic of the situation and the evidence presented in Chapter 6 tell a more complicated story. The potential effect of both textbooks and tests on content coverage is contingent on the decision-making process of the teacher. It is not as if these two prescriptions are automatically followed by teachers. This point is made even more evident when we consider that the implied content coverage of tests and textbooks is not necessarily the same, since they are typically developed separately.

In addition to these two mixed signals, teachers have to deal with state and district standards as well as school-related curriculum guides. Even state standards and state assessments are not in perfect accord (Porter et al., 2011). This is why Schwille et al. (1983) described teachers as *content brokers*, because they must act as the intermediary negotiating among these multiple definitions of which content to cover and with what emphasis (instructional time), using their own professional judgments, beliefs, and mathematics backgrounds. Chapter 6 provides further evidence for such content brokering: Even after controlling for state and district, we found that over 80% of the total variation in content coverage among classrooms at the same grade level within schools was due to teacher decisions. At this level of classrooms within a school, textbooks and tests are invariably the same, yet there remained substantial classroom variation in content coverage. In this chapter, we examine both of these school-related materials and their potential impact on inequalities in content coverage in mathematics.

## TEXTBOOKS: THE POTENTIALLY IMPLEMENTED CURRICULUM

Textbooks are probably the most ubiquitous feature of U.S. classrooms after teachers. In this book, we have written about intended curriculum—state, district, and school standards, as well as curriculum guides that express what officials intend to be taught in various subjects at various grades. We have also written about implemented curriculum—the way in which teachers turn these intentions into what is actually done in real classrooms through decisions about which topics to teach, when to teach them, how long to teach them, and how to teach them. Textbooks fall somewhere between the intended and the implemented curriculum, acting as a bridge between intentions and implementation. We might call them the potentially implemented curriculum or the semi-implemented curriculum (Schmidt et al., 1996; Schmidt, McKnight, Valverde, et al., 1997).

Textbooks are important because they translate the formal academic disciplines into forms that are appropriate for presentation to students of a given age or grade. They help define school subjects such as mathematics as students will experience them. A great deal of school funding goes toward the purchase of such materials. They are designed by authors to translate the abstractions of curriculum policy and standards into instructional tasks that can be carried out by teachers and students (Valverde, Bianchi, Wolfe, Schmidt, & Houang, 2002).

Teachers often do not have time to make decisions about how to present each topic or in what sequence topics should be covered in a way that will be effective for their students. Textbooks can be a resource in making those decisions. Many teachers will go beyond what the textbooks suggest, but it is much easier to leave something out that a textbook covers than it is to add something else. In these ways, textbooks can impact content coverage.

Textbooks and other instructional materials can also affect the quality of learning opportunities. It matters a great deal how well the material on a given topic is developed. The important issue of focus in instruction is affected by how deeply textbooks go into a given topic. The order in which topics are covered in a textbook has an impact on the coherence of instruction at a given grade level—that is, on whether the topics relate to one another so as to present an understandable picture of mathematics as a whole.

We believe there are three different roles that the textbook can play in influencing opportunity to learn. In the United States, the textbook can sometimes play an even stronger role, as it becomes essentially the *de facto* curriculum in a district (scenario I). For such districts, the textbook *is* the curriculum—it is simply followed page by page from the first page, with few exceptions, to however far a teacher can reach by the end of the school year. What the book covers or does not cover essentially defines the content learning opportunities that students in such a district will have, no matter what the district or state standards say about intentions. But again, teacher decisions become central. Since the textbooks are too large to be covered in 1 year, where teachers start in the book is important, as is deciding which sections of the book can be skipped. Furthermore, the teacher must decide how much time to spend on different topics in the book, which has implications for how far into the book the class will go. This often precludes coverage of topics at the end of the book. The textbook becomes closest to what is actually implemented in teaching. It is much closer to shaping actual teaching than any formal document that states what students are intended to learn.

In other districts where the textbook is not treated as a curricular "bible," it affects the quality of learning opportunities just as the teacher does. In those cases where the state and district standards really do define the curriculum (scenario II), the textbook is used only as a supplement to other materials to implement those topics that the standards say should be covered. If a topic is not in the standards, it may well not be covered, even though it is found in the textbook. If a topic is in the standards but is not covered in the selected textbook, then other materials that cover the topic must augment the textbook. The standards define the curriculum in this scenario. Clearly, the use of textbooks to support standards is very difficult. It involves determining which sections of the book should be covered, which should be omitted, and what other materials are needed to supplement the textbook. This kind of very limited use of textbooks is likely to be quite rare.

The most typical case is neither of the above, but one in which the textbook neither defines the curriculum nor serves only a limited role. Rather, it is a combination of the two where the textbook plays a major role but only as one of several sources, including state and district standards and tests (scenario III). Textbooks still play a prominent role in this model, but remain the "potentially implemented curriculum" because teachers use the textbooks but do not necessarily follow them strictly (Chávez, 2006; Remillard, 2005; Stein, Remillard, & Smith, 2007). They serve as a foundation, but, in response to state standards or through their own initiative, teachers skip some topics contained in their textbooks, add other topics that are not in the book, reorder the sequence in which topics are covered, or do other things than what the textbook suggests when it comes to covering a topic. It is here where teachers make decisions that somehow balance across what are often disparate content prescriptions. It is why Schwille et al. (1983) referred to teachers as content brokers.

In all three scenarios, textbooks have a significant impact on learning opportunities. They influence whether certain learning opportunities are available, affect the quality of those learning opportunities, or both. At a minimum, textbooks influence the quality of content coverage (OTL) as the teachers use the book and its particular representation or development of the topics being covered, including the depth to which the topic is addressed. Textbooks also have the potential to strongly define the topics to be covered, the sequence in which they are covered, and the amount of emphasis the topics will receive by the number of pages allocated to the topic. However, in all three scenarios, but especially in scenarios II and III, the teacher also plays a significant role by the decisions he or she makes on how to use the book and which parts of it to cover with a particular class of students. This is consistent with the analyses in Chapter 6, which indicated that the vast majority of variation across classrooms in content coverage was related to such teacher decisions.

## MATHEMATICS TEXTBOOKS

The pervasive and systematic use of textbooks by mathematics teachers and the fact that there is such a variety of textbooks, as well as a variable number of ways that teachers use textbooks, raises the possibility of another source of variation in content coverage. With respect to educational equality we should ask: Do different textbooks provide similar content coverage? We coded 353 mathematics and 153 science textbooks to answer this question. They included the most popular commercial textbooks used extensively in 7th- through 12th-grade classrooms, as well as textbooks whose development was supported by the National Science Foundation (NSF).[1] The textbooks were coded using procedures developed as a part of the curriculum work done in TIMSS (Schmidt, McKnight, Valverde, et al., 1997; Schmidt, Raizen, Britton, Bianchi, & Wolfe, 1997).

### The Topics Included in Mathematics Textbooks

We first considered mathematics by examining each of the 44 topics in the mathematics framework (see Appendix B), used throughout this book, to examine which were included in the various textbooks. The textbooks were classified into eight categories: (1) general or basic mathematics, (2) pre-algebra, (3) algebra I, (4) geometry, (5) algebra II, (6) precalculus, (7) calculus, and (8) integrated mathematics.[2] We calculated the percentage of the books in each category that covered each of the 44 topics. It would be reasonable to expect that content coverage would be very similar within a category, given that those books are focused around a single area of mathematics. Most of the topics should either be covered by virtually all or by virtually none of the books, with the exceptions of basic and integrated mathematics books. The distributions of the 44 percentages are summarized in Figure 8.1, where each topic is treated as an observation.

The median coverage of topics in each of the eight categories of textbooks ranged from 33% to 74%—that is, between a third and three-fourths of the textbooks covered the typical topic for that textbook type. The substantial variation indicated little agreement across books within any of the eight categories. For example, as an advanced topic, calculus books would not be expected to cover many of the 44 topics. The median percentage was only 33% for these books and ranged from 0% to 70% for the middle half of the topics.

As one would expect, all algebra books—both algebra I and algebra II—covered equations. All the algebra II books covered functions and slope. Not all of the algebra I books covered these two topics. For instance, about 17% of the algebra I books did not cover the idea of slope. One important question about algebra books is how much coverage they gave to the more elementary arithmetic topics (those supposedly left behind for the most part in a first

**Figure 8.1. Distributions of the percentage of textbooks covering each of 44 mathematics topics by textbook type.**

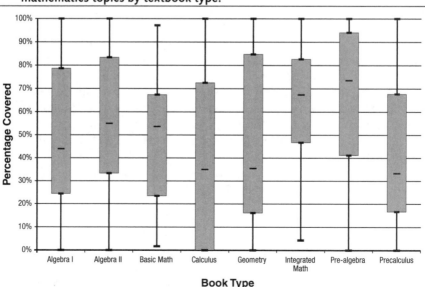

**Book Type**

*Note.* For an explanation of how to interpret box and whisker plots, see Figure 2.1.

algebra course). In fact, many elementary topics are included in algebra textbooks. For example, fractions and decimals were included in about 40% to 60% of both algebra I and algebra II textbooks. The topic of percentages was in 78% of the algebra I books and 67% of the algebra II books.

General or basic mathematics textbooks also varied considerably in the content they covered. Such books were typically used in 7th and 8th grades; however, they were also used for high school courses in many schools and districts. Since they were dealing with mathematics more generally, one would expect them to vary considerably in the topics covered. This is especially clear when we consider the range in the percentage of textbooks for the middle 50% of the topics. Topic coverage ranged from 23% to 67% for the middle half of the topics. The median value was about 54% of the books.

Perhaps most remarkable was topic coverage in geometry books. These books were by far the most variable in their content coverage. (The apparent variability of calculus books is an artifact.)[3] The interquartile range for the geometry books was almost 70% and the median 35%. That is, a typical topic was only covered in around one-third of the geometry books. The cases that were not at either extreme of coverage—the middle 50% of topics—ranged from less than one-fifth (16%) to over four-fifths (85%) coverage in the geometry books. Even if we consider only the nine geometry topics in the framework, there is still a great deal of variation across the geometry textbooks. Coverage of these nine topics ranged from around one-half to 100% of the geometry textbooks. For example, only half of the geometry textbooks covered vectors. All of the geometry textbooks covered the coordinate system, two- and three-dimensional geometry, and congruence and similarity. Basic geometric constructions were covered in only a small number of the books.

If the different textbooks were followed strictly by teachers, they would lead to very different content coverage and learning opportunities, even when the title of the book suggests that the material should be identical. Not all algebra I books were alike in what they covered mathematically, nor were all geometry books alike. Not even all calculus books covered the same content. To the extent that the textbook influences what is actually taught in classrooms, algebra I courses, Geometry courses, and Calculus courses would all be profoundly different, based solely on the choice of textbook. Textbooks are, therefore, just one more way in which inequalities in content coverage arise.

## The Topic Categories That Get Space in Mathematics Textbooks

A second way to examine this issue is to categorize the 44 topics into different areas, and then determine the number of topics within a category that are found in a textbook. For example, five topics in the mathematics framework are classified as algebra. We determined the percentage of algebra textbooks that covered zero through five of these topics.

There were few differences among the Algebra I and Algebra II books in the number of the five algebra topics included. Almost all of the Algebra II books covered all five topics. There was a little more variability in the Algebra I books, but this was mostly due to whether the topic of functions was included. By contrast, general mathematics books were highly variable in how many of the five algebra topics they covered. About one-third of these general mathematics textbooks did not cover any of the algebra topics or covered only one of them. Just over half (56%) covered two of the five algebra topics. About 10% covered four or five of the algebra topics. Obviously, these differences have implications for subsequent success in an Algebra I course, depending on which general mathematics textbook was used.

The same sort of differences existed among the general mathematics books for the nine geometry topics. About half of the general mathematics textbooks covered five or fewer of the geometry topics. By contrast, the geometry books all covered at least nine of the ten geometry topics. A similar pattern held for precalculus and calculus books. Such specialized high school mathematics textbooks tended to cover most, if not all, of the relevant topics. However, general mathematics books (including pre-algebra books) tended to vary more in what they covered.

To study the variability in content coverage among advanced high school mathematics textbooks, we must look for a different explanation because those textbooks, although somewhat variable, are much more similar in terms of content coverage. They may be less similar, however, in terms of what topics they emphasize, as indicated by the number of pages given to a particular topic. A more refined examination of content opportunities would then focus on the number of pages given to various topics, since this is most likely related to the number of days a teacher will give to covering those same topics. More pages of coverage may not always be better, but more pages tend to indicate more content exposure and perhaps more in-depth coverage of a topic, although, strictly speaking, this is a measure of quantity and not of quality.

The 44 mathematics topics were divided into six broader categories—arithmetic, transition arithmetic, geometry, algebra, calculus, and data/statistics. We calculated the total number of pages associated with each category for each book and then calculated the mean. Figure 8.2 displays the results of the analysis and gives an indication of a typical book of each type. Clearly, the books that focus on a particular topic generally covered that topic. This was true for books for Algebra I, Algebra II, geometry, and calculus. By contrast, integrated mathematics, basic mathematics, and pre-algebra books covered a broader range of mathematics topics.

We made the point earlier that Algebra I books covered most of the algebra topics. However, here we examine how this varied among different books. On average, 57% of the Algebra I texts covered the five algebra topics.

**Figure 8.2. Mean percentage of textbook pages spent on seven broad categories of mathematics by type of book.**

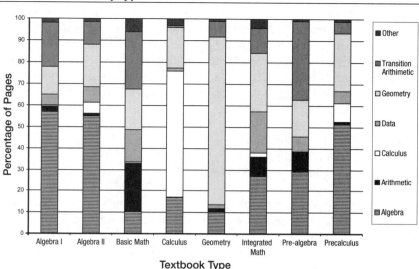

Yet there were marked differences among them. One book used only 16% of its pages to cover these five algebra topics. Another book used 74% of its pages to cover them. This much variation devoted to the five algebra topics in two Algebra I textbooks makes it hard to imagine that using these two books would result in equal content exposure.

The Algebra I textbooks also varied in how much they covered transition arithmetic. Some spent no pages at all on this topic. Another spent almost 60% of the book on transition arithmetic, which represents 480 pages in a typical 800-page Algebra I textbook.

Unsurprisingly, 75% of the Algebra II books spent between 50% and 70% of their pages on algebra-related topics. Similarly, geometry books used most of their pages for geometry topics. About 75% of the geometry textbooks devoted between 78% and 97% of their pages to the 10 geometry topics we investigated.

Basic mathematics books were very different, which should not be a surprise given the earlier results showing wide variation in topics covered among books from this category. They varied greatly in their coverage of almost any topic. For example, they ranged from no coverage at all to almost a whole book (84%) covering algebra topics. They ranged from no coverage to almost 90% of the textbook devoted to arithmetic. This pattern also held for the way transition arithmetic was covered.

As we might expect, precalculus textbooks focus mainly on algebra, not trigonometry or calculus. However, even here there are differences.

Mathematically, it would make sense for most of the pages in a precalculus book to focus on functions. Algebra I books focus mostly on equations. As mathematics advances, there should be a transition from a focus on equations to a focus on functions in order to express similar ideas in a more powerful, sophisticated form. Some precalculus books split their pages somewhat evenly among functions and equations (both are algebra topics). Others focused more heavily on functions. However, some of the books still concentrated more on equations. Of the 24 precalculus textbooks we examined, the breakdown was as follows:

- greater emphasis on equations—14
- roughly equal emphasis—5
- greater emphasis on functions—5

One book spent over 50% of its pages covering equations but only 10% covering functions. Another devoted a third of its pages to covering fractions. It covered less algebra in general than the previous book and markedly fewer pages on equations in favor of what was a transition arithmetic topic, not even an algebra topic. Another book used only 17% of its pages for algebra.

## THE TOPICS INCLUDED IN SCIENCE TEXTBOOKS

School science is based on many different science disciplines. Most science textbooks at the 7th through 12th grades are written around one specific topic area based on one or more of these disciplines. The exception is general science textbooks, which draw from many parts of science and do not focus on any specific area or discipline. Normally, high school science textbooks are specialized for physics, chemistry, biology, anatomy, astronomy, geology, and so on. Middle school science books are similarly organized, usually as life, earth, or physical science. Each of these middle school textbooks can, however, draw from different areas of scientific study—physics, biology, microbiology, biochemistry, chemistry, geology, astronomy, anatomy, materials science, engineering, and others.

Some areas of science are strongly interrelated. This presents obvious difficulties when it comes to organizing school science and picking the topics to include in textbooks, both for general science textbooks and for more specialized texts, such as a high school physics textbook. Even for specialized textbooks, choices must be made about which related topics to include from other parts of science (for example, chemistry).

For each type of science textbook, we calculated the percentage of the books that covered each of the 79 topics in the science framework. The percentages are summarized in Figure 8.3. Here, we can see the enormous

**Figure 8.3. Distributions of the percentage of textbooks covering each of 79 science topics by textbook type.**

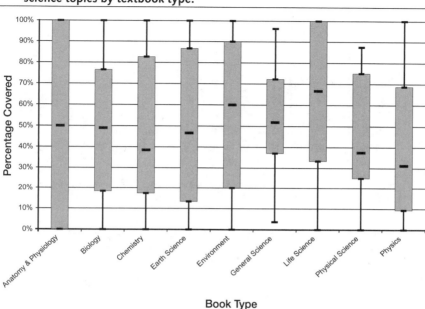

**Book Type**

*Note.* For an explanation of how to interpret box and whisker plots, see Figure 2.1.

range of coverage for the 79 topics (see Appendix C). For each of the main categories of high school science textbooks (physics, chemistry, and biology), the percentage of textbooks covering a topic ranged from 0% to 100%, while the middle part of the distribution (the interquartile range) varied from around 10% to 90% for seven of the nine categories of books.[4] A typical topic (represented by the median) was covered by about 50% of the biology textbooks, 40% of the chemistry textbooks, and 30% of the physics textbooks.

In general, there were smaller differences among those topics that are traditionally considered part of the subject indicated by the title of the textbook. For example, 94% of physics textbooks covered the typical physics topics. Similar results also held for chemistry and biology, with over 90% of the textbooks covering these topics. The 79 science topics from the school science framework were combined into 24 broader categories representing larger areas of school science in order to simplify the analysis of the number of pages allocated to each topic. Figure 8.4 shows the percentage of pages that were devoted to each of the 24 major categories of topics averaged over all textbooks of a particular type. About 20% of the pages for a typical high school biology textbook were allocated to non-biology areas, including physics, chemistry, and earth science

# Figure 8.4. Mean percentage of textbook pages spent on 25 broad categories of science by type of book.

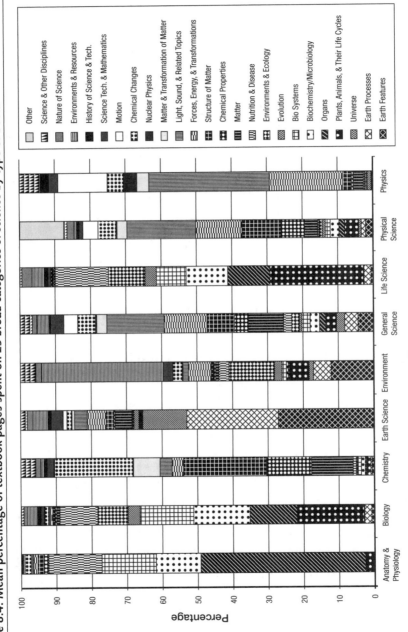

topics. In high school chemistry books, this percentage was also about 20%. In high school physics books, the percentage of other material was over 25%. These results support the earlier characterization of U.S. science curricula as being "a mile wide." General science textbooks devoted space across all four of the major disciplines. Physics was the most prominent, typically covering around 35% of a general science textbook.

The previous discussion characterized the content covered in typical science textbooks in each of the major categories. Although this is interesting in itself, what we are more interested in is the differences among textbooks in each category. For example, consider biology textbooks. Typically, these books devoted about 15% of their space to the topic of biological systems. However, some books devoted only 4% of their space to this area, while others devoted almost a third of the book to it. Biological systems includes the study of the basic systems through which life functions. Unless the content is totally trivial or redundant, a textbook that devoted eight times more space to such a central topic than did another would provide a different level of coverage of the content. Another equally important area is a biochemistry area that focuses on topics such as DNA and the processes by which cells generate their energy and carry out their reproductive functions. In biology textbooks, the differences for this subject were equally large, ranging from 6% to 40% of the textbook.

In chemistry textbooks, an important topic is the nature of chemical changes. Chemistry textbooks typically allocated about one-fourth of their pages to this area. Chemical change is obviously important for understanding chemistry; however, the different books ranged from devoting virtually no coverage to this area to devoting almost half of the book (43%) to it. Central topics in physics textbooks include energy and the forces of nature, together with light, sound, electricity, and magnetism. On average, about half of physics textbooks focused on these topics, but some did not even cover them at all. Simply put, science textbooks appear to be just as highly variable in content coverage as mathematics books, even for the essential topics suggested by the books' titles.

## TEXTBOOK FACTORS THAT INFLUENCE THE QUALITY OF LEARNING OPPORTUNITIES

In this section, we consider the form and style of mathematics textbooks. Every textbook has a structure, and a basic orientation to teaching (pedagogical orientation). These factors are very important because they provide the context in which the content is embedded and determine how it is presented. We believe pedagogical orientation is likely to influence the quality of learning opportunities. The results reported here are from the TIMSS study for which the U.S. sample included the most commonly used textbooks in the United States at the time of the study (1996). The same criterion was used in selecting textbooks from the other countries in the study.[5] What follows is a summary of the study's results as presented in the book *According to the Book: Using TIMSS to Investigate the Translation of Policy into Practice in the World of Textbooks* (Valverde et al., 2002).

### Number of Pages

One of the most obvious physical characteristics of a textbook is the number of pages it contains. This has the potential to affect both the nature and the quality of the learning opportunities related to the book's use. The size of a textbook can translate directly into a measure of time devoted to various parts of instruction when that book is used in classroom instruction. This is why it is likely that the very large size of U.S. textbooks contributes directly to a "mile wide, inch deep" characterization of topic coverage in the U.S. curriculum (Schmidt et al., 2001).

Internationally, the average number of pages for a 4th-grade mathematics textbook was 125 pages. U.S. 4th-grade textbooks were around 500 pages long. U.S. high school textbooks were over 100 pages longer than the average of an international sample of high school textbooks (Valverde et al., 2002). The average number of pages in an 8th-grade international mathematics textbook was 225. U.S. 8th-grade mathematics textbooks, on the other hand, typically averaged around 800 pages.

Such large textbooks almost certainly have an effect on learning opportunities. For example, it is likely that all topics in most U.S. textbooks cannot be covered because of the significant length of the books. If this is the case, then the topics the teacher chooses essentially define the content to which students will be exposed. It is also very likely that the topics included at the end of a textbook often are not covered—a notion for which there is some evidence—following from the fact that teachers often cover the topics in a book in order (Schmidt, 2011).

The size of a textbook also directly affects the occurrence (or lack thereof) of an opportunity to learn specific topics. Differing lengths can also impact how long an opportunity is to learn those specific topics, and thus, the quality of the learning opportunity. Further, the size of a textbook has other influences on the quality of learning opportunities for specific topics. If a teacher perceives that she or he needs to cover the entire book, then little time will be spent on any one topic, ensuring that the coverage of any one topic will be rather shallow. Such superficial study could well explain why children forget much of the mathematics they study and, perhaps, why teachers often cover the same redundant material year after year that students apparently have never learned or have forgotten.

Based on the size of mathematics textbooks, a typical U.S. 9-year-old is expected to cover four times as many pages as her peers in the other countries studied in TIMSS. This has the potential to affect greatly not only whether learning opportunities for specific content occur but also the quality of those opportunities. It is also likely that the negative effects of large-sized textbooks will be felt more by disadvantaged children. Given that they often have reading difficulties and that they often struggle more with mathematics than those who are more privileged, how could they not be discouraged by the task of taking on an 800-page textbook?

## Textbook Structure

Mathematics textbooks are designed to influence how teachers and students use their instructional and study time, including both time in the classroom and study time out of the classroom (e.g., student use at home). For this reason, the structure of textbooks represents the authors' convictions about the best way to present the content.

One structural feature concerns content flow—how content is organized across the whole book. It represents a plan for the sequencing of content coverage designed to influence actual classroom coverage of the content. For example, a Swedish mathematics textbook had only ten topic themes, which were developed in a sequence. In effect, these are different sections, each focusing a major portion of the book on a topic or a combination of related topics. There is a clear progression of content covered as students progress through the book. U.S. mathematics textbooks, on the other hand, are typically not organized in this blocked, sequential way. They are more fragmented, moving among many topics in what appears to be a disconnected manner. Rarely did U.S. books sustain coverage of any particular topic. The pattern was brief coverage of a topic interrupted by similar short coverage of other topics, only to return to the original topic.

To analyze formally the structure of the textbooks, we characterized the number of breaks (changes from one topic to another) found in textbooks. Breaks were defined relative to the flow of content. *Content flow* was defined as successive textbook material that shares the same content focus. What interests us is the number of times such a focus changes from the beginning to end of the book. Such a change is defined as a break in the content flow of the textbook.

Large numbers of breaks indicate a pattern of short, non-continuous coverage of a topic. This would show a frequent occurrence of leaving and then subsequently returning to a topic. The topics covered in such a textbook would be constantly changing, with a very fragmented, interrupted flow of content throughout the book and a high degree of repetition. Books with few such interruptions in their flow would indicate that they cover content more coherently. This would likely provide a more supportive context for the learning opportunities presented through the textbook—one from which students would be more likely to learn. In textbooks with fewer breaks and more flow, content themes would be built in a focused way. Each new content area would be built on a foundation that is developed by the content preceding it. These two different textbook structures—sustained versus fragmented coverage of the same content—likely would have an effect on the quality of learning opportunities for the students who use the books.

TIMSS countries' textbooks, on average, had around 50 breaks in content flow at the three grade levels studied: 4th grade, 8th grade, and high school. Those countries with high average achievement scores used textbooks with few such breaks. For example, 4th-grade textbooks from South Korea, Hong Kong, Singapore, the Netherlands, and Japan each had fewer than 30 breaks. One Singapore textbook had only ten breaks, while one Korean textbook had only five breaks.

Three leading U.S. 4th-grade textbooks were analyzed, and they showed 307, 202, and 122 breaks, respectively. That is, the U.S. textbooks had from three to ten times more breaks than the textbooks from high-achieving countries. Contrast the 307 breaks of one U.S. textbook with the five breaks of one of the South Korean books and the difference is obvious. Of course, this partly reflects the fact that the U.S. books were longer and covered more topics than other countries. Even so, there are only 44 topics in the entire mathematics framework, many of which are inappropriate for 4th grade. Therefore, 307 breaks implies that the U.S. textbook kept changing back and forth among a small number of topics.

At 8th grade, U.S. mathematics textbooks also had many breaks—215, 195, 151, and 129—while most of the textbooks from the top-achieving countries had fewer than 25 breaks. One 8th-grade mathematics textbook from the Czech Republic and one from Japan each had fewer than 15 breaks. These were both high-achieving countries in 8th-grade mathematics. There were two exceptions among the high-achieving countries. A South Korean mathematics textbook and one from Hong Kong had around 50 to 60 breaks each, which is still less by far than the number of breaks in U.S. 8th-grade mathematics textbooks.

U.S. 12th-grade textbooks for advanced mathematics—mostly calculus and precalculus—were more similar to those found in the other countries. However, one U.S. advanced textbook had 174 breaks. Other advanced U.S. textbooks had around 60 breaks, which compares favorably with some of the 12th-grade mathematics textbooks for the high-achieving countries like Singapore (79 breaks) and Hong Kong (63 breaks). However, one South Korean mathematics textbook had 130 breaks.

Science textbooks were even more fragmented. The U.S. 4th-grade science textbooks analyzed had 240, 240, and 145 breaks. This does not compare well with the books of high-achieving 4th-grade-science countries, which had fewer than 25 breaks (South Korea, Japan, Singapore, and Hong Kong—except for one Hong Kong book that had 44 breaks). The number of breaks in 8th-grade science textbooks increased radically compared with 4th-grade books, including 633, 494, and 342 breaks. The high-achieving 8th-grade-science countries (Hong Kong, Singapore, Japan, and South Korea) had textbooks with 88 or fewer breaks. This likely reflects the fact that school science at this level is represented by at least four science disciplines—physics, chemistry, biology, and geology. More subjects being covered would likely result in more breaks, even if the content were not covered in a completely fragmented way. Even U.S. 12th-grade physics textbooks (including Advanced Placement Physics) had many breaks, certainly more than the books in the high-achieving science countries. The two U.S. physics textbooks examined had 268 and 186 breaks. The four Asian countries—Japan, Hong Kong, South Korea, and Singapore—each had textbooks with 80 or fewer breaks.

## The Implications of Textbook Size and Structure

Both U.S. mathematics and science textbooks were physically very large and had extremely large numbers of breaks in their content flow. A suggestion of what this means is stated in an analysis of textbooks for the TIMSS countries:

> One way to understand a textbook structure laden with content strand breaks is to consider this as a degree of compositional complexity. Textbooks with more than one strand must coordinate a number of distinct content elements into a presentation that makes sense to teachers and students. Textbooks with greater numbers of strands appear to be attempting to incorporate many more distinct elements. The challenges for sense making would seem greater. (Valverde et al., 2002, p. 121)

That is, as books come to have more breaks than topics, the challenge of making sense of the content becomes greater and the composition and structure of the books becomes more complex. The fragmented, bulky character of U.S. science and mathematics textbooks is a challenge for students and teachers as they try to make sense of the content. Considered together with complex topics or groups of topics, U.S. textbooks make learning science and mathematics more difficult for most students in the United States, especially compared with similar students in other countries. The problem is likely to be greater for disadvantaged students, such as those from low SES families.

Furthermore, the differences among U.S. textbooks of the same level and type were very striking. In U.S. 4th-grade mathematics textbooks, the number of breaks ranged from more than 122 for one to more than 300 for another. Both were large compared with other countries' books. Even so, the difference in size between them was also large, which has the potential to make differences in the quality of learning opportunities for students even larger if the teachers using the two books followed them closely. Moreover, the topics in the books were not even the same. Such complex textbooks, already fraught with the potential for unequal content coverage, were even more likely to produce differences in opportunities to learn. Such differences in the complexity of composition were found in mathematics textbooks at other levels and for science textbooks as well. The differences were especially large for 8th-grade science textbooks, where the number of breaks ranged from 342 for one book to 633 for another.

U.S. textbooks appear to offer the worst of all worlds. The complexity was greater than all the other countries' books we analyzed. Compared with other countries, the United States is unnecessarily increasing the difficulties of learning science and mathematics by using books such as these. The bad situation is further complicated by the fact that this increased difficulty is not consistent among U.S. classrooms, since some U.S. books were much more complex than others. Already unequal learning opportunities in science and mathematics are made more so by adding unnecessary difficulty to topics that already vary in different books and, thus, for different students.

## ASSESSMENTS AND TESTS

This section examines state assessments, standardized achievement tests, and high school exit exams to determine their role in creating inequalities in content coverage. Those who make educational policies, choose textbooks, or decide what is going to happen in their own classrooms are often keenly aware of the implications that such external tests have. In this section, we examine the role that such tests play in creating variation related to content coverage.

There is a sort of *chicken-and-egg paradox* in talking about tests. It may seem strange to think of tests as something that could influence content coverage. Tests are more naturally thought of as a way to measure student attainments that result from the learning opportunities students have had. They clearly serve this *egg* role of measuring attainments and outcomes. However, not all mathematics (or other content area) tests give us the same information. On the surface, one might expect that "a mathematics test is a mathematics test"—that is, all tests of the same type are pretty much alike. However, upon more careful analysis, not all mathematics tests of the same type are alike in their content coverage (Schmidt, Jakwerth, & McKnight, 1998). As a consequence, using test scores to make decisions about what content to cover or to emphasize can lead to different decisions depending on the assessment chosen. Although two mathematics tests may both assess mathematics, they will likely differ in their focus on particular mathematics content, even for the same grade.

However, tests also play the role of a *chicken*. They can influence what content will be covered in the future. Past tests can shape future opportunities. Once again, the operative word is *can*, because the extent of this influence likely varies depending on the teacher and how strongly other influences impact his or her content decision making. Many teachers do "teach to the test," as knowledge of the content covered on tests taken in the past influences what they teach in the future. This is especially true for tests that have a great deal riding on their results (so-called *high-stakes* tests). In some districts, it is not uncommon for teachers to spend some limited time preparing students to take their state's assessment test, especially with the advent of NCLB. Today, low performance on a state assessment can place a school in a precarious position with respect to NCLB regulations. Since school principals are well aware of this, they can put great pressure on teachers to focus on the content that is expected to be on the test. Many critics of the No Child Left Behind Act focus on this issue as one of their major concerns. Test results can also affect state curriculum policymakers and, eventually, those who design textbooks. In this way, tests directly shape learning opportunities.

As with textbooks and standards, tests give teachers another signal concerning content coverage. This can evolve into "noise" if the multiple signals are not consistent with each other, which they often are not. It is hard to make reasonable decisions in a noisy environment. For that reason, we look at three types of tests in this chapter—state assessments, commercially available standardized achievement tests, and high school exit exams.

State assessments are comparable in their role of influencing learning opportunities to state curriculum standards (as discussed in Chapter 2). They may also be an even greater source of inequalities than standards when it comes to learning opportunities across states. State assessments tend to drive teachers' choices and decisions more than state standards. State standards are often vague in specifying what content should be covered and for how long. In comparison, tests give a very concrete picture of which content to cover, emphasize, and spend more time on. Here, we examine state mathematics assessments for 14 states, focusing on 4th and 8th grade.[6]

Standardized (achievement) tests can have similar effects, although they play very different roles within the educational system. Districts typically use them as an additional source of information about their students' performance. Not all districts do this, but those that do use such achievement tests are interested in comparing their students' performance with national benchmarks—that is, to determine how well similar students do nationally. State assessments only indicate student performance levels relative to students in other schools in the same state. Standardized tests permit results to be compared against a national sample.[7] Inevitably, the content of these tests also helps shape future learning opportunities in the states or districts in which they are used. This potentially contributes further to the differences among districts that we discussed in Chapters 2, 3, and 6. In this section, we present results for seven of the standardized tests sold in the United States that cover 3rd through 8th grade.

Finally, many states want to increase the rigor of their high school programs. To do this, they have initiated high school exit examinations. These are sometimes linked to whether students will receive their high school diplomas, which makes them a very high-stakes examination for the students involved. As a result, they have a powerful impact on shaping learning opportunities.

One further point about tests needs to be made. Clearly, tests have the potential to contribute to inequality in learning opportunities among districts and states because they have an influence through administrators and teachers on what content might be covered and emphasized and because they can shape how much time is devoted to covering particular topics. However, they also can dilute the effectiveness of other policy instruments that shape learning opportunities, such as state and district standards. Studies have shown that state assessments do not necessarily align well with state standards (Porter et al., 2011; Rothman, Slattery, Vranek, & Resnick, 2002).

Tests cannot cover all the content in an area that students are expected to learn. They sample the content on which they will test, defining only a representative sample of that content. Teaching to the test, therefore, has the potential to dilute content coverage that is not included on the test (often based on past experience with the tests). Different teachers within the same district or state are likely to interpret signals from past tests differently. Some will ignore the test results in determining what to teach. Others will use the tests to shape their instructional plans. Both reactions exacerbate the differences in content coverage among states and districts—and even within districts. Tests provide just one more varied signal of which learning opportunities should be included in the classroom.

### State Assessments

We will first consider the results of an analysis of the state assessments for 14 states that were in place in early 2000.[8] The results indicated how much emphasis different topics received on each state assessment. *Emphasis* is defined as the percentage of test items focusing on a particular topic. We examined only 4th- and 8th-grade tests. These were typically the only grades tested before the No Child Left Behind Act introduced mandatory testing for all students in 3rd through 8th grades.

Consider the 4th-grade results first (see Table 8.1). We used seven broad categories of content to look at the percentage of items on each of the 14 state assessments that focused on each category of content. The differences among topics emphasized were very large, especially for a grade level so early in the education process. For example, consider simple arithmetic, which focuses mainly on the four operations with whole numbers—addition, subtraction, multiplication, and division. The percentages of test items devoted to simple arithmetic on the 14 state assessments ranged from 15% to 66%.

Imagine being a teacher in the two states with the greatest and least emphasis, respectively, on simple arithmetic. The state assessment tests for 4th-graders would drive teachers in these two states in two entirely different directions in teaching mathematics. If students had taken each of these two tests, what would the teacher think should be emphasized the next year in 4th-grade mathematics? In one state, you would focus on arithmetic. This would include transition arithmetic—fractions, decimals, percentages, and so on—since simple arithmetic and transition arithmetic, combined, represented about 90% of the items on the test. The test would send a clear signal to 4th-grade teachers in that state. Arithmetic is king; the rest of mathematics is not particularly important.

Another state's assessment focused almost entirely (86%) on measurement and data. Parents in this state, unaware of this unique definition of 4th-grade mathematics, would assume that if their child did well on the state test, then he or she was mastering basic arithmetic concepts and computation, since this is what most parents think that 4th-grade mathematics is all about.[9]

**Table 8.1. Percentage of content coverage (by items) for 4th-grade state assessments.**

| | | | | | Topic Area | | |
|---|---|---|---|---|---|---|---|
| State | Arithmetic | Transition Arithmetic | Data | Geometry | Measurement | Functions | Equations |
| 1 | 15 | 18 | 57 | 25 | 29 | 8 | 3 |
| 2 | 66 | 23 | 47 | 43 | 13 | 17 | 11 |
| 3 | 49 | 5 | 10 | 9 | 10 | 28 | 1 |
| 4 | 56 | 11 | 14 | 28 | 17 | 3 | 8 |
| 5 | 18 | 10 | 23 | 32 | 30 | 12 | 3 |
| 6 | 54 | 18 | 11 | 10 | 10 | 4 | 24 |
| 7 | 51 | 24 | 19 | 16 | 19 | 6 | 16 |
| 8 | 38 | 16 | 24 | 27 | 16 | 7 | 2 |
| 9 | 50 | 44 | 17 | 31 | 10 | 17 | 4 |
| 10 | 25 | 11 | 18 | 25 | 22 | 12 | 1 |
| 11 | 45 | 15 | 15 | 20 | 35 | 5 | 5 |
| 12 | 56 | 14 | 18 | 17 | 15 | 15 | 2 |
| 13 | 58 | 30 | 13 | 19 | 19 | 5 | 8 |
| 14 | 48 | 6 | 13 | 17 | 12 | 2 | 8 |

Most of these state assessments covered whole number arithmetic in a substantial percentage of their items. This percentage reached about half of the test for ten of the states. Four states included a much smaller number of simple arithmetic items. The percentage of items covering transition arithmetic ranged from about 5% of one's state assessment to almost half of another state's assessment. Geometry was also a category that differed among these 14 state assessments.

Among the 14 states, 8th-grade assessments differed even more in the content they covered (see Table 8.2). We used the same seven content categories as we used for the 4th-grade mathematics tests. However, the results showed that the emphasis at 8th grade had shifted to two areas of algebra—linear equations and functions. One state had essentially no coverage of linear equations on its 8th-grade mathematics assessment (literally, 1% of the test items). Another state had around one-half of the test devoted to this content. About half of the states had assessments with 10% or fewer of the items focusing on algebra. The other half varied between 12% and 32% (excluding the state already mentioned that had 48% of its items devoted to this).

Clearly, the differences in state assessments were as variable as the differences in state standards described in Chapter 2. That is, both state assessments and state standards varied among the states, although not necessarily in the same ways. These findings pose a problem for issues of equality. Teachers who make decisions about what to cover and for how long tend to pay more

**Table 8.2. Percentage of content coverage (by items) for 8th-grade state assessments.**

| | | | | Topic Area | | | |
|---|---|---|---|---|---|---|---|
| State | Arithmetic | Transition Arithmetic | Data | Geometry | Measurement | Functions | Equations |
| 1 | 4 | 15 | 64 | 10 | 7 | 22 | 1 |
| 2 | 73 | 80 | 40 | 33 | 48 | 10 | 15 |
| 3 | 12 | 27 | 37 | 20 | 27 | 17 | 8 |
| 4 | 39 | 51 | 12 | 15 | 11 | 22 | 5 |
| 5 | 24 | 37 | 19 | 28 | 16 | 0 | 14 |
| 6 | 3 | 19 | 22 | 35 | 51 | 8 | 19 |
| 7 | 18 | 60 | 17 | 13 | 12 | 2 | 31 |
| 8 | 38 | 50 | 25 | 33 | 17 | 4 | 12 |
| 9 | 6 | 18 | 32 | 34 | 74 | 6 | 10 |
| 10 | 1 | 27 | 25 | 39 | 15 | 11 | 6 |
| 11 | 7 | 18 | 23 | 23 | 22 | 8 | 5 |
| 12 | 55 | 82 | 17 | 27 | 18 | 4 | 32 |
| 13 | 19 | 25 | 18 | 22 | 16 | 3 | 10 |
| 14 | 13 | 29 | 23 | 39 | 29 | 2 | 48 |

attention to state tests than they do to state standards. If there are great differences among tests from state to state, it will have even more impact than differences among state standards. Consider a child in a state where 50% of the state assessment is about algebra and another 40% is about geometry. Now consider a second child who lives in a state where 13% of the items are devoted to algebra and 23% are devoted to geometry. If the first child does well on her assessment, then she is likely to have an easier time in future mathematics courses in high school and college than the second child, even if both children do well on their state's assessment. The parents of both children would assume that their child is well prepared for further mathematics work, since each did well on the state's assessment. Parents usually do not have access to the more technical information about what the content of their state's assessment is or how demanding it is, compared with the assessments of other states. In a sense, this is a lack of *truth in advertising*, a lack of which the state officials themselves may not be aware of. However, it is a lack with consequences—possibly very serious consequences—for at least one of the children involved.

These differences carry another powerful implication: They make it impossible for parents or policymakers to know which states are doing a better job in mathematics instruction. The content of the assessments in our study varied dramatically from state to state. A child's score and official conclusions as to the child's proficiency in mathematics could well change if that child were to move to another state. When the measuring stick changes from state to state, it becomes very hard to tell what the measurement means, even if it says that a child is standing tall. In response to this problem, the Obama administration has funded the development of two new assessments as part of the Race to the Top program, which will become available in 2014 for states that have adopted the Common Core State Standards.

## Standardized Achievement Tests

We now look at the same sort of results for seven major standardized test series available for purchase in early 2000 by districts and schools.[10] Many school districts use standardized tests to determine how well their students achieve relative to a nationally representative sample of similar students. This use of standardized tests is likely more widespread in wealthier districts, since they have the financial resources to use such tests. More important, the parents of students in such districts want to have these results available as they begin to assess their children's chances of going to a good college or university. Obviously, these districts want their students to perform well so that parents will remain pleased with the district's performance. Thus, it is possible that the content covered on these tests will have an impact on the content that is covered by teachers in that district.

The decision about what content the tests will cover is not made by state officials or any elected body. Firms that develop tests, item writers, and others hired by these firms make the decisions about what to cover and what to emphasize. Table 8.3 summarizes the results of our analyses of these tests. As we expected, the tests differed from one another in the content covered at both 4th and 8th grade. What these tests cover is also at odds with what is covered in other countries, especially at 8th grade.

Basic whole number arithmetic dominated the 4th-grade content, which comprised half or more of the items on all these 4th-grade tests. However, there were substantial differences among the 4th-grade tests. Items devoted to basic whole number arithmetic ranged from 56% to 89% of the items on the eight tests. Even larger differences existed at 4th grade for transition arithmetic. Two tests devoted less than 10% of their items to fractions, decimals, percents, and so on. Another had almost 30% of its items focused on this content. There were also large differences in the area of measurement, for which the percentage of the items ranged from around 5% to around 24% of the items.

These differences were just as pronounced at 8th grade, especially as the focus of 8th grade turns to algebra. Four of the seven tests had less than 10% of their items focused on linear equations, a key algebraic topic. Another test had 26% of its items devoted to this same content. One test had over 80% of its items focused on whole number arithmetic and less than 10% on algebra. However, another test that could have been purchased by the same districts had only about 35% of its items on whole number arithmetic and about 40% of its items focused on geometry and algebra.

## High School Exit Examinations

High school exit examinations have a different character from the other two kinds of examinations. They often have a role in certification, as in many

**Table 8.3. Percentage of coverage (by items) for 4th- and 8th-grade published standardized tests.**

| Topic Area | 4th-Grade Publisher | | | | | | | | 8th-Grade Publisher | | | | | | | |
|---|---|---|---|---|---|---|---|---|---|---|---|---|---|---|---|---|
| | 1 | 2 | 3 | 4 | 5 | 6 | 7 | 8 | 1 | 2 | 3 | 4 | 5 | 6 | 7 | 8 |
| Arithmetic | 64 | 63 | 65 | 56 | 89 | 83 | 63 | 67 | 40 | 44 | 37 | 65 | 79 | 33 | 82 | 55 |
| Transition Arithmetic | 19 | 25 | 9 | 12 | 9 | 23 | 29 | 26 | 63 | 64 | 46 | 44 | 54 | 71 | 59 | 63 |
| Data | 23 | 19 | 9 | 17 | 8 | 22 | 11 | 15 | 18 | 10 | 19 | 17 | 23 | 15 | 12 | 15 |
| Geometry | 10 | 13 | 8 | 21 | 3 | 16 | 10 | 5 | 18 | 20 | 10 | 29 | 7 | 14 | 14 | 14 |
| Measurement | 10 | 13 | 12 | 19 | 5 | 24 | 7 | 14 | 13 | 11 | 12 | 23 | 5 | 6 | 15 | 9 |
| Functions | 2 | 0 | 5 | 2 | 0 | 0 | 3 | 6 | 4 | 3 | 4 | 0 | 1 | 2 | 2 | 4 |
| Equations | 4 | 8 | 9 | 2 | 0 | 0 | 7 | 8 | 8 | 18 | 26 | 17 | 9 | 3 | 3 | 14 |

cases, they determine whether students ending high school will be certified by receiving a high school diploma. In that sense, they indicate the completion of high school with successful mastery of important content. We present results for these examinations similarly to those for the other two types of tests that we studied.

We analyzed high school exit examinations for eight states. The tests were designed to ensure that students graduating from high school in the state in which the test was given had mastered the mathematics they would need for work or for university study. As with the other tests analyzed in this chapter, they differed from one another in the content they covered. One state exit examination focused around 50% of its items on algebra and only around 15% of its items on arithmetic (both whole number arithmetic and transition arithmetic topics such as fractions and percentages). Another state used an exit examination that had about 30% of its items on arithmetic and about 30% on algebra. One state had an exit examination that was almost dominated by geometry (80% of its items) while another had very little geometry on it (about 6% of its items). Students who took these examinations successfully would all be certified as having mastered basic high school mathematics and would graduate supposedly ready for further mathematics study in college, or for taking jobs that required a high school education in mathematics, but their "mastery" was certified for very different content.

## A LAST THOUGHT ON THE INFLUENCE OF TEXTBOOKS AND TESTS

By this point, it should hardly be a surprise that, just as with other sources such as standards and textbooks that can have an impact on content coverage, there is considerable variation among the different mathematics tests, for all three types we examined. This diversity has two major consequences. First, tests, like textbooks, contribute to inequalities in learning opportunities observed at the state, district, school, and classroom levels. Both send signals to the teachers as to which content they should cover, to what depth, and in the case of textbooks, in what sequence. The two sets of signals are not necessarily aligned with each other, nor are they necessarily aligned with state, district, and school standards. Because of the fragmented nature of the U.S. educational system, teachers are faced with multiple, varied, and often conflicting messages about which content they should cover. As a consequence, teachers are being placed in a complex and difficult decision-making situation, especially if their backgrounds did not prepare them to deal with such curriculum issues. Given the inconsistency of the messages, different teachers—even those teaching the same grade in the same school—will likely arrive at different decisions, resulting in inequalities in content coverage.

The second consequence is unique to tests and assessments. Because of the differences in the mathematics content emphasized in different tests, they also add confusion in the assessment of student learning. In using a particular test, administrators and teachers believe they have a precise and scientific measure of the attainments of the students being tested and a measure of the school's success in teaching mathematics. However, what has been measured is actually very different. When they go on to later grades, college, or work, the students will differ greatly in their preparation and they will be surprised by those differences, as will their parents. These differences among important tests not only add confusion about what content should be covered and emphasized in schooling, but they also create confusion in understanding how effective schooling has been.

# Part III

# FACING THE CONSEQUENCES

## CHAPTER 9

# Content Coverage Matters

The previous chapters have laid out in detail a fundamental truth of American education: Children do not receive equal content coverage or equivalent learning opportunities in mathematics. The data indicated that such inequalities can occur because of the state and local community in which the child lives, which school within the community he or she attends, who the teacher is, what textbook is used, and what tests are taken. In this chapter, we look at the consequences of such a system of schooling. More specifically, the fundamental issue of this chapter is whether differences in content exposure are related to what children actually learn. If content coverage does vary—if schools do matter—then the differences we discuss are of more than theoretical interest. They are signs of a system in which opportunities are driven more by chance than by design, and that these differences have real consequences in terms of what mathematics children learn in school.

Some would suggest that schooling does not matter. In their formulation, cognitive ability and its distribution in the population and in various subpopulations defined by SES, as described in *The Bell Curve*,[1] is what matters. *The Bell Curve*'s authors have claimed that schooling has little real impact on such abilities. If, however, observed differences in learning opportunities *are* related to mathematics learning, which itself is a component of cognitive ability, then these observed differences in learning opportunities (especially those found in Chapter 3—differences in content coverage related to the SES of the district) suggest that the opportunities provided by schooling are an important lever by which the impact of social class can be lessened. They are a means by which at least *some* of the achievement gaps that plague our society can be *lessened*. Murray (2008) calls this "educational romanticism" and regards it as naïve, dangerous, and something to be avoided (p. 1). If, contrary to such beliefs, these relationships are matters of empirical facts—if the idea that school does not matter is rebutted by the evidence—then equalizing content learning opportunities becomes one of our best and most visible means for establishing the level playing field for all of America's children. Schooling will be returned to its rightful role as the means to a better life that has so long been a part of the American dream and of America's vision of itself.

The truth is that there is a large amount of evidence that content coverage resulting from formal schooling—that is, learning opportunities—does, in fact, relate to academic achievement. What follows is an elaboration of this point.

## ACHIEVEMENT AROUND THE WORLD

Numerous studies (including reviews of *The Bell Curve*) have provided strong evidence that OTL is related to academic achievement (Brophy & Good, 1986; Floden, 2002; McDonnell, 1995; Smith, 2002; Suter, 2000). Recent research has contributed to the evidence, including the work of Rowan and colleagues and Porter and colleagues (Hill, 2005; Porter, 1989, 1991, 2002; Porter, Floden, Freeman, Schmidt, & Schwille, 1986, Porter et al., 1988; Rowan, Camburn, & Correnti, 2004; Rowan, Harrison, & Hayes, 2004). A review of this work can be found in the *AERA Handbook of Education Policy Research* (Schmidt & Maier, 2009, Chapter 44). In this chapter, we focus on another body of work—that related to data from the 1995 Third International Mathematics and Science Study (TIMSS) exploring the relationship of OTL to achievement across some 30 countries. We used measures of content coverage defined at the national level (the counterparts of the state and district standards discussed earlier) as well as at the classroom level, including analyses of the textbooks used, to provide an inter-country analysis of content opportunities and their relationships to achievement.[2]

With respect to variation in OTL, we found much the same situation among countries that we found among classrooms, districts, and states within the United States. The national mathematics standards of different countries were quite varied in the content that was intended to be covered. There were differences in what was available in each country's textbooks and also in what was covered in each country's classrooms. Various aspects of the curriculum always differed when we looked across countries. They differed for various topics within a country as well, but not in the same way in each country. The variations in OTL at all levels were large across the countries we studied.

The cross-national differences in achievement gains from 7th to 8th grade[3] were found to be related to country differences in the content covered. This result held even when we controlled for economic and social differences among countries (e.g., in their GDP). We concluded that schools do matter among nations around the world (or at least in the "TIMSS world"). We also found evidence that social and economic factors (such as SES) were related to student learning in all countries. However, the effects of social and economic factors were not so strong that they excluded the effects of differences in curriculum.

In another set of analyses, we examined how different aspects of the curriculum worked together to influence student learning and achievement in each of the TIMSS countries (Schmidt et al., 2001). We found a variety of patterns, and we present two of them here: one in Japan and the other in the United States—both at the 8th-grade level (Schmidt et al., 2001). In Japan, the content defined in the national standards was directly related to the textbook content used in a majority of that nation's classrooms. That is, the topics covered in the textbooks were derived from the national standards. Both the national standards and what content was covered in textbooks had a direct impact on how Japan's teachers allocated their instructional time to topics; more instructional time, on average, given to a topic related to higher student achievement gains for Japan's 8th-grade students on that topic. We conducted our analysis across the 20 8th-grade mathematics topics available in TIMSS.[4]

Put differently, if a mathematics topic was found in Japan's national standards, then it was related to the amount of coverage it received in Japan's textbooks. Both national standards and textbook coverage of the topic were related to how much time Japanese teachers allocated, on average, for instruction on that topic. Greater instructional time was related to greater achievement gains during that year of schooling for typical 8th-grade Japanese students. This relationship pattern and the influence of content coverage it suggests are summarized in Figure 9.1. The Japanese pattern seems to be what one would expect. It reflects an educational system where the various aspects of content coverage work together and toward greater achievement.

As a contrast, the U.S. pattern is illustrated in Figure 9.2. The only relationship of content coverage to achievement gains at the national level

**Figure 9.1. Estimated structural model of curriculum and achievement for 8th-grade mathematics in Japan.**

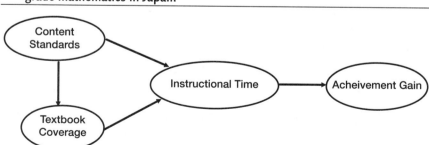

*Note.* Figure from *Why Schools Matter: A Cross National Comparison of Curriculum and Learning* (p. 283), by W. H. Schmidt, C. C. McKnight, R. T. Houang, H. A. Wang, D. E. Wiley, L. Cogan, & R. G. Wolfe, 2001, San Francisco: Jossey-Bass. Copyright 2001 by Jossey-Bass. This material is reproduced with permission of JohnWiley & Sons.

came from differences in textbook coverage. The amount of space allocated to covering a topic in a student textbook was directly related to the size of the achievement gain for a typical U.S. 8th-grade student on that topic. The amount of space allocated to covering the topic in a textbook was also related to the average amount of instructional time allocated to that topic. However, apart from the content differences in textbooks being related to average gains in achievement, there was no separate relationship of teacher allocated time to learning (gains in achievement).

This implies that content coverage in textbooks has a powerful relationship in the United States to student learning, more important than the relationship of teacher instructional time on a topic to such gain. It must be kept in mind that this analysis was done at the country level, and therefore, the relationship should not be generalized to similar relationships at the school or classroom level. Further, there is no statistically significant relationship of the presence of a topic in the content standards to the textbook coverage of it or the amount of instructional time related to it or to average student achievement gains. This most likely reflects the absence of clearly articulated national standards at the time of the study. The differences among state and district standards did not present a unified *national* picture of content standards and the aggregate covered virtually every topic. Thus, it is not surprising that there is no relationship between "national" (combined state) standards and student performance. Perhaps this will change over time as the new Common Core State Standards become the "national" standards.

The absence of a relationship in the United States between teacher instructional time for a topic and student learning for that same topic may

**Figure 9.2. Estimated structural model of curriculum and achievement for 8th-grade mathematics in the United States.**

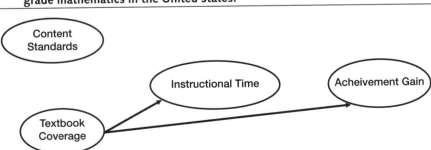

*Note.* Figure from *Why Schools Matter: A Cross National Comparison of Curriculum and Learning* (p. 283), by W. H. Schmidt, C. C. McKnight, R. T. Houang, H. A. Wang, D. E. Wiley, L. Cogan, & R. G. Wolfe, 2001, San Francisco: Jossey-Bass. Copyright 2001 by Jossey-Bass. This material is reproduced with permission of John Wiley & Sons.

seem unusual; however, it is understandable when we realize that the analysis statistically controlled for textbook coverage of the topic. The answer may well lie in the relationship of the number of pages allocated to a topic in the textbooks to teachers' instructional time related to that topic. That is, teacher time and textbook space were highly correlated. Of the two, textbook space related to a topic dominated the relationship to achievement gains. Compared with Japan, in the United States the textbook has a stronger relationship to how teachers allocated instructional time.

The significant relationship of different aspects of the curriculum to learning (achievement gains) as illustrated for Japan and the United States was replicated in virtually all of the TIMSS countries and for at least some of the 20 topics in mathematics in almost every country. Which topics differed significantly varied from country to country. What was universally true among these countries was that there was a relationship between content coverage and achievement gain. The topics might differ for which this was true. The aspect of the curriculum—whether the textbook, standards, or teacher coverage—might be different. What did not change was the relationship between content coverage and achievement. The detail of these analyses and the nature of the relationships are too complex and numerous to discuss in this book, but they are discussed in detail elsewhere (Schmidt et al., 2001).

## CLASSROOM-LEVEL ANALYSIS AND U.S. ACHIEVEMENT

We earlier posed the question, are inequalities of content coverage across U.S. classrooms related to differences across classrooms in achievement gains? The international results of the previous section show that the kinds of variations in content coverage found in the United States also existed among nations. Further, it showed that these differences were related to achievement gains. The analyses were done at the country level, averaging over the schools and classrooms for the country. The relationships are therefore defined at the country level. In this section, we ask: If we restricted our attention to what happens in individual classrooms in the United States rather than for the United States as a whole, would we see evidence of a similar relationship?

We present evidence from three sources to help answer this question. First, we summarize two analyses done using the 7th- and 8th-grade classrooms that were a part of the U.S. sample in the 1995 TIMSS study. For each of the 8th-grade classrooms, a summary of the amount of instructional time allocated by the teacher to cover each of 20 mathematics topics was created from the teacher responses to the survey questionnaire.[5] In addition, each student's SES and several instructional variables were included in the analyses to control for student background, motivational factors, and instructional practices. The outcomes were measures of residual gain in achievement for 20 topic areas of mathematics.[6, 7]

These analyses resulted in a general conclusion: Content coverage—that is, the amount of allocated time to a topic—was significantly related to achievement gain for U.S. 8th-grade mathematics students. This was true even when we used statistical methods to adjust for differences in SES. What follows is a quotation from Schmidt et al.'s *Why Schools Matter* that discusses some of the specifics of these analyses. The degree to which the relationships found were logical strengthens the general conclusion, but also contributes to a deeper understanding of how mathematics learning develops from student's exposure to school mathematics content:

> The analyses were formulated to include the curriculum opportunity topic variables directly aligned with the sub-test together with the appropriate prerequisite topic areas (those that were logically related to learning in the target topic area). For example, this included the further learning of whole number arithmetic and fractions at 8th grade. Algebra involves the manipulation of equalities involving whole numbers as well as rational numbers (and thus fractions). Thus, algebra gave additional practice that could have led to improvements in whole number arithmetic and fractions. . . .
>
> For most of these thirteen areas, the relationship was straightforward logically. That is, more time (as a percent of total instructional time) that a teacher spent on a topic was related to a greater achievement score for that topic, given equal achievement in the topic at the seventh grade. That is, this was a measure of learning or achievement change because seventh grade achievement was also included in the model. . . .
>
> Relations of fractions had rational and real numbers as a topic area in which opportunity to learn had a marginally significant relationship to achievement. The same was true for estimating quantity and size, rounding and estimating computations. For perimeter area and volume, the corresponding opportunity variable was not significant but time spent in one and two-dimensional geometry was. This makes sense since these measurements are usually done for the same geometric figures that were studied in the geometry areas. (Schmidt et al., 2001, p. 342)

A second set of analyses we used to explore this issue used data from the Longitudinal Study of American Youth (LSAY). LSAY is a longitudinal study that follows the same students from 7th through 12th grade for a nationally representative set of students (Reynolds, 1991; Reynolds & Walberg, 1992). The data allowed us to examine achievement gains for individual students. This is different from the cohort longitudinal analyses done with TIMSS data, where the longitudinal unit of analysis was the classroom. The data on content coverage were not as detailed as the TIMSS data, nor was the measure of achievement detailed with respect to specific topics. However, LSAY offers the advantage of following students over several years and provides an opportunity for a different kind of evidence to support the conclusions from the TIMSS analyses.

We used a test focused on algebra and geometry from the LSAY achievement data to set up a series of analyses that related the content of the textbooks used by each student in each of the courses they took over the 6 years to their gain in achievement over the same period of time. We used several different models. Each looked at the exposure each student had with particular mathematics content for a 1-year period, such as 10th grade, and then related this to achievement gain on the algebra-geometry test, defined as the difference in the achievement score from the beginning of 10th grade to the beginning of 11th grade (which, ignoring summer, is essentially the end of 10th grade).

In these analyses, content coverage (OTL) was defined as the amount of textbook coverage given to each of the topics in the TIMSS mathematics framework (that is, the LSAY textbook data were analyzed and grouped into the TIMSS content categories). This makes these analyses parallel to those just described from the TIMSS data, since the categories of topic coverage were the same. Of course, this assumes that the number of pages devoted to a topic in the textbook gives a good indication of how much time was spent covering the topic in the actual classrooms, an assumption that is supported by other TIMSS analyses.[8]

The results were consistent with those for TIMSS. Significant relationships existed between content OTL (measured by textbook coverage) and achievement gains on the algebra-geometry test at all but one grade level. These results using longitudinal data on individual students support the conclusions from the previous TIMSS analyses using classroom cohort longitudinal data. In TIMSS, the content coverage data and test areas were more detailed and specific to the mathematics curriculum covered in particular classrooms, but LSAY provides longitudinal results, which are better for estimating learning. Both studies were based on nationally representative samples for the United States. The fact that we obtained similar results with two different indicators of content coverage (textbook space and teacher reports of how much instructional time they spent teaching each topic) makes a stronger argument that mathematics content coverage is related to student achievement. In addition, the fact that the relationship at the country, classroom, and individual student levels were all significant, together with other studies' results, strongly suggests that OTL is related to learning. It is also consistent with our conclusion that textbooks play a prominent role in determining instruction in U.S. classrooms.

The third set of analyses looked at the corresponding relationship between content coverage and achievement at the district level. In Chapter 3, we characterized the relationship between the SES of a school district and the mathematics content coverage for 8th-grade students (using data from the Third International Mathematics and Science Study-Repeat [TIMSS-R] for a sample of 13 districts). Districts with the highest percentage of parents with university degrees had, on average, the largest percentage of students taking classes that focused on algebra and geometry content (see Figure 3.1).

Figure 9.3 shows how the 13 districts performed, on average, on the TIMSS test. It also portrays the strong linear relationship between SES and achievement at the district level, with the higher SES districts having, in general, higher achievement scores. Figure 9.4 shows a similar pattern for the 13 districts as to the relationship of content coverage, defined by their course-taking, to average student achievement (Schmidt, Cogan, Houang, & McKnight, 2011). The relationships were strong in both cases—around 75% of the variance in average student achievement at the district level was attributed to differences in SES in both analyses. What do the three figures (including Figure 3.1 from Chapter 3) imply about the relationship of content coverage and achievement at the district level?[9]

There were substantial differences in content coverage among the 13 districts (as was also demonstrated for the 100-plus districts analyzed in Chapters 2, 3, and 6), reflecting the practice of local control of the curriculum with state standards that can be enforced only relatively weakly. An undesirable consequence of this policy in the United States is that the differences in

**Figure 9.3. Scatterplot with estimated regression line relating SES to the TIMSS mathematics achievement score for 13 districts.**

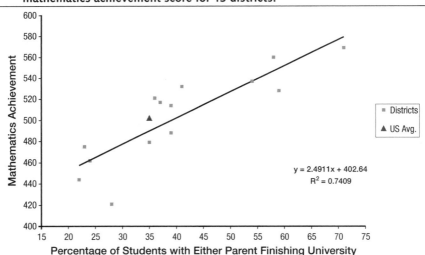

*Note.* Figure adapted from "Equality of Educational Opportunity: Myth or Reality in US Schooling," by W. H. Schmidt, L. S. Cogan, & C. McKnight, 2010, *American Educator, 34*(4), p. 15.

**Figure 9.4. Scatterplot with estimated regression line relating content coverage to the TIMSS mathematics achievement score for 13 districts.**

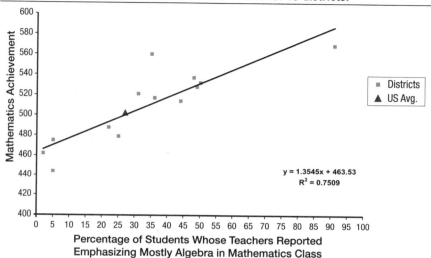

Percentage of Students Whose Teachers Reported
Emphasizing Mostly Algebra in Mathematics Class

content coverage end up being related to the demographics of the districts. The prominent district characteristic that influenced content coverage was the average parental education level. That this occurs reflects the homogeneous nature of housing patterns in the United States along social class lines, combined with the practice of local control of the curriculum.

As a result, the influence of SES on student achievement is further exacerbated. SES is related to achievement, not only through family (and the well-established impacts of human capital), but also through the aggregate effect that the community has on the district's specification of its content expectations. SES has both a direct family effect on achievement and an indirect community effect through community SES's impact on district content coverage.[10] The indirect effect occurs because schools and content coverage, in particular, are related to achievement, as illustrated in Figure 9.4. This can be summarized in Figure 9.5.

We did a more formal hierarchical linear model (HLM) statistical analysis based on the IGP index using the 13 districts.[11] The original data for the districts were collected as random samples of schools and their classrooms. This enabled an analysis that permitted us to examine the relationship of content coverage to learning for classrooms (within schools) and for districts.[12] The estimated classroom relationship was consistent with those described using the TIMSS and LSAY data. What was new was that there was an additional relationship at the district level such that, for a one-grade-level increase in the rigor of the content coverage, the projected increase in achievement would be a 30-point gain on the TIMSS mathematics test.

**Figure 9.5. Hypothesized model relating SES, content coverage, and student learning at the district level.**

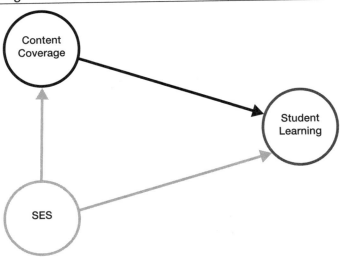

This result suggests that achievement gains at the district level were related to differences in content coverage at the district level (even after controlling for the same relationship at the classroom level), which itself was related to the SES of the district.[13, 14, 15] The combination of the three analyses suggests that achievement gains are related to content coverage at the district level as well as at the national and classroom levels. These district analyses reveal that district-level achievement gains reflect inequalities in OTL, which are related to SES (Schmidt, Cogan, Houang, & McKnight, 2011).

## RELATING TRACKING TO ACHIEVEMENT

One of the arguments we made in Chapter 5 was that tracking in the 8th grade has a pronounced effect on learning opportunities (content coverage). It accounted for about 40% of the variance in content coverage.[16] In this section, we analyze the relationship of tracking to achievement gain using the same U.S. TIMSS sample described earlier in this chapter. Students were not randomly distributed across the different tracks within schools, which made it difficult to examine the relationship of tracking to achievement gain. The differences in achievement across tracks could be related to the differences in the mathematics ability of those who are selected into various tracks or who selected tracks for themselves.[17, 18] We first examined the means on the TIMSS 7th- and 8th-grade mathematics test according to the three tracks we used in Chapter 5—Regular Mathematics, Pre-algebra, and Algebra I.

The average performance in the regular mathematics track classrooms in the U.S. 7th-grade sample was about 60 points lower than that for the pre-algebra classrooms. There was an almost 100-point difference on average achievement between the 8th-grade regular mathematics track classrooms and the 8th-grade algebra track classrooms. The difference between the two 8th-grade tracks represented a difference of one standard deviation and was approximately equal to the difference between average U.S. student achievement and the achievement of students in South Korea and Japan, the two countries that had the second and third highest achievement scores in these grades, respectively.[19]

However, we are not simply interested in differential achievement by tracks. We want to know whether the mean achievement differences across the three tracks were related to the mean differences across the tracks in content coverage, or whether they merely reflected differences in ability, which is how membership in the various tracks is usually determined.

There were large differences in mathematics achievement according to differences in the tracks students were in when they studied mathematics. This was true even after statistical methods were used to eliminate differences in SES and in prior mathematics achievement. Therefore, U.S. 8th-grade mathematics students differed in what they achieved in mathematics, a difference that was related not just to their socioeconomic status or to a measure of achievement in 7th grade.

In Chapter 5, differences in content covered for each of the three tracks were characterized in considerable detail. We noted large differences in the learning opportunities provided by the different tracks. Clearly, these differences in learning opportunity were related to what the students learned (gained) when they had those differing learning opportunities during 8th grade.[20, 21] The differences between the algebra track and the regular track were large and statistically significant—over 60 points on the TIMSS test.[22] There were also significant differences between the pre-algebra and the regular mathematics track, about a 30-point difference.[23] In terms of predicting how students will score from the content covered, a typical U.S. 8th-grade mathematics student exposed to the content of the algebra track would have a mean achievement similar to that of students from two of the top five 8th-grade achievement countries in TIMSS.[24] Once again, the evidence is overwhelming that content coverage is indeed related to student learning in mathematics.

## RELATING INEQUALITIES IN CONTENT COVERAGE TO ACHIEVEMENT

In this chapter, we examined the relationship of opportunity to learn and mathematics learning. The first eight chapters of this book established empirically that, taken as a whole, the American educational system did not, and still does not, provide equality of content coverage even though the system was built on the concept of schooling as the great equalizer—providing equal opportunity for all.

This chapter has examined the consequences of that reality. We found that at multiple levels of the system, including districts, schools, tracks, and classrooms, there were statistically significant relationships between opportunity and student learning. We defined opportunity to learn in terms of content rigor and the amount of instructional time allocated to specific topics. It is this reality—that schooling matters to student learning—that makes the inequalities characterized throughout this book fundamentally important both to the nation and to individual students.

## CHAPTER 10

# From Inequality to Equality:
# The Road We Must Follow

We have told many stories in this book—both about people and about data. But what is the main story? It is a story of schooling in America and the consequent inequalities—a story of what has been and what is, but hopefully not what will be. In Chapter 2, we asked whether, educationally, the United States really was "one nation," as stated in the Pledge of Allegiance. Sadly, the simple but clear answer found in the data is *no*.

## WHAT IS AND WHAT HAS BEEN

The inequalities in content coverage begin with the state and local community in which a child is to attend school—a reality over which many adults (let alone their children) have no control—and continue with the neighborhood school to which the child is assigned. Furthermore, two children, even from the same family and attending the same school but with different teachers for each of the first five grades, are not likely to have the same learning opportunities. When these children reach middle school, tracking and course choices begin to enter the picture. These placement decisions further exacerbate the differences in learning opportunities over their next seven grades through the end of high school.

The opportunities for learning mathematics can differ in several ways. A topic can be covered or not covered. Topics can be studied in different sequences, some of which may not make any sense from the point of view of the content itself. Students can receive more or less time for instruction, depending on the teacher's decision. All of these differences in content coverage can be found in the varying experiences of children from different families who live in different regions of the state or country. They also can be found for children who attend different schools within the same district. Schools are community-based—representative of the community in which the schools are found—and they set individual policies and practices related to content coverage. Furthermore, schools are only somewhat influenced by district and state policies, and even less by any kind of national policy. As a result, the chances for equivalent content coverage are small. They become even smaller for some groups of children, given the role that social class plays in neighborhood housing patterns and thus in different districts or schools within districts.

Whatever their genesis, it is at the classroom level that intentions are shaped into real opportunities, and as a result, it is here that issues of equality in content coverage play out. Differences among standards—whether these are defined at the state, district, or school level—exist merely on paper. It is in classrooms that teachers make the critical decisions about content: deciding what to cover, for what amount of time, and in what sequence topics will be presented. These professional decisions vary from one teacher to another, even if they teach in the same state, the same district, or the same school. In other words, the observed differences in content coverage derive only in part from the fact that different states, districts, and schools have different content standards. Differences in standards at any of these levels are merely one contributing factor to the large variations observed in classroom content coverage.

Further complicating the expression of clear and coherent intentions for classroom content coverage is that textbooks and tests instantiate their own sense of which topics should be learned. Chapter 8 demonstrated that the major differences between textbooks and assessments compound the documented differences among standards at the state, district, and school levels. These various expressions of intentions for student learning ultimately play out in a particular classroom. As such, they may give rise to national inequalities in classroom content coverage either through differences in intentions across various sources (e.g., standards, textbooks, and assessments) or through differences in the various implementations of the sources (e.g., New York standards versus Texas standards or textbook series A versus textbook series B).

In every neighborhood school in the United States, teachers are confronted with the complex task of formulating a classroom content coverage plan informed by the many different and often conflicting expressions of intentions by their state and district standards, the school curriculum guide, their adopted textbook series, and state assessments and standardized tests. However, as reported in Chapter 7, most teachers, particularly at the elementary level, are not likely to have the mathematics background and the preparation needed to make such complex decisions. The fact that teachers with varying mathematics expertise must make these complex decisions exacerbates the inequalities that stem from diverse curricular intentions. Aggregating the differences in teacher content decisions to the national level only increases the variation that results from where the child attends school.

This provides a reasonable explanatory hypothesis for the observation that anywhere from 60% to 95% of the variation in classroom content coverage was at the classroom—that is, teacher—level. Nonetheless, teachers cannot be blamed for this; they cannot be blamed for being placed in such an incoherent system as what we have in the United States, where, by design, little agreement exists between different definitions of intended content coverage. Put another way, teachers can hardly be blamed for being products of a system in which they experience a relatively weak mathematics curriculum in their own K–12 schooling and then experience relatively weak preparation to teach mathematics (see Center for Research in Mathematics and Science Education, 2010, *Breaking the Cycle*).

For U.S. children, the nation is by no means indivisible. The data we presented in the preceding chapters show the extent to which the nation's children are divided by differing content exposures in mathematics and science. These content learning opportunities define the core of schooling. Since there are so few guarantees for equivalent learning opportunities, public schooling has become more like a game of chance. It clearly does not embody "equality for all," but instead "inequality for all."

Nowhere is this more evident than in 7th and 8th grades, where children are arbitrarily divided into tracks offering different mathematics content learning experiences. The consequences of these seemingly harmless divisions represent further inequalities in opportunities and achievement that can have major economic and social repercussions. For the last 10 years, the *de jure* educational policy of the United States may have been No Child Left Behind and the vision that lies behind that legislation, but the *de facto* policy and practice is quite antithetical, with very different, unintended educational consequences from those envisioned by the legislation.

Sometimes disparities in educational opportunities appear to be insignificant, such as leaving out one topic at a specific grade. However, given the cumulative nature of learning, especially in areas such as mathematics, such differences in opportunities at a specific grade will not necessarily disappear over time. Things will not necessarily "even out." In fact, the opposite is more likely. In education, the "educationally rich" get richer and the "educationally poor" get poorer. This is especially true for the more than 70% of people who never graduate from college, although it is not limited to them.

Economic inequality has recently been a focus of heated public debate, among policymakers, scholars, and the general public. There is an income gap between Wall Street and Main Street workers (Khatiwada, 2010; Philippon & Reshef, 2009) and between corporate staff and their workers (Economic Policy Institute, 2011; Krantz & Hansen, 2011). In education, addressing the achievement gap between White and African American or Hispanic students has dominated the discussion (Chubb & Loveless, 2002; Daily Mail Reporter, 2011; Gabriel, 2010). We are suggesting yet another type of inequality, one with equally serious consequences: inequality in opportunity to learn. We have devoted this book to describing these inequalities, what influences them, and their likely consequences. For example, Chapter 4 suggested that the White versus African-American and Hispanic achievement gap could well be related to inequalities in content coverage. However, this must remain a hypothesis that awaits further study, as it is beyond the scope of this book.

The American ideal of a level playing field has been subverted by a confused, tangled lottery of different opportunities, the differences of which are almost invisible to the eyes of students, parents, and the public. Does schooling provide a way up within society? That is far less likely than we want to believe. More often, students become entangled in different possibilities and are victimized by decisions that they (or others on their behalf) have made without any knowledge of their ultimate consequences. The vision of NCLB—to leave no child behind—faces deadly threats in such an environment, yet this is the real world of U.S. schools.

The consequences of such differences for our society are frightening. The book *The Bell Curve* (Herrnstein & Murray, 1994) suggests that people with less cognitive ability have a greater chance of ending up on welfare, in prison, or being some other burden on society through crime, family structure, unemployment, being injury prone, and the absence of civility and good citizenship. We believe that the authors' controversial conclusions stem at least in part from students' lower-quality education, a consequence of the kinds of inequalities in content coverage we discussed in the preceding chapters. Of course, the consequences they discuss are those that affect our society as a whole. The consequences for these individuals are even more devastating.

The confusing lottery of differing learning opportunities is unacceptable. If we take "freedom" and "equality" seriously, then such large differences in society are unacceptable. Such large differences, as characterized in Chapter 4, among ethnic groups and social classes in the basic opportunities to learn important subject matter are just as unacceptable. This was especially true for content coverage related to algebra and geometry at 7th and 8th grade.

Without arguing too much about what makes a "liberal," we might say that when a liberal considers the phrase "with liberty and justice for all," the essential word in that phrase for him or her is *justice*. A thoughtful liberal likely would argue that such inequalities in content coverage are inherently unjust. These inequalities would be seen as at odds and inconsistent with the fundamental philosophy of social justice and individual rights. For a "conservative," the key word is likely *liberty*, a freedom from constraint within the bounds of an organized and civil society. A thoughtful conservative might argue that such inequalities have consequences for the economy, both in having schools provide an adequately prepared workforce (especially for those not entering professions) and in placing a burden on society through the provision of welfare, prisons, and the like. This would introduce undesirable constraints on what might be done in that society. He or she might feel that this would have not only an economic cost but also a social cost. The social cost would be realized in a strain on the nation's social fabric and in decreased political participation that is essential to democracy, making it harder for economic liberty to be realized. Only a deeply cynical or nihilistic ideologue would not be troubled by these differences.

How does a nation founded on democratic principles and populated by immigrants arrive at educational structures, policies, and practices that encourage if not create inequalities in exposure to important content in public schools? Certainly, it is not a part of our official beliefs. Believing that "all men are created equal" has been a goal, although an elusive one. The answer is, in all probability, part historical and part ideological. America has supported public education as a means to inculcate immigrants with the American way of life. The United States has also supported public education as a way toward a better life for all citizens.

Immigrants flooded this nation during the 19th and the early 20th century. Immigrant parents often worked multiple jobs in order for their children to get a better education. This was seen as the means for those children to "move up" in our society, both economically and socially. Such motives continue to drive many parents to immigrate to the United States in the 21st century. It drives those who are already here to better their lot and that of their descendants.

It is at least in part from this perspective that the concept of a level playing field grew. This is the notion that education is the great leveler and that it helps, in part, to create a meritocratic society. The positions of importance in our society should go to those of merit who can do those jobs and have been prepared to do so, regardless of their original background. It is a part of most Americans' beliefs that if one works hard enough and takes advantage of all opportunities, and in particular educational opportunities, then a better life is there to be had. No barriers should stand in the way of those of real merit and ability who are willing to learn and to work hard. Each individual should be responsible for his or her own success. These beliefs are, at least in part, a consequence of our Puritan predecessors, whose experience helped shape our culture and commonly held beliefs.

This is a strongly individualistic orientation, ideology, or set of beliefs. Historically, during the formation of the United States, there was resistance to the creation of a strong federal government. As a result, the U.S. Constitution left many responsibilities to the states. It did not yield to the federal government any more responsibilities than were thought necessary at the time for the protection of the country and the provision for the common good. States and local regions were left with the responsibility to provide for common public schooling. The result has been almost 15,000 individual local school districts based in local communities and resisting the cession of any authority to states and even more so to the federal government. These structures, policies, and practices were set in place, driven almost exclusively to serve the needs of individual children and groups of children with similar demographic characteristics provided by a relatively homogeneous local community.

The humorist Garrison Keillor likes to talk about the mythical community of Lake Wobegon where "all the women are strong, all the men are good-looking, and all the children are above average." This idea that "all the children are above average," with its self-contradictory irony, is a wonderful statement for humor. The wit pales when it shows up in ways that are seriously believed by American citizens. Many parents seem to believe that this is true—at least for their own children. As a result, parents and others have encouraged all kinds of advanced courses and alternatives in schools such as tracking. This only generates further differences in content learning opportunities for different children.

We have an educational system that in many ways reflects traditional American values. It is widely believed that this system is based on merit, and that an individual's advancement depends on his or her own efforts. Americans, at least in principle, also value equality. However, we have an educational system based on local control (especially of concern here is the control of the curriculum) that allows parents who are the most well-off to pass their advantages to their children through the quality of education that is available to them, regardless of talent and effort. David Brooks, a columnist for the *New York Times*, in discussing economic inequalities, raised a question, writing, "Income inequality is on the rise. The rich are getting better at passing their advantages on to their kids. Lifestyle and values gaps are widening between the educated and uneducated. So the big issue is: Will Americans demand new policies to reverse these trends—to redistribute wealth, to provide greater economic security?" (Brooks, 2007, para. 1).

A similar question can be posed about inequalities in content learning opportunities. Will Americans demand new policies to redistribute content learning opportunities to provide greater equality? Will they reverse this trend and reestablish schools as the level playing field that grants to all a chance at the American dream? Sociologist Seymour Martin Lipset recognized the tension between achievement and equality as a major theme in American history (Lipset, 2003). Brooks draws the implication again with respect to income inequality, that in the tension between achievement and equality, the "achievement ethic reshapes the definition of equality. When Americans use the word 'equality' they really mean 'fair opportunity'" (Brooks, 2007, para. 7).

Considering Lipset's ideas and Brooks's interpretations suggests that Americans do believe in fair opportunity and that this should be the basis for founding an educational system. Perhaps most Americans believe that that is how our schools really work. If so, they are badly deceived.

Are these two types of inequalities related? Economics is usually in the background of debates about education, whether we are discussing the opportunities afforded to individuals or the overall competitiveness of the U.S. economy. Science and mathematics have had a privileged place in these discussions, in part because these subjects are seen to have a more direct impact on finding a job, opening a business, or creating a strong labor force. But educational inequality is about much more than making sure that a few more people have employable skills. The failure of the U.S. educational system to provide equal opportunities to learn for every student—no matter where they live, what school they go to, how much money their parents make, or their ethnicity—makes a mockery of our claims to live in a just society.

It is increasingly clear that the United States has become a highly unequal society in economic terms, as Brooks points out. A smaller proportion of the citizenry controls an ever-greater share of the country's wealth, with income concentrating to a degree not seen since the days of the robber barons. The United States is now one of the most economically unequal societies in the industrialized world (Smeeding, 2005), an inequality that has steadily intensified (McCall & Percheski, 2010). This inequality has been justified on the grounds of economic efficiency, but has been *politically* sustainable principally due to the perception that individual wealth is the result of merit, that those who have garnered great wealth from the free operation of the market have done so through their own talents and hard work. This defense rests on a very specific foundation, however: the principle of equal opportunity. If economic inequalities are due to differences in effort and skill, it might be possible to defend them (Roemer, 2004). However, if there is unequal access to the means for cultivating individual talent, if the educational system fails to provide equal content exposure to develop the skills of all children, then any justification of economic inequality will fail.

Unfortunately, we have strong reasons to believe that equal opportunity for all does not, in fact, hold. The idea of the United States as the land of opportunity, where individual rewards are based on our own efforts, is in all likelihood a myth (Esping-Anderson, 2004). A key piece of evidence is intergenerational mobility. If success in an economy were really based on individual talents and effort, then we would expect a low correlation between the economic position of the father in comparison with the daughter. Historically, the United States has been a country with relatively high rates of intergenerational mobility (Long & Ferrie, 2007); hence, the archetypal Horatio Alger "rags to riches" tale—a story that no longer holds true. Today, the United States is not only one of the world's more unequal societies, but it also has *lower* rates of intergenerational mobility than other advanced democracies (Beller & Hout, 2010; Sawhill & Morton, 2008).

The two dynamics, of unequal distributions of wealth and low rates of mobility, interact with each other in a negative feedback loop, with increasing concentration of wealth in the first generation passing intact to a second generation, witnessing steadily growing divisions of wealth over time (Beller & Hout, 2010; Esping-Anderson, 2004). This phenomenon is not one that takes place just at the top of the income scale, with a few fabulously wealthy families residing atop a prosperous middle-class society. In truth, the incomes of middle-income families have stagnated over the last generation, increasing only because of the entry of women into the workforce (Sawhill & Morton, 2008). At the same time, the U.S. poverty rate has remained unusually high and persistent across generations (Jäntti, 2009).

And why is it that social mobility is so low? Why is it that parental incomes predict between 40% and 60% of their children's incomes? A host of reasons have been presented, from family structure to cultural capital to the nature of the welfare state, but among these must certainly be inequalities in opportunities to learn. Given the gateway function that education serves in providing coverage of content related to important skills, knowledge, problem solving, and reasoning abilities (such as mathematics), it is only logical that inequalities in the provision of such opportunities would reduce the prospects for students from modest economic backgrounds to excel and hence undermine social mobility. The fact that we found higher-income (mostly suburban) districts have consistently greater coverage of rigorous content, especially in grades 6 through 8, and students in low-income districts consistently have fewer such learning opportunities, paints a dire picture for the prospects for upward mobility for some 40% of U.S. children living in low-income families (Chau, Thampi, & Wight, 2010).

The resources given to primary and secondary education, and the guarantees that education is equitably provided, are strongly related to social mobility across countries (Ichino, Karabarbounis, & Moretti, 2010; McCall & Percheski, 2010). Long and Ferrie (2007) demonstrate that the tremendous educational advantage enjoyed by the United States played a major role in its relatively high rate of social mobility in the 19th century. As the returns to education in the economy have grown (going increasingly to affluent children), and as public investment in education has declined, social mobility has declined as well (Beller & Hout, 2010; Mayer, 2001). While practices like tracking are still common in the United States (see Chapter 5), countries that have abolished them, such as Finland, have enjoyed not only superior educational performance on international assessments but have also experienced dramatic increases in social mobility (Pekkarinen, Uusitalo, & Kerr, 2009).

The relationship between socioeconomic status, race, and residency further complicates the picture. Lack of equal educational opportunities has been identified as both one of the chief causes of economic inequality between Blacks and Whites (Bertocchio & Dimico, 2010) and a contributor to lower upward mobility among Blacks (Mazumder, 2008). The decentralized character of U.S. schooling exacerbates these educational and economic inequalities. Although legal segregation has been eliminated in the United States, *de facto* racial segregation has increased over the last several decades (Frankenberg & Chungmei, 2002). A new trend is residential segregation by income as well as race, resulting in the economic and social homogenization of neighborhoods

(Massey, Rothwell, & Domina, 2009). The consequence of such stratification is that low-income and minority students are very likely to attend schools with other low-income and minority students, with all of the attendant ills of school segregation (social ostracism, inadequate learning opportunities, and so forth) (Anderson, 2010). Children who attend schools without equal content coverage and with poorly trained and dispirited teachers can hardly be judged as having an equal chance at life.

Sharp economic cleavages coupled with inequalities in content coverage of important areas such as mathematics and science is no recipe for a healthy society. As far back as Aristotle, a healthy middle class has been identified as a key ingredient for any stable political order. Lack of equal opportunities, on the other hand, strike at the core of our democratic convictions. In discussing the broader problem of segregation, Elisabeth Anderson (2010) argues that social equality is the normative basis for democracy. We might ask ourselves what the consequences would be for democracy and social order if we fail to support that equality. If a substantial number of citizens decided that their life opportunities, including those related to schooling, were not equal, that success in life had more to do with who one's parents are than what one does, would they continue their obligations to the society that they would view (with some justice) as exploiting them? Whatever other benefits they might have, the Common Core State Standards would embody an explicit public commitment that all children, whatever their origin, should have an equal chance to succeed.

We personally do not believe that we can eliminate all differences in achievement among children. Children differ in backgrounds, motivation, and other factors. When they are left free to achieve on their own in comparable circumstances, unequal results will likely follow. This, too, is an American belief and a valuing of individual differences. The key phrase here is "in comparable circumstances." Schools must provide equal content coverage for children of all backgrounds at least through the first 8 years of schooling. If children of different backgrounds are given different content coverage, and if those opportunities are less rigorous over a period of years, the children who receive lesser opportunities are probably destined for lower achievement. Even the most motivated and striving student in those circumstances will achieve less, likely even less than other students in different circumstances who are not as motivated or do not work as hard. This situation fundamentally violates another American value—that of fairness. Letting life's chance occurrences play a major role in determining whether a child has access to high-quality content learning opportunities violates America's sense of fairness and justice. Put simply, a child's entry into school should not be likened to being a player in a game of chance. The stakes for that child and for society are too high, and to base an educational system on the vicissitudes of life not only is unfair but also cruel, shortsighted, and morally questionable.

We set out in this book to tell the story of schooling in America and how very far it is from being a level playing field. We have tried to show the unexpected variation in learning opportunities that lie under the surface of seemingly similar circumstances. It may seem surprising that what appears to be a somewhat mundane issue around the nuts and bolts of schooling such as what content topics get taught and for how long has implications for fundamental democratic principles such as liberty and justice, as well as for policy and ideological issues including local school control of the curriculum, tracking, and the role of national standards. Such opportunities also have implications for economic issues, such as the growing wealth and income gaps, and similarly for decreases in intergenerational mobility, which have implications for the importance of maintaining a strong middle-class democracy.

As we have tried to show, this is not just an issue for racial and ethnic minorities. It is not just an issue for children of poorer families. This issue can affect any American child, even one from majority racial and ethnic backgrounds and middle and higher socioeconomic status. To any parent, we would say, "It is not just a matter that affects students who are 'different.' It is a matter for your child as well." In fact, we found the greatest variation in content coverage for schools that serve children from the middle class. It is an issue of inequalities in opportunity that can affect all children—hence, the title of this book.

Parents concerned for their child's safety have often been asked, "Do you know where your child is?" Modifying that phrase, parents should also be asked, "Do you know what your child's learning opportunities are?" Or more specifically, "Do you know what mathematics content your 4th-grade child is studying? Is it what she should be studying at that grade?" Beneath the surface similarities among American schools and classrooms lie differences in content coverage. In these times of increasing international competition (given our troubled economy and fierce competition within the United States), this should be a pressing issue for every parent because it affects every child. The parents of school-aged children may not be aware that they are participating in an educational lottery, but their children will bear the risk of losing that lottery all the same.

## WHAT CAN BE

This book is the story of what has been and what is with respect to opportunities to learn. But we as a nation have an opportunity to change the story of the future. The good news is that we can reach for lofty goals such as equality of mathematics content coverage and thereby significantly improve the mathematics knowledge of American children.

First, we need to develop and maintain the political will to do something about the hidden inequalities in content coverage in U.S. schools. We believe that the United States must make a public commitment about what content *all* students are going to be exposed to—summoning the political will to guarantee equality of educational opportunity. The road to achieving this goal is full of political and ideological potholes, not the least of which is the current system of fragmented and uncoordinated decision making involving 50 states, around 15,000 local school districts, and approximately 137,000 schools. This fractured system is both deeply entrenched and a major source of inequality.

Second, the nation must marshal its resources in support of the implementation of the Common Core State Standards, adopted by more than 40 states, in order to establish a strong foundation upon which to build educational equality. What is critical to our argument about the importance of the Common Core State Standards is that they are *common*. These standards define uniformly and for all children in these states what is important to be learned at each grade of schooling. The United States is quite unique among most developed countries in not having national standards and in expecting teachers to decide what content they will teach. This might be fine if the consequences of such a system were more advantageous than other approaches, but we believe there is overwhelming evidence that the current system has severe negative consequences both in terms of mediocre performance on international assessments such as the Programme for International Student Assessment and the Trends in International Mathematics and Science Study and in terms of equality of opportunity and fairness. That reality will continue through simple inertia until some force for change moves us in a different direction. The Common Core State Standards are potentially such a force, but they are already under attack by various political and ideological forces and threatened by organizational features of the school system and attendant policies.

It is difficult to imagine how equality of opportunity and fairness could be achieved in an educational system with a curriculum as fragmented as ours. The consequence of not implementing rigorous, internationally benchmarked *common* standards would be the continuation of such inequalities. The No Child Left Behind (NCLB) Act was a bipartisan attempt to address this issue. However, the political process that produced this act preserved the essential feature that foreshadowed its inevitable failure: Each state was left to define its own standards, which is hardly a way to end the fragmentation presented in Chapters 2 and 3.

The internationally benchmarked Common Core State Standards were, in a politically astute way, developed by the nation's governors and the chief state school officers in a way that avoids being designated as nationally mandated federal standards. It is believed by some that the federal government would only mire the process of setting standards in a political and ideological battle that would be subject to continued and changing political pressures. By contrast, with the National Governors Association (NGA) and the Council of Chief State School Officers (CCSSO) leading the effort, the Common Core State Standards (Common Core State Standards Initiative, n.d.) are truly state and not federal standards.

Even with the Common Core State Standards being developed at the state level and with federal support only for their development, there is a tendency by some to think of them as *national* standards, or at least voluntary national standards. There have been sharp criticisms against the idea of having such national standards. For example, it has been argued that more aggressive federal involvement might violate the Constitution (McCluskey, 2010).

Even if the constitutional concerns related to education being under the control of state and local policy could be addressed, a number of other substantive issues have been raised with respect to national education standards (not specifically focused on the Common Core State Standards). First, there is the claim that national standards will not achieve their stated aim of improving educational quality. Darling-Hammond (1994) and McCluskey (2010) argue that there is a lack of solidly grounded empirical research justifying the effectiveness of national standards. A "one-size-fits-all" approach to educational standards could ignore the benefits of individualized learning within particular, local contexts needed to relate educational materials to students' everyday lives (Darling-Hammond, 1994; Gibbs & Howley, 2001; Zhao, 2009). There is also a concern that homogenized national standards would fail to take into account the increasing diversity of the student body (Barton, 2009; Darling-Hammond, 1991; Gittell, 1996).

National standards, particularly when combined with high-stakes testing, have been criticized as focusing far too much on the economic gains associated with particular areas of the curriculum (such as mathematics), reducing the educational process to an excessively narrow, utilitarian calculus (Gibbs & Howley, 2001). In addition, Ravitch (2010b) and others (e.g., Darling-Hammond, 1991) have criticized shifting authority away from local school boards as violating the spirit of democratic governance and actually reducing public accountability and transparency. As Barton (2009) and Darling-Hammond (1991) have suggested, the possible benefits of national standards may simply have been oversold.

Although impassioned, the critique of the notion of national standards is not persuasive. The idea that education has always been a strictly local affair is somewhat naïve. As Hirschland and Steinmo (2003) note, the federal government has long taken an active role in subsidizing public education. Fears that federal involvement in education might cause inequalities ignore the very poor track record of localities in guaranteeing equal content coverage as this book portrays. Further, the Common Core State Standards, as a voluntary project organized by states, can hardly run afoul of the Constitution, and there is evidence that more aggressive state interventions can promote more equal educational outcomes (Fuller & Johnson, 2001; Fusarelli, 2009).

When we weigh the benefits and costs of the Common Core State Standards, it is important to remain focused on the subject at hand. Critics of national standards frequently conflate standards with high-stakes testing, privatization, and funding scarcity, lumping all of these very different elements together to paint a very dark picture. However, there is no necessary connection between the very real concerns about high-stakes testing, market-based reforms, or lack of funding on the one hand and common standards on the other. It is also a mistake to assume that national standards, especially in subjects like mathematics and science, allow no room for creative teaching. Standards identify which topics should be learned and in what order. It answers the question of what and when—the *how* remains very much in the hands of teachers, consistent with what is done in most countries' educational systems (Schmidt et al., 2001). In fact, we would argue that common educational standards would facilitate creativity in instruction by freeing teachers to focus on *how* to teach, rather than *what* to teach.

The Common Core State Standards will not remove all inequalities in content coverage. The present fact of inequality, along with the traditions that created it, has a long history in the United States, and will not disappear quickly. Local district control of the curriculum and curricular decision making by teachers have been a part of America's educational system for many decades. It is that reality that is a threat to the hope that the future need not reflect the present. However, the Common Core State Standards would define a standard toward which all players in the educational system, at least in the 40-plus states that have adopted them, could and should move in a coordinated way. This includes states, districts, schools, and teachers. Teachers would no longer be placed in a complex and difficult decision-making situation to determine what content to cover from among the many varied and often conflicting messages. Districts would no longer have to spend time defining the curriculum. The most important impact of the Common Core State Standards might well be the removal of such conflicting messages so that textbooks, tests, district standards, and teacher preparation requirements all align themselves to the Common Core State Standards. It is perhaps this alignment, which is not assured by any means, that must be undertaken in order to ensure the successful implementation of the new standards.

As a result, teachers' very important decisions would not be what to teach but how to best teach the content effectively to students in their classrooms. This is, in fact, the case in most countries in TIMSS (Schmidt et al., 2001). Under the standards, local school boards could still address important local policy issues. In fact, by focusing on instructional practices to which they are much better suited, teachers and school boards might have more real day-to-day autonomy—and certainly exhibit more effectiveness—than they do at present. However, they would need to leave the specification of what content is to be taught and in what sequence and to what depth to the Common Core State Standards.

The Common Core State Standards represent a sacrifice of local control over one aspect of educational policy—but is that not better than a sacrifice of many local children's opportunities to learn mathematics? A balance can be struck among competing principles, one that respects the capacities of all parties. Local control of the curriculum is a long-standing principle with broad support. But we as a nation also claim to be in favor of justice and fairness for all. In educational policies and our education system, these values have come into conflict. To date, one basic American value (fairness for all) has taken second place to another value (decentralization). The result of our choices is a disastrously unequal educational system, especially in the imbalance in content coverage between the wealthy and the rest of society, particularly the poor.

These choices have consequences that affect our nation's most precious resource—not our petroleum or mineral reserves—but our future workforce and future fellow citizens, for this is exactly what our children are. They represent a resource that will affect our economic and political future in an increasingly "flat world" of interlocking economies and societies. An imbalanced educational system will likely affect the health of our democratic society as well, for as Plutarch was quoted as saying, "An imbalance between rich and poor is the oldest and most fatal ailment of all republics." Perhaps this is true of schooling as well.

Not to act is a sign of shortsightedness. Even more, not to act is a sign of political ineptitude and gross irresponsibility. Not to act would be the final surrender of public education to political ideology and policy inertia—of accepting injustice in the name of "doing things as we always have." Failing to act is the same as choosing to imperil our future. Can we afford those consequences? Can our children? If we think that they and we cannot, then we should be very, very determined. We should apply pressure on policymakers until reasonable actions are taken to guarantee successful implementation of the Common Core State Standards and the improvement of teacher preparation programs that prepare future teachers to teach the standards. The United States was founded on the idea that an unacceptable status quo presents, not a bar to progress, but a challenge to overcome. What we insist is that America live up to that tradition.

# Data Sources Used in This Book

The bulk of the data included in this book come from six large-scale research projects conducted over the past 20 years. In each case, the concept of educational opportunity to learn specific content—for example, mathematics and/or science—has been an organizing theme. The model identifies three aspects of the school curriculum: the *Intended*, *Implemented*, and *Attained*. These led to three of the research questions forming the conceptual framework for the Third International Mathematics and Science Study (TIMSS) conducted by the International Association for the Evaluation of Educational Achievement (IEA) in the mid-1990s: What are students expected to learn? (*Intended*); How is instruction organized? (*Implemented*); and What have students learned? (*Attained*) (Schmidt & Cogan, 1996). A fourth research question for the 1995 TIMSS—Who delivers the instruction?—required instruments that focused on teachers' background, professional training, and professional competence. This last construct became the focus of the recent IEA-sponsored project, the Teacher Education and Development Study—Mathematics (TEDS-M), that investigated the professional preparation and knowledge of future mathematics teachers in 17 countries (Tatto et al., 2008). The four other projects represented in this book are the 1999 TIMSS-Repeat Benchmark study (TIMSS-R), the Longitudinal Study of American Youth (LSAY), the National Longitudinal Study of Adolescent Health (Add Health), and the Promoting Rigorous Outcomes in Mathematics/Science Education (PROM/SE).

The 1995 TIMSS remains the largest, most comprehensive study of education yet conducted. It focused on two school subjects, mathematics and science, and three student populations: 9-year-old students (typically those in either grade 3 or grade 4, and heretofore referred to as Population 1); 13-year-old students (typically those in either grade 7 or grade 8, and heretofore referred to as Population 2); and students in their final year of secondary school (Population 3). TIMSS included a comprehensive analysis of curriculum materials—textbooks and curriculum guides—for students in all three populations. Internationally, 45 countries participated in the curriculum analysis aspect in which nearly 500 textbooks were coded and analyzed. For Population 1 (grades 3 and 4), more than 190,000 students from 28 countries completed surveys and assessments in more than 4,000 schools. For Population 2 (grades 7 and 8), the main focus of the study, nearly 290,000 students from 44 countries in more than 6,000 schools participated.

Population 3 (end-of-secondary) was composed of nearly 86,000 students from 25 countries in nearly 3,100 schools. In addition, the teachers of the participating students from Populations 1 and 2 also completed surveys about their professional background and what they taught. Internationally, nearly 9,300 Population 1 teachers completed surveys; more than 31,000 Population 2 mathematics and science teachers participated. The instrumentation and analytic methodologies developed for TIMSS were adapted for use in the other five projects included in this book. In addition, the 1995 TIMSS international results provide measurement benchmarks for understanding results obtained in the United States in each of the projects included here.

Students who participated in the 1995 TIMSS were sampled so as to be representative of all such students in each participating country. In the United States, participating students were selected using a stratified two-stage random sampling methodology. Schools, students, and teachers representing the United States as a whole came from all six census regions. In total, more than 12,000 students in grades 3 and 4 from 186 schools and their over 600 teachers represented the United States. Nearly 11,000 students in grades 7 and 8 from 183 schools and their over 1800 mathematics and science teachers participated. More than 10,000 students from over 200 schools represented the United States in the end-of-secondary portion of the TIMSS.

Four years after the 1995 TIMSS, the TIMSS-R Benchmark study was conducted both in the United States and internationally. The goal was to evaluate the performance of the youngest cohort from the 1995 TIMSS (Population 1) as they were expected to be in the 8th grade at the time of TIMSS-R (Eighth grade had been the main focus of the 1995 TIMSS). In addition, participation in TIMMS-R was opened up to allow entities other than countries, such as U.S. states and school districts, to participate in the study as "countries." In the United States, 14 states and 13 school districts or consortia of districts chose to do this. The results included in the book come from the more than 36,000 students and their nearly 1,700 teachers from the participating states and districts—13 districts/consortia and 9 states.

The Longitudinal Study of American Youth (LSAY) is a longitudinal study that provides a comprehensive description of the major factors that influence mathematics student achievement in the United States. LSAY selected a national probability sample of more than 3,100 public school students in grade 7 and approximately 3,000 public school students in grade 12 in the fall of 1987 (Miller, Kimmel, Hoffer, & Nelson, 2000). Students in both cohorts were followed for a period of over 7 years. LSAY Cohort Two began with 3,116 7th-grade students from 50 public middle schools that were feeder schools to the high schools included in Cohort One. Each student in Cohort Two was asked to take a mathematics achievement test and a science achievement test each fall, using a set of tests developed from the item pools of the National Assessment of Educational Progress (NAEP). Mathematics and science teachers for each student completed surveys each year about their professional background and indicated which textbooks were used for classroom instruction. All of these texts were coded and analyzed using the TIMSS curriculum analysis methodology.

In Chapter 8, data were also included from the National Longitudinal Study of Adolescent Health (Add Health), a nationally representative longitudinal sample of 20,746 students in grades 7 through 12 from 80 high schools or the high schools' feeder schools. More than 145 mathematics textbooks were identified and coded from a subsample of 3,523 high school students in 110 high schools.

Promoting Rigorous Outcomes in Mathematics/Science Education (PROM/SE) is a comprehensive research and development effort to improve mathematics and science teaching and learning in grades K–16 funded by the National Science Foundation. The project was headquartered at Michigan State University in cooperation with more than 60 districts organized by five consortia in two states, Michigan and Ohio. These districts represented more than 300,000 students; about 37% were in urban or rural poor contexts. Participating districts had nearly 600 schools from which almost 6,000 teachers responded to PROM/SE surveys modeled after the TIMSS survey instruments. The PROM/SE demographics closely mirrored those of the country as a whole. In addition to student assessments in both mathematics and science, all mathematics and science teachers were asked to complete professional background surveys, detailed surveys of what they taught in each of their classes, measures assessing their preparedness to teach specific topics, and measures regarding their knowledge related to teaching mathematics or science. Designed as a multiyear project with multiple data collections and professional development initiatives, initial data collection began in the spring of 2004 and continued into 2011.

The Teacher Education Study in Mathematics (TEDS-M) was an international study conducted in 17 countries sponsored by the IEA that focused on the preparation of teachers of mathematics at the elementary and middle school levels. The project built on the results of TIMSS and broke new ground as the first large-scale international study to examine how teachers are prepared to teach. Future teachers near the end of their final year of teacher preparation were the focus of the study. In the United States, more than 100 public and private colleges and universities were randomly selected to participate. Following standardized IEA sampling guidelines, nearly 3,300 future teachers of mathematics completed background surveys and an assessment of their knowledge of mathematics related to teaching mathematics in schools. This assessment was neither a test of school mathematics nor one addressing concepts covered in advanced college mathematics courses, but one that sought to measure the more advanced understanding of mathematics that supports the teaching of school mathematics (Center for Research in Mathematics and Science Education, 2010).

## REFERENCES

Center for Research in Mathematics and Science Education (CRMSE). (2010). *Breaking the cycle: An international comparison of U.S. mathematics teacher preparation.* East Lansing: Michigan State University.

Miller, J. D., Kimmel, L. G., Hoffer, T., & Nelson, C. (2000). *Longitudinal study of American youth: User's manual.* Chicago: Northwestern University.

Schmidt, W. H., & Cogan, L. S. (1996). Development of the TIMSS context questionnaires. In M. O. Martin & D. L. Kelly (Eds.), *Third international mathematics and science study technical report* (Vol. I: Design and Development, pp. 5-1–5-22). Chestnut Hill, MA: Boston College.

Tatto, M. T., Schwille, J., Senk, S. L., Ingvarson, L., Peck, R., & Rowley, G. (2008). *Teacher education and development study in mathematics (TEDS-M): Conceptual framework.* East Lansing: Teacher Education and Development International Study Center, College of Education, Michigan State University.

# Mathematics Content Topics

List of Mathematics Content Topics

- Whole Number Meaning
- Whole Number Operations (Adding, Subtracting, Multiplying, Dividing)
- Properties of Whole Number Operations
- Fractions
- Decimals
- Relation of Fractions & Decimals
- Percentages
- Properties of Fractions & Decimals
- Negative Numbers, Integers, & Their Properties
- Rational Numbers & Their Properties
- Real Numbers & Their Properties
- Binary Arithmetic &/or Other Number Bases
- Exponents, Roots, & Radicals
- Complex Numbers & Their Properties
- Number Theory Including Primes & Factorization
- Systematic Counting
- Estimating Quantity & Size
- Rounding & Significant Figures
- Estimating Computations
- Orders of Magnitude & Scientific Notation

- Measurement Units
- Length, Perimeter, Area, & Volume
- Measurement Estimation & Errors
- 2-D Coordinate Geometry
- 2-D Geometry Basics
- Polygons & Circles
- 3-D Geometry
- Vectors & Matrices
- Transformations, Patterns, & Tessellations
- Congruence & Similarity
- Constructions Using Straightedge & Compass
- Proportionality Concepts
- Proportionality Problems
- Slope & Trigonometry
- Linear Interpolation & Extrapolation
- Patterns, Relations, & Functions
- Equations & Formulas
- Data Representation & Analysis
- Uncertainty & Probability
- Infinite Processes
- Change
- Validation & Justification
- Structuring & Abstracting
- Other Content

# Science Content Topics

List of Science Content Topics

- Earth's Composition
- Landforms
- Bodies of Water
- Atmosphere
- Rocks & Soil
- Ice Forms
- Weather & Climate
- Physical Cycles
- Building & Breaking
- Earth's History
- Earth in the Solar System
- Planets in the Solar System
- Beyond the Solar System
- Evolution of the Universe
- Plants & Fungi
- Animals
- Microorganisms
- Organs & Tissues
- Cells
- Organism Energy Handling
- Organism Sensing & Responding
- Biochemical Processes in Cells
- Life Cycles
- Reproduction
- Variation & Inheritance
- Evolution, Speciation, & Diversity
- Biochemistry of Genetics
- Biomes & Ecosystems
- Habitats & Niches
- Interdependence of Life
- Animal Behavior
- Human Biology & Health
- Human Nutrition
- Human Disease
- Classification of Matter
- Physical Properties of Matter
- Chemical Properties of Matter
- Atoms, Ions, & Molecules
- Macromolecules & Crystals
- Subatomic Particles
- Energy Types, Sources, & Conversions
- Heat & Temperature
- Wave Phenomena
- Sound & Vibration
- Light
- Electricity
- Magnetism
- Physical Changes
- Explanations of Physical Changes
- Kinetic Molecular Theory
- Quantum Theory & Fundamental Particles
- Chemical Changes
- Explanations of Chemical Changes
- Rate of Change & Equilibria
- Energy & Chemical Change
- Organic & Biochemical Changes
- Nuclear Chemistry

- Electrochemistry
  - Types of Forces
  - Time, Space, & Motion
  - Dynamics of Motion
  - Relativity Theory
  - Fluid Behavior
  - Nature or Conceptions of Technology
  - Influence of Mathematics & Technology in Science
  - Applications of Science in Mathematics & Technology
  - Influence of Science & Technology on Society
  - Influence of Society on Science & Technology
- History of Science & Technology
  - Pollution
  - Land, Water, & Sea Resource Conservation
  - Material & Energy Resource Conservation
  - World Population
  - Food Production & Storage
  - Effects of Natural Disasters
  - Nature of Scientific Knowledge
  - The Scientific Enterprise
  - Science & Mathematics
  - Science & Other Disciplines

# Notes

## Chapter 1

1. Public Law 107-110, which is to be cited as the "No Child Left Behind Act of 2001," was actually signed into law on January 8, 2002, "to close the achievement gap with accountability, flexibility, and choice, so that no child is left behind." See http://www.ed.gov/policy/elsec/leg/esea02/index.html for a copy of this law.

2. Statistically significant, $p < .01$.

3. See, for example, Apple, 1990, 1996; Beyer & Apple, 1998; Bockarie, 1993; Lave, 1988, 1990; Porter, Archbald, & Tyree, 1990; Ravitch, 1985, 1995a, 1995b; Saxe, 1985, 1988, 1990; Sears, 1998; Young, 1998.

4. This distinction between "intended" and "implemented" curriculum was first set out in 1979. (See McKnight, 1979.) For an online discussion, see Valverde, 2002.

5. See, for example, Burtless, 1996; Cohen, Raudenbush, & Ball, 2003; Dee & Levine, 2004; Elliott, 1998; Greenwald, Hedges, & Laine, 1996; Hoxby, 2001; Murray, Evans, & Schwab, 1998; Ucelli, Foley, & Emdon, 2002.

## Chapter 2

1. The 2000–2001 data were collected as a part of the 1995 TIMSS study (Schmidt, McKnight, Valverde et al., 1997). The 2008–2009 data were part of the international study of teacher preparation—Teacher Education and Development Study (TEDS) (Center for Research in Mathematics and Science Education, 2010).

2. The framework and coding procedures were developed in the Third International Mathematics and Science Study (TIMSS) and reflect the input of almost 50 countries (Schmidt, McKnight, Valverde et al., 1997).

3. One state only had very general categories of topics listed in its state standards and is excluded from these analyses.

4. The median is an indication of what is typical in the sense that 50% of the group (states in this case) would be at or below this number and 50% would be at or above that number. It is a much more reliable indicator of what is typical in this case than is the arithmetic average since it is less affected by unusually high and low numbers than is the average. Throughout our discussions, we will focus on the median as an indicator of what is typical.

5. This work can be found in detail in the *Journal of Curriculum Studies* (Schmidt et al., 2005).

6. Using data from TIMSS, we did a country-level regression analysis relating measures of coherence (based on the benchmark model of coherence) and focus

(number of topics intended for coverage), both derived from the country standards and student achievement. The estimated regression coefficients were both statistically significant (Schmidt & Houang, 2007).

7. This characterization of the intended curriculum was found to also be characteristic of textbooks and what teachers actually taught—see Schmidt, McKnight, & Raizen, 1997.

8. The district data were obtained from the TIMSS-Benchmarking Study (Schmidt, Cogan, & McKnight, 2010), PROM/SE (http://promse.msu.edu/), and a special study for the California Department of Education.

9. In Michigan and Ohio, using the TIMSS national achievement results as a base, we compared those results with the results from the testing of children in grades 3, 4, 7, and 8 in the PROM/SE project. The results were not statistically significantly different. We also compared the districts in terms of demographics and similarly found no significant differences from national estimates.

10. Ohio, although the sample is not random, represents a large percentage of the state's student population and, with both Cleveland and Cincinnati (and most of the surrounding suburbs) included, is a reasonably representative sample. Michigan's sample does not include the two largest cities and is less representative, especially of the urban population. The sample did include most of the districts in three counties: Ingham, Calhoun, and St. Clair. This included Lansing and its suburbs, small urban areas, and small rural areas. In California, the districts were sampled with probabilities proportional to the size of the district, as indicated by the total student enrollment.

11. At one level, this is the question of alignment between standards and assessments. This has become a large educational policy issue. Porter and others have explored this issue, especially the alignment between state standards and tests (Porter, 1995; Porter, McMaken, Hwang, & Yang, 2011).

12. Similar to what was done in mathematics, a model of coherence was developed for science based on the high-achieving counties. They included Singapore, Czech Republic, Japan, and South Korea. The procedures were the same, and a detailed description can be found in Schmidt et al., 2005.

## Chapter 3

1. More fully, this case was *Oliver L. Brown et al. v. the Board of Education of Topeka (KS) et al.*, with the decision rendered by the U.S. Supreme Court in 1954. The legal team that represented the plaintiff was led first by Charles Houston, and later by Thurgood Marshall (later to be a longtime justice of the Supreme Court). This was not the first challenge to school segregation. The first came as early as 1849, before the U.S. Civil War. Brown was not the only plaintiff at the time of the 1954 decision. More than 200 plaintiffs from several states were part of NAACP cases brought to the Supreme Court in 1951. Brown was chosen as a main plaintiff for the Kansas case, perhaps as a strategy to give the case a personal face. A good source of further information is http://brownvboard.org/summary/.

2. Much has been written about *Brown v. Board of Education* and what its legacy has been. Some sources that might be consulted are Carroll, Fulton, Abercrombie, & Yoon, 2004; Hanushek, Kain, & Rivkin, 2004; Lagemann & Miller, 1996; Orfield

& Lee, 2004; "Promoting Educational," 1999; Raudenbush, 2009; Strum, 2002; Walker, 2004; Willie & Willie, 2005.

3. Regarding school finance, see, for example, Ahlin & Mörk, 2008; Aud et al., 2011; Baicker & Gordon, 2006; Burtless, 1996; Downes & Shah, 2006; Fernandez & Rogerson, 2003; Figlio, Husted, & Kenny, 2004; Ladd, Chalk, & Hansen, 1999; Lee & Burkam, 2002; Zhang, Mizunoya, You, & Tsang, 2011. Regarding teacher quality, see, for example, Almy & Theokas, 2010; Boyd, Lankford, Loeb, Rockoff, & Wyckoff, 2008; Clotfelter, Ladd, Vigdor, & Wheeler, 2007; Darling-Hammond, 2000; Lankford, Loeb, & Wyckoff, 2002.

4. The California districts had to be dropped from the analyses in this chapter, as we did not have the comparable SES data.

5. This program, administered by the U.S. Department of Education, is intended to provide additional support for districts with substantial numbers of students in poverty to ensure that adequate nutritional needs are met for all students.

6. Statistically significant, ($p < .01$).

7. Statistically significant, ($p < .05$).

8. This is the group with the largest number of districts. Although the concept of "all" districts covering a combination is theoretically the same as for groups with fewer districts in them, in practice it is more difficult to achieve unanimity among many districts than it is to achieve unanimity among fewer districts. This does not negate the differences within Group III, but it is a caveat that needs to be considered. The fact that the differences are quite large (184 in Group I versus 49 in Group III) tends to lessen the concern about differing numbers of differences within the group.

9. The Council of the Great City Schools.

10. These data come from the Benchmarking Study, a special component of the TIMSS-R study. The Benchmarking Study included 13 school districts and 14 states, which were over-sampled to allow their comparison with the countries in TIMSS.

11. The estimation of a regression line, using district as the unit of analysis, does not take into account the hierarchical nature of the data. More formal analyses, considering the data structure, are presented in Chapter 5.

## Chapter 4

1. The Michigan and Ohio data were from the PROM/SE Project and the Seattle data were collected as a separate project. The data collection instruments were the same in both studies and were slightly modified versions of the original TIMSS instruments.

2. For these analyses, those teachers who do not teach a topic are recorded as providing no time. In statistical terms, for those who are interested in the technical details, this means that these time estimates are not conditional on coverage.

3. Technically, we are, in effect, estimating the distribution of the 90%-range over all the 29 topics. The potential for misinterpretation here is that the units of the distribution—that is, the topics—are not equal in size. Not all of the 29 topics are equal in terms of the amount of mathematics involved. They are certainly not equal in the time needed for their coverage in school. We call this the grain-size issue, which is only a problem when we try to summarize the distribution over topics. From the data, it appears that this is only a problem for one to three of the topics, but not for

the majority. We will caution readers where appropriate and point out the topics that might be causing the large values. One approach might be to give the distribution of the ratio of the 90%- range to the mean, but this also can mask the absolute value of variability for those topics with large mean values. Since the total instructional time is limited, such large absolute values have powerful impacts that need to be understood.

4. The variation is fairly even across all the topics by 4th and 5th grades. Therefore, the grain size is not likely to be a factor in interpreting the distributions presented in Figure 4.1.

5. The topics included in the TIMSS questionnaires were essentially the same as those used in obtaining the classroom level data reported on in this chapter. Only 7th- and 8th-grade data were available (none from the 6th grade). We used the 7th-grade data to provide an estimate for the 6th grade. The extent of the error in using this average for 6th grade would seem small, as there is not much difference in the estimated variances between 7th and 8th grade, relative to the mean across the topics.

6. This was estimated by looking at the ratio of the two estimated standard deviations—that is, 3.46 for Singapore divided by 6.14 for the United States.

7. The Flemish-speaking schools in Belgium (a separate system from the French-speaking schools) also have a centralized curriculum. It has inspectors to ensure that its curriculum is implemented properly in all classrooms. These schools had a slightly higher estimated variation for transition arithmetic than did Singapore. However, it was still only about two-thirds of the U.S. variation. Belgium was also a top-performing country.

8. An IGP is assigned for all topics typically taught in school mathematics in 1st through 12th grades. These values indicate the grade at which the topic is covered most extensively throughout the world (or at least the world as defined by the almost 50 countries that participated in TIMSS). Using data from TIMSS, each country's coverage of each of the typical mathematics topics was mapped onto 1st through 12th grades. At each grade, it was noted whether a topic was covered and, if so, how extensively. A value was assigned for each topic, placing it at a particular grade taking into account the grade at which the topic received the most focus among the TIMSS countries as well as the grade at which it was first introduced. This procedure reflected the hierarchical nature of mathematics as topics were placed along the "continuum" of 1st through 12th grades. Place value, an elementary topic, had an IGP value of 1.75, implying that over the 50 countries, this topic was mostly the focus of 1st grade. Differential calculus, an advanced topic, had a value of 11, indicating that it was placed internationally at around the 11th grade.

9. Differences were statistically significant, ($p < .05$).

10. Differences were statistically significant, ($p < .05$).

11. To estimate these differences, we used the estimated mean at each grade and then cumulated the differences. This represents the typical student but only from cross-sectional data. To do this more precisely would require longitudinal data that we do not have. Estimating these quantities as an approximation to the correct solution creates a hypothetical student assuming that children in cohorts within a district will have the same general curricular exposure in the next grade as the cohort of children currently in the next grade did have. To make this assumption more viable, we also assume that the children have the same basic demographics across the grades within a district.

12. See the American Diploma Project (ADP) as an example of one point of view (Achieve, Inc., 2004).

13. This was true even after eliminating the smallest 5% of the cases.

## Chapter 5

1. As a part of PROM/SE, a parent survey was undertaken in 26 districts, including several urban districts. Preliminary findings of the survey support our contention. Forty-two percent of parents in the low SES group considered their children's mathematics program to have done a fair to poor job, compared with about 16% of parents in the high SES group. In contrast, 13% of low SES parents wanted mathematics classes to challenge their children. For the high SES parent group, 22% of the parents indicated the need for challenging mathematics courses.

2. The discussion presented in this section is drawn from Cogan, Schmidt, and Wiley, 2001.

3. Actually, the correct way to report these estimated percentages is that 27% of the nation's 8th-graders attended a school in which only one mathematics course was offered.

4. Data are from the 1995 TIMSS U.S. national sample.

5. The data are drawn from a 1995 sample of U.S. schools. There is some evidence, although not as reliable, that these percentages may have changed.

6. In the 1995 study from which these results came, there were 6,405,756 8th-grade students.

7. This was done as a series of regression analyses using a threshold approach to define the coding for the opportunity variable (Cogan et al., 2001).

8. A multivariate analysis of variance (MANOVA) of the amount of time teachers devoted to each of the 21 mathematics topics and the total number of topics taught by course type and textbook type yielded significant overall effects for the course type–textbook type interaction as well as the main effect of course type ($F = 1.46$, $p < .001$ $F = 1.61$, $p < .001$, respectively). Five out of the 21 topics demonstrated a significant course-textbook interaction, as indicated by the univariate F ratios: whole numbers, common and decimal fractions, estimation and number sense, equations and formulas, and sets and logic. This suggests that the type of textbook employed in a course has an impact on the structure of students' learning opportunities beyond the differences attributable to the particular course in which students are enrolled. Two of the topics exhibiting significant interactions—whole numbers and common and decimal fractions—also exhibited main effects for course type, along with four additional topics: number theory, basics of one- and two-dimensional geometry, slope, and functions.

9. Specific-topic differences are further described among the various tracks in Cogan et al., 2001.

10. This is consistent with reports using other data from TIMSS, suggesting the U.S. curriculum to be from 1 to 2 years behind other countries (Schmidt et al., 1999; Schmidt, McKnight, & Raizen, 1997; Stigler, Gonzales, Kawanaka, Knoll, & Serrano, 1999).

11. Statistically significant differences were evident in the IGP index across the three tracks—regular, pre-algebra, and algebra ($F = 35.01$; $p < .0001$). The estimated contrast of the algebra track with the pre-algebra and regular track combined was statistically significant using a 95% confidence interval.

12. The difference was not statistically significantly different from zero, (p < .08).

13. These data were collected as a part of PROM/SE in 2005.

14. These results presented here and in the next sections are drawn from PROM/SE Research Report 3 (PROM/SE, 2008) and were presented in "Equality of Educational Opportunity: Myth or Reality in US Schooling" in the *American Educator* (Schmidt et al., 2010).

15. Examples we found for beginning algebra include: Applied Algebra, Algebra I, Algebra I Honor, Introductory Algebra, and First Year Fundamental Algebra, among others. For geometry, we found Elementary Geometry, Geometry, Plane Geometry B, Informal Geometry, and Fundamental Geometry, among others. For advanced algebra, we found Algebra II General, Enriched Algebra II, Integrated Algebra II, Advanced Algebra II, Essentials of Algebra II, and even Algebra II.

16. Perhaps here the titles best illustrate the tremendous variation in learning opportunities all these course offerings suggest. We found Fundamental Math, Technical Math, Transitional Math I, Contemporary Math I, Practical Math, Math Junior, Intervention Math I, Final Math Topics, Corrective Math, Alternative Math, Life Skills Math, and Vocational Math, among others.

17. One of the problems with past research in this area is that courses are usually classified into broader categories such as algebra, geometry, and so on. We believe, based on this sample, that national estimates of the percentage of U.S. students who take Algebra that people interpret as standard Algebra I is an overestimate. Assuming this sample is representative, that estimate might be better put at only less than 20%.

18. District Z is not in Figure 5.2 since these data were not available for it. Thus, this figure shows 17 districts rather than the 18 that the other figures show.

19. One additional district's data was available and was included in this figure.

20. The students' courses were recorded at each grade as was the textbook used in the course. The textbooks were coded using the TIMSS coding procedures. This gave an estimate of content coverage at each grade for each student. An adjustment to the content coverage of the book was made based on the teacher statement as to how much of the textbook was covered during the year.

21. The percentages for each year were added together, resulting in the cumulative percentage totaled over all content areas over all 6 years. If a student took 6 years of mathematics, this would result in 600%. This was rescaled to 100% by dividing by six. If a student did not take a mathematics course at some grade, that year's content coverage would be zero. However, the potential of taking a course that year would add another 100% to the total. When this was divided by six, the average would be less than 100%.

22. Two of the 18 districts did not provide us with their science data.

## Chapter 6

1. Data were not available that distinguish among the alternative ways that schools are involved in the joint decision making but it is very likely that the *de facto* model might be the most common. What we did was simply aggregate among teachers the coverage of topics as reported by each teacher in a school. If there were school standards, the aggregated data would reflect those standards, at least as implemented.

2. In sampling terms, what we have is a nested hierarchical design from which we want to estimate the variance components at each of the levels in the design. Since these are only two states, we treat this as a fixed effect. The districts are assumed to be a sample of the population of districts within each state. As such, they are considered random. Even though all schools and all classrooms within schools were included, we also assume these to be random effects in the model.

3. The yearly time allocations for each topic as reported by the teacher were weighted by the relevant IGP value. These weighted values were then summed to represent the topic coverage in that classroom for the year. This is essentially what was done and reported on in Chapter 4. These weighted classroom estimates were then aggregated to the school level, which were then further aggregated to the district level and finally to the state level. This was done at each of the first eight grades. The data used were from the 60 Michigan and Ohio districts. Since only two states were involved, we simply used the estimated mean differences between the states as an indication of variability at the state level. Variance component estimation for the remaining three levels was done using HLM techniques.

4. Statistically significant, ($p < .05$).

5. Statistically significant, ($p < .01$).

6. Statistically significant, ($p < .01$).

7. For each of the five grades, the estimated district variance was statistically significant, ($p < .02$, $.00$, $.00$, $.03$, $.003$ for each of the five grades, respectively).

8. These estimated variance components at the district level were statistically significant at each grade level, ($p < .001$).

9. Statistically significant, ($p < .02$).

10. Statistically significant, ($p < .002$).

11. Statistically significant, ($p < .001$).

12. Track would be confounded with classroom when not formally specified in the variance component model.

13. Unless the sampling frame is done carefully to stratify on track, the estimation of the variance components is very difficult. In PROM/SE, although we took all classrooms at the 8th grade in each school, the school identification of the track designation for each class was not accurate enough to study the track effect. The TIMSS U.S. sample gave us the data necessary to derive the best estimates of the tracking variance. Although not the perfect design from which to correctly estimate the components—no stratification for track was built into the TIMSS U.S. sampling frame—this provided the best available data to date. This was true because all classrooms within the sampled schools were identified.

14. This represented 73% of the 8th-grade schools.

15. The U.S. TIMSS sample was for the United States as a whole. Thus, the estimation of district-level effects was not possible with acceptable standard errors.

16. Only at 6th and 3rd grade were the district variance components statistically significant, ($p < .05$).

17. The data available in the U.S. TIMSS sample also included non-tracked schools. In those schools, the total variance of the IGP weighted index of teacher coverage at 8th grade was estimated at 0.45. The total variance for the tracked schools was 0.85. The school variance increased to about a third (33%) of the total variance and the estimated variance component of classrooms or teachers was 67% of the total. This

is close to the estimated relative projection of variance attributable to classrooms for the tracked schools. Combining tracks and classrooms gives an estimate of 75%, compared with 67% in the untracked schools.

## Chapter 7

1. The difficulty of being able to give a test to teachers is well understood.

2. For additional information, see Center for Research in Mathematics and Science Education, 2010; Schmidt, Blömeke et al., 2011; Schmidt, Cogan, & Houang, 2011; Schmidt, Houang et al., in press; Schmidt, Houang et al., 2011; Schmidt, Tatto, Bankov et al., 2007; Schmidt, Houang et al., 2008.

3. The list of topics came from the PROM/SE research report *Knowing Mathematics: What We Can Learn from Teachers* (PROM/SE, 2006).

4. There were no topics that met the (75%) criterion for the whole group of PROM/SE teachers. This is consistent with these district-level results. Both topics were close overall, and these results are based on districts. The result implies that the larger districts likely had lower rates and, when taken over all PROM/SE teachers, this would make the percentage less than the average over all districts where the size of the district is not taken into account.

5. The TIMSS data do not represent a sample of teachers but a sample of students, so the indicator is expressed in terms of the percentage of students who have a teacher with a major/minor in either mathematics or science. The TIMSS data do not allow an estimation of the number of teachers with only a mathematics major or minor.

6. Actually, teachers should be acknowledged for having had insight into their own limitations and the integrity to report them honestly.

## Chapter 8

1. The books were coded as a part of three projects. The first were NSF-supported materials analyzed as a part of a TIMSS-R related grant (NSF Award Number 9814042). The second were textbooks used by students in a nationally representative study of high school students, Add Health (NSF Award Number 0120282). The third were textbooks used by a nationally representative sample of 7th- through 12th-graders who were studied longitudinally through high school as a part of the LSAY study (NSF Award Number 9346762).

2. For these and all the analyses in this section, there were 353 mathematics textbooks coded. These included:

|   | Textbook | # Coded |
|---|----------|---------|
| 1 | Basic Math | 177 |
| 2 | Pre-algebra | 17 |
| 3 | Algebra I | 41 |
| 4 | Geometry | 31 |
| 5 | Algebra II | 30 |
| 6 | Precalculus | 24 |
| 7 | Calculus | 10 |
| 8 | Integrated | 23 |

3. A further look shows that this mostly has to do with the large number of topics not included in only a few or even only one of these books or included in only one of them. This was true for 18 of 44 topics.

4. For these and all analyses in this section, there were 153 science textbooks coded. These included:

|   | Textbook | # Coded |
|---|----------|---------|
| 1 | Anatomy & Physiology | 4 |
| 2 | Biology | 49 |
| 3 | Chemistry | 26 |
| 4 | Earth Science | 15 |
| 5 | Environment | 5 |
| 6 | General Science | 27 |
| 7 | Life Science | 3 |
| 8 | Physical Science | 8 |
| 9 | Physics | 16 |

5. The actual criterion for the selection of textbooks was to select those textbooks that collectively would account for at least 50% usage at that grade level (see Schmidt, McKnight, Valverde et al., 1997).

6. These data were part of a set of analyses done for Achieve in early 2000.

7. Technically, they are "normed" against a national sample.

8. The emphasis here is on the variation in content coverage, not on a characterization of what was tested by each state. That might have changed over the decade, but most likely not the amount of variation.

9. Items could be classified into more than one content category and are counted that way in determining the percentages. This is an accurate portrayal of topic coverage—the only consequence is that the percentages do not add to 100.

10. The tests that were analyzed included Iowa Tests of Basic Skills (ITBS), Stanford Achievement Test (SAT), Comprehensive Test of Basic Skills (CTBS), California Achievement Test (CAT), TerraNova Achievement Tests, SUPERA Achievement Test (Spanish version of the TerraNova), Metropolitan Achievement Test (MAT), and Northwest Evaluation Association Test (NWEA).

## Chapter 9

1. Herrnstein & Murray, 1994; to this, we might add the writings of Charles Murray such as those in his op-ed piece "Intelligence in the Classroom" in the January 16, 2007, edition of the *Wall Street Journal* or his feature article "The Age of Educational Romanticism" in the May 2008 issue of *The New Criterion* (Murray, 2007; 2008).

2. The instruments and methodologies were much the same as the ones used to generate the data described in Part I of this book. In fact, the modifications made after TIMSS were done to provide a more detailed characterization of opportunity but ones that were consistent with the TIMSS methodology and falling within the same measurement system. Put simply, the new instrumentation was always designed to "collapse back" to the original TIMSS instrumentation.

3. Actually, in TIMSS, the grade was not "the 8th grade" officially. It was the upper of the two grades containing the majority of 13-year-olds. This was the 8th year of schooling (not counting preschool or kindergarten) in most countries. The gain was a pseudo-gain based on a cohort longitudinal design that measured both 7th and 8th grade (see Schmidt et al., 2001).

4. The regression analysis was done with topic as the unit of analysis. There were 20 topics. Adjustments were made to the standard errors to account for correlated units of analysis.

5. The questionnaire used in the analyses described in Chapter 4 was derived from the original TIMSS questionnaire and differed only in having a greater elaboration of several topics into various subareas. The creation of more topics for teachers to respond to was done such that the results could be collapsed to the original TIMSS framework.

6. The following excerpt describes the variables we used:

> . . . mother's and father's education; the number of books in the home; student's age, sex and race; several indices related to the possessions found in the student's home; the educational expenses of parents for their child; the student's own educational aspirations; the size of the family; and the number of adults living in the home. These variables were included to allow statistical control in order to hold SES constant in examining the relationship of achievement and opportunity to learn.
>
> In addition, . . . other variables describing instructional practices were used in the analyses. These included variables describing lesson activities—for example, the percentage of a class period that was devoted to instruction, seatwork, and homework (both to initial coverage of the homework as well as to its review and correction after it was collected). A variable characterizing additional aspects of pedagogy was also included. One question asked teachers in the TIMSS questionnaire was how often certain practices (e.g. "explaining the reasoning behind an idea") were used in their classroom. An index was developed to characterize activities that could be viewed as moving beyond routine procedures to demand more complex performances from students. This index included (a) explaining reasoning behind an idea; (b) representing and analyzing relationships using tables, graphs, and charts; and (c) working on problems for which there was no immediately obvious method of solution.
>
> The basic achievement measures used for the analyses were at the tested topic area level and for individual students. These were the . . . 20 tested topic areas of mathematics (Schmidt et al., 2001, pp. 340–344).

7. The appropriate analysis had to take into account the hierarchical nature of the data—classrooms that were located within schools and students who were located within classrooms. This was necessary since the SES and sub-test achievement score variables were defined at the student level and the curriculum implementation (as well as other instructional variables) was defined at the classroom level (Schmidt et al., 2001).

8. The unit of analysis for the regression analyses was the individual student. LSAY had a national probability sample of the United States and each student took a different set of courses, as Chapters 4 and 5 indicated was typical for U.S. students. The study followed students, not classrooms. The textbook coverage was adjusted as to the amount of the textbook that was covered in the class the student took. The difficulty of the tests varied by grade level, and a one-parameter IRT model was used to scale the different tests so they were comparable across the grades.

9. These analyses are not properly adjusted or modeled correctly, but are descriptive and borne out by formal analyses.

10. The use of the term *effect* does not necessarily imply causality.

11. We examined the nature of the relationship both with and without states and found no substantial differences other than the power of the statistical tests. Significant effects for content coverage as represented by the IGP index were found at the classroom, school, and district levels.

12. The statistical significances were classroom level ($p < .0001$) and district level ($p < .02$).

13. At the district level, the adjustment was in terms of the percentage of students in the district eligible for free and reduced-price lunches. (Schmidt, Cogan et al., 2008).

14. HLM methods were used to examine the relationship of aggregate IGP to district-level mathematics achievement, controlling for SES at each level in the hierarchy. In addition, a cohort-defined measure of prior achievement (7th grade) at the classroom level was included.

15. One methodological problem encountered in carrying out these analyses is the small number of districts or consortia (13). This greatly reduces the power for analysis done at the district level. As a part of the same benchmarking study that produced the data for the 13 districts, identical data were collected on a set of volunteer states. Eight of those states agreed to be a part of this work. Treating each of those eight states as a sort of "super district" brings the total for analysis to 22. Of course, states are aggregates of districts and differ from consortia of districts by being much larger aggregates. Treating states as districts is not desirable. Because of this, analyses first explored how the relationship in Figure 3.1 and Figures 9.3 and 9.4 would look if one made the methodologically necessary assumption to treat states as "super districts." Two of the corresponding patterns are almost identical. For the other, the estimated coefficient of determination was .31, compared with .51 for Figure 3.1. If two questionable districts with data were removed, the coefficient of determination was .46, which is far more comparable to the .51.

16. Actually, the measure was one of the rigor of the coverage.

17. How to disentangle those effects from the curricular ones is difficult as well as complex. We explored this relationship in several ways, using various kinds of statistical adjustments in an attempt to find the least biased estimate (and hence, remove the selection bias) of the nature of the relationship between curriculum tracking and student achievement in mathematics.

18. We assumed no major cohort differences within the same school for students following the same track other than the additional year of schooling. Using this assumption, we paired 8th-grade classrooms in each school with their feeder 7th-grade classrooms as defined by the school course-offering structure.

19. This analysis used the TIMSS IRT score and a 100-point difference represents a difference of one standard deviation. These analyses were not adjusted for potential selection bias effects, nor were they adjusted for the hierarchical nature of the data (Schmidt, Cogan et al., 2008).

20. Although not a perfect solution, adjusting for the prior achievement at the class level and the SES both at the class and individual levels should remove most of the likely student selection bias. This makes the estimated track effect less biased and, therefore, most likely to reflect differences in the curriculum associated with the various tracks.

21. To explore this issue more fully, a three-level HLM analysis was done separately for the tracked schools. The three levels included schools, classrooms nested within schools, and students nested within classrooms. The dependent variable was the TIMSS international mathematics score (this scale was not the same as the one referred to in endnote 13—the standard deviation for this scale was 100), which was modeled at the individual student level. The full three-level model included several covariates at the appropriate level. The student-level model included race and the composite SES measure. The class-level model included the appropriate 7th-grade pre-measure, mean SES, and track indicators. The school-level model included the school-level mean SES, the percentage of minority enrollment at the school, the location of the school (rural, suburban, or urban), and the size of the school as measured by the number of the 8th-grade students.

22. Statistically significant, $p < .0001$.

23. Statistically significant, $p < .0001$.

24. The difference of 60 points is approximately two-thirds of a standard deviation on the TIMSS test.

# References

Achieve, Inc. (2004). *Do graduation tests measure up? A closer look at state high school exit exams: A report from the American Diploma Project.* Washington, DC: Author.

Ahlin, Å., & Mörk, E. (2008). Effects of decentralization on school resources. *Economics of Education Review, 27*(3), 276–284.

Almy, S., & Theokas, C. (2010, November). *Not prepared for class: High-poverty schools continue to have fewer in-field teachers.* Washington, DC: The Education Trust.

Anderson, E. (2010). *The imperative of integration.* Princeton, NJ: Princeton University Press.

Apple, M. W. (1990). *Ideology and curriculum* (2nd ed.). New York: Routledge.

Apple, M. W. (1996). Power, meaning, and identity: Critical sociology of education in the United States. *British Journal of Sociology of Education, 17*(2), 125–144.

Aud, S., Hussar, W., Kena, G., Bianco, K., Frohlich, L., Kemp, J., & Tahan, K. (2011). *The condition of education 2011* (NCES 2011-033). U.S. Department of Education, National Center for Education Statistics. Washington, DC: U.S. Government Printing Office.

Baicker, K., & Gordon, N. (2006). The effect of state education finance reform on total local resources. *Journal of Public Economics, 90*(8–9), 1519–1535.

Baker, S. (2006, January 23). Math will rock your world [electronic version]. *Business Week, 6*(4). Retrieved from http://www.businessweek.com/magazine/toc/06_04/B3968magazine.htm

Ball, D. L., & Bass, H. (2000). Interweaving content and pedagogy in teaching and learning to teach: Knowing and using mathematics. In J. Boaler (Ed.), *Multiple perspectives on the teaching and learning of mathematics* (pp. 83–104). Westport, CT: Ablex.

Ball, D. L., Hill, H. C., & Bass, H. (2005, Fall). Knowing mathematics for teaching: Who knows mathematics well enough to teach third grade, and how can we decide? *American Educator,* 14–22.

Barr, R. (1988). Conditions influencing content taught in nine fourth-grade mathematics classrooms. *The Elementary School Journal, 88*(4), 387–411.

Barton, P. E. (2009). *National education standards: Getting beneath the surface.* Educational Testing Service. Retrieved from http://www.ets.org/research/pic

Baumert, J., & Kunter, M. (2006). Stichwort: Professionelle kompetenz von lehrkräften [Keyword: Professional competencies of teachers]. *Zeitschrift für Erziehungswissenschaft [Journal of education science], 9,* 469–520.

Beller, E., & Hout, M. (2010). Intergenerational social mobility: The United States in comparative perspective. *The Future of Children, 16*(2), 19–36.

Berlin, I. (1969). Two concepts of liberty. In I. Berlin (Ed.), *Four essays on liberty* (pp. 118–72). Oxford, England: Oxford University Press.

Berliner, D. C. (1990). What's all the fuss about instructional time? In M. Ben-Peretz & R. Bromme (Eds.), *The nature of time in schools* (pp. 3–35). New York: Teachers College Press.

Bertocchio, G., & Dimico, A. (2010). *Slavery, education, and inequality* (Report Number 051). Modena, Italy: University of Modena e Reggio Emilia, Department of Economics, Center for Economic Research (RECent).

Beyer, L. E., & Apple, M. W. (Eds.). (1998). *The curriculum: Problems, politics, and possibilities* (2nd ed.). Albany, NY: State University of New York Press.

Bidwell, C. E., & Kasarda, J. D. (1980). Conceptualizing and measuring the effects of schools and schooling. *American Journal of Education, 88*(4), 401–430.

Blömeke, S. (2002). *Universität und lehrerausbildung [University and teacher education]*. Bad Heilbrunn, Germany: Klinkhardt.

Blömeke, S. (2005). *Lehrerausbildung—lehrerhandeln—schülerleistungen: Perspektiven nationaler und internationaler empirischer bildungsforschung [Teacher education—teacher performance—student achievement: Perspectives of national and international empirical research in education]*. Public Lecture on December 10, 2003, at Humboldt University. Berlin, Germany: Humboldt-Universität.

Bockarie, A. (1993). Mathematics in the Mende culture: Its general implication for mathematics teaching. *School Science and Mathematics, 93*(4), 208–211.

Boyd, D., Lankford, H., Loeb, S., Rockoff, J., & Wyckoff, J. (2008). The narrowing gap in New York City teacher qualifications and its implications for student achievement in high-poverty schools. *Journal of Policy Analysis and Management, 27*(4), 793–818.

Bromme, R. (1992). *Der Lehrer als Experte. Zur Psychologie des professionellen Lehrerwissens [The teacher (seen) as an expert. On the psychology of professional teacher knowledge]*. Göttingen, Germany: Hans Huber.

Brooks, D. (2007, January 14). The American way of equality. *The New York Times.* Retrieved from http://www.nytimes.com/2007/01/14/opinion/14brooks.html

Brophy, J., & Good, T. (1986). Teacher behavior and student achievement. In M. C. Wittrock (Ed.), *Handbook of research on teaching* (pp. 328–375). New York: Macmillan.

Bruner, J. S. (1995). On learning mathematics. *Mathematics Teacher, 88*(4), 330–335.

Burtless, G. (Ed.). (1996). *Does money matter? The effect of school resources on student achievement and adult success.* Washington, DC: Brookings Institution Press.

Carroll, J. B. (1963). A model of school learning. *Teachers College Record, 64*(8), 723–733.

Carroll, T. G., Fulton, K., Abercrombie, K., & Yoon, I. (2004). *Fifty years after Brown vs. Board of Education: A two-tiered education system.* Washington, DC: National Commission on Teaching and America's Future.

Center for Research in Mathematics and Science Education. (2010, April). *Breaking the cycle: An international comparison of U.S. mathematics teacher preparation.* East Lansing, MI: Michigan State University. Retrieved from http://www.educ.msu.edu/content/default.asp?contentID=710

Chau, M., Thampi, K., & Wight, V. R. (2010). *Basic facts about low-income children, 2009: Children under age 18.* New York: National Center for Children in Poverty, Mailman School of Public Health, Columbia University.

Chávez, O. (2006). From the textbook to the enacted curriculum. In S. Alatorre, J. L. Cortina, M. Sáiz, & A. Méndez (Eds.), *Proceedings of the 28th annual meeting of the North American Chapter of the International Group for the Psychology of Mathematics Education.* Mérida, México: Universidad Pedagógica Nacional.

Chubb, J. E., & Loveless, T. (2002). *Bridging the achievement gap.* Washington, DC: Brookings Institution.

Clotfelter, C. T., Ladd, H. F., Vigdor, J. L., & Wheeler, J. (2007). High-poverty schools and the distribution of teachers and principals. *North Carolina Law Review, 85*(5), 1345–1379.

Cogan, L. S., Schmidt, W. H., & Wiley, D. E. (2001). Who takes what mathematics and in which track? Using TIMSS to characterize U.S. students' eighth grade mathematics learning opportunities. *Educational Evaluation and Policy Analysis, 23*(4), 323–341.

Cohen, D. K., Raudenbush, S. W., & Ball, D. L. (2003). Resources, instruction, and research. *Educational Evaluation and Policy Analysis, 25*(2), 119–142.

Coleman, J. S. (1966). *Equality of educational opportunity.* Washington, DC: Government Printing Office.

Common Core State Standards Initiative. (n.d.). Retrieved from http://www.corestandards.org/

Connelly, M., Phillion, J., & He, M. F. (Eds.). (2008). *Handbook of research on curriculum.* New York: Sage.

Daily Mail Reporter. (2011, June 24). *"Sobering" report shows education achievement gap between Hispanics and Whites remains unchanged in two decades.* Retrieved from http://www.dailymail.co.uk/home/index.html

Darling-Hammond, L. (1991). The implications of testing policy for quality and equality. *The Phi Delta Kappan, 73*(3), 220–225.

Darling-Hammond, L. (1994). National standards and assessments: Will they improve education? *American Journal of Education, 102*(4), 478–510.

Darling-Hammond, L. (1999). *Teacher quality and student achievement: A review of state policy evidence.* Seattle, WA: University of Washington, Center for the Study of Teaching and Policy.

Darling-Hammond, L. (2000). New standards and old inequalities: School reform and the education of African American students. *Journal of Negro Education, 69*(4), 263–287.

Darling-Hammond, L., & Bransford, J. (Eds.). (2005). *Preparing teachers for a changing world: What teachers should learn and be able to do.* San Francisco: Jossey-Bass.

Davis, J. D. (2009). Understanding the influence of two mathematics textbooks on prospective secondary teachers' knowledge. *Journal of Mathematics Teacher Education, 12*(5), 365–389.

Dee, T. S., & Levine, J. (2004). The fate of new funding: Evidence from Massachusetts' education finance reforms. *Educational Evaluation and Policy Analysis, 26*(3), 199–215. doi:10.3102/01623737026003199

Dillon, S. (2011, August 14). State challenges seen as whittling away federal education law. *The New York Times.* Retrieved from http://www.nytimes.com/2011/08/15/education/15educ.html?_r=2&ref=nochildleft

Downes, T. D., & Shah, M. P. (2006). The effect of school finance reforms on the level and growth of per-pupil expenditures. *Peabody Journal of Education, 81*(3), 1–38.

Economic Policy Institute. (2011). More compensation heading to the very top: Ratio of average CEO total direct compensation to average production worker compensation, 1965–2009. *The State of Working America.* Washington, DC: Author.

Elliott, M. (1998). School finance and opportunities to learn: Does money well spent enhance students' achievement? *Sociology of Education, 71*(3), 223–245.

Elmore, R. F. (1983). Complexity and control: What legislators and administrators can do about implementing public policy. In L. S. Shulman & G. Sykes (Eds.), *Handbook of teaching and policy* (pp. 318–369). New York: Longman.

Elmore, R. F. (2000). *Building a new structure for school leadership.* Washington, DC: The Albert Shanker Institute.

Esping-Anderson, G. (2004). Unequal opportunities and the mechanisms of social inheritance. In M. Corak (Ed.), *Generational income mobility in North America and Europe* (pp. 289–314). Cambridge, UK: Cambridge University Press.

Fan, L., & Kaeley, G. S. (2000). The influence of textbooks on teaching strategies: An empirical study. *Mid-Western Educational Researcher, 13*(4), 2–9.

Fernandez, R., & Rogerson, R. (2003). Equity and resources: An analysis of education finance systems. *Journal of Political Economy, 111*(4), 858–897.

Figlio, D. N., Husted, T. A., & Kenny, L. W. (2004). Political economy of the inequality in school spending. *Journal of Urban Economics, 55*(2), 338–349.

Finn, C. E., Jr., Julian, L., & Petrilli, M. J. (with Broad, E., Brown, C., Cohen, M., Gordon, R., Hess, F. M., Hickok, G, Kress, S., et al.). (2006). *To dream the impossible dream: Four approaches to national standards and tests for American schools.* Washington, DC: The Thomas B. Fordham Institute.

Floden, R. E. (2002). The measurement of opportunity to learn. In A. C. Porter & A. Gamoran (Eds.), *Methodological advances in cross-national surveys of educational achievement* (pp. 231–266). Washington, DC: National Academy Press.

Floden, R. E., & Meniketti, M. (2005). Research on the effects of coursework in the arts and sciences and in the foundations of education. In M. Cochran-Smith & K. Zeichner (Eds.), *Studying teacher education: The report of the AERA Panel on Research and Teacher Education* (pp. 261–308). Mahwah, NJ: Lawrence Erlbaum Associates.

Floden, R. E., Porter, A. C., Alford, L. M., Freeman, D. T., Irwin, S., Schmidt, W. H., & Schwille, J. R. (1988). Instructional leadership at the district level: A closer look at autonomy and control. *Educational Administration Quarterly, 24*(2), 96–124.

Floden, R. E., Porter, A. C., Schmidt, W. H., Freeman, D. J., & Schwille, J. R. (1981). Responses to curriculum pressures: A policy-capturing study of teacher decisions about content. *Journal of Educational Psychology, 73*(2), 129–141.

Frankenberg, E., & Chungmei, L. (2002). *Race in American public schools: Rapidly resegregating school districts.* Cambridge, MA: The Civil Rights Project, Harvard University.

Freeman, D. J., & Porter, A. C. (1989). Do textbooks dictate the content of mathematics instruction in elementary schools? *American Educational Research Journal, 26*(3), 403–421.

Friedman, T. (2005). *The world is flat: A brief history of the twenty-first century.* New York: Farrar, Straus and Giroux.

Fuller, E. J., & Johnson, J. F., Jr. (2001). Can state accountability systems drive improvements in school performance for children of color and children from low-income homes? *Education and Urban Society, 33*(3), 260–283.

Fusarelli, L. D. (2009). Improvement or interference? Reenvisioning the 'state' in education reform. In B. C. Fusarelli & B. S. Cooper (Eds.), *The rising state.* Albany, NY: SUNY Press.

Gabriel, T. (2010, November 9). Proficiency of Black students is found to be far lower than expected. *The New York Times.* Retrieved from http://www.nytimes.com/2010/11/09/education/09gap.html

Gibbs, T. J., & Howley, A. (2001). "World-class standards" and local pedagogies: Can we do both? *Thresholds in Education, 27*(4), 51–55.

Gittell, M. (1996). National standards threaten local vitality. *The Clearing House, 69*(3), 148–150.

Gootman, E. (2009, March 23). Children face rejection by neighborhood schools in Manhattan. *The New York Times.* Retrieved from http://www.nytimes.com/2009/03/24/education/24schools.html

Greenwald, R., Hedges, L. V., & Laine, R. D. (1996). The effect of school resources on student achievement. *Review of Educational Research, 66*(3), 361–396.

Hamilton, L. S., Stecher, B. M., Marsh, J. A., McCombs, J. S., Robyn, A., Russell, J. L., Naftel, S., & Barney, H. (2007). *Standards-based accountability under No Child Left Behind: Experiences of teachers and administrators in three states.* Santa Monica, CA: RAND Corporation. Retrieved from http://www.rand.org/pubs/monographs/MG589

Hanushek, E. A., Kain, J. F., & Rivkin, S. G. (2004, February). *New evidence about Brown v. Board of Education: The complex effects of school racial composition on achievement.* Palo Alto, CA: Stanford University, Hoover Institution.

Hanushek, E. A., & Rivkin, S. G. (2006, October). *School quality and the Black-White achievement gap.* (Working Paper No. 12651). National Bureau of Economic Research. Retrieved from www.nber.org/papers/w12651

Hanushek, E. A., & Woessmann, L. (2007, February). *The role of education quality for economic growth.* (Policy Research Working Paper No. 4122). Washington, DC: World Bank, Human Development Network Education Team.

Herrnstein, R. J., & Murray, C. (1994). *The bell curve: Intelligence and class structure in American life.* New York: The Free Press.

Hill, H. C. (2005). Content across communities: Validating measures of elementary mathematics instruction. *Educational Policy, 19*(3), 447–475.

Hill, H. C., & Ball, D. L. (2004). Learning mathematics for teaching: Results from California's mathematics professional development institutes. *Journal for Research in Mathematics Education, 35*(5), 330–351.

Hill, H. C., Rowan, B., & Ball, D. L. (2005). Effects of teachers' mathematical knowledge for teaching on student achievement. *American Education Research Journal, 42*(2), 371–406.

Hirschland, M. J., & Steinmo, S. (2003). Correcting the record: Understanding the history of federal intervention and failure in securing U.S. educational reform. *Educational Policy, 17*(3), 343–364. doi:10.1177/0895904803017003003

Hoxby, C. (2001). All school finance equalizations are not created equal. *The Quarterly Journal of Economics, 116*(4), 1189–1231.

Ichino, A., Karabarbounis, L., & Moretti, E. (2010). *The political economy of intergenerational income mobility.* (Working Paper No. 15946). Retrieved from the National Bureau of Economic Research website: http://www.nber.org/papers.html

Imazeki, J. (2005). Teacher salaries and teacher attrition. *Economics of Education Review, 24*(4), 431–449.

Ingersoll, R. M., & May, H. (2010). *The magnitude, destinations and determinants of mathematics and science teacher turnover.* Philadelphia: University of Pennsylvania, Consortium for Policy Research in Education. Retrieved from http://www.gse.upenn.edu/pdf/rmi/MathSciTeacherTurnover.pdf

Jackson, A. (1997). The math wars: California battles it out over mathematics education (Part I). *Notices of the American Mathematical Society, 44*(6), 695–702.

Jäntti, M. (2009). Mobility in the United States in comparative perspective. *Focus, 26*(2), 38–42.

Khatiwada, S. (2010). *Did the financial sector profit at the expense of the rest of the economy? Evidence from the United States.* (Discussion Paper No. dp206_2010). Geneva, Switzerland: International Institute for Labor Studies. Retrieved from the International Labour Organization website: http://www.ilo.org/public/english/bureau/inst/download/dp206_2010.pdf

Krantz, M., & Hansen, B. (2011, April 4). CEO pay soars while workers' pay stalls. *USA Today.* Retrieved from http://www.usatoday.com/money/companies/management/story/CEO-pay-2010/45634384/1

Ladd, H. F., Chalk, R., & Hansen, J. S. (Eds.). (1999). *Equity and adequacy in education finance: Issues and perspectives.* Washington, DC: National Academy Press.

Lagemann, E. C., & Miller, L. P. (1996). Brown v. Board of Education: *The challenge for today's schools.* New York: Teachers College Press.

Lankford, H., Loeb, S., & Wyckoff, J. (2002). Teacher sorting and the plight of urban schools: A descriptive analysis. *Educational Evaluation and Policy Analysis, 24*(1), 37–62.

Lave, J. (1988). *Cognition in practice: Mind, mathematics and culture in everyday life.* New York: Cambridge University Press.

Lave, J. (1990). Views of the classroom: Implications for math and science learning research. In M. Gardner, J. G. Greeno, F. Reif, A. H. Schoenfeld, A. Disessa, & E. Stage (Eds.), *Toward a scientific practice of science education* (pp. 251–263). Hillsdale, NJ: Lawrence Erlbaum.

Lederman, L. (1996, April). Getting high school science in order. *Technology Review, 3,* 61–63.

Lee, V. E., & Burkam, D. T. (2002). *Inequality at the starting gate: Social background differences in achievement as children begin school.* Washington, DC: Economic Policy Institute.

Leithwood, K., Edge, K., & Jantzi, D. (1999). *Educational accountability: The state of the art.* Gutersloh, Germany: Bertelsmann Foundation.

Lewin, T. (2010, July 10). *Many states adopt national standards for their schools.* New York Times. Retrieved from http://www.nytimes.com/2010/07/21/education/21standards.html

Lincoln, A. (1989). Message to Congress in special session, July 4, 1861. In D. E. Fehrenbacher (Ed.), *Speeches and writings, 1859–1865* (p. 259). Washington, DC: Library of Congress.

Lipset, S. M. (2003). *The first new nation: The United States in historical and comparative perspective.* Edison, NJ: Transaction Publishers.

Long, J., & Ferrie, J. (2007). The path to convergence: Intergenerational occupational mobility in Britain and the US in three eras. *The Economic Journal, 117*(519), C61–C71.

Mass Insight Education and Research Institute. (2004). *More math please: The surprising consensus on math among parents, the public, and business leaders in two "new economy" states.* Boston: Author.

Massey D. S., Rothwell, J., & Domina, T. (2009). The changing bases of segregation in the United States. *The ANNALS of the American Academy of Political and Social Science, 626*(1), 74–90. doi:10.1177/0002716209343558

Mayer, K. U. (2001). How did the increase in economic inequality between 1970 and 1990 affect children's educational attainment? *American Journal of Sociology, 107*(1), 1–32.

Mazumder, B. (2008). *Upward intergenerational economic mobility in the United States.* Washington, DC: Economic Mobility Project, Pew Charitable Trusts. Retrieved from http://www.economicmobility.org/reports_and_research/

McCall, L., & Percheski, C. (2010). Income inequality: New trends and research directions. *Annual Review of Sociology, 36,* 329–347.

McCluskey, N. (2010). *Behind the curtain: Assessing the case for national curriculum standards* (Policy analysis no. 661). Washington, DC: CATO Institute. Retrieved from http://www.cato.org/pub_display.php?pub_id=11217

McDonnell, L. M. (1995, Autumn). Opportunity to learn as a research concept and a policy instrument. *Educational Evaluation and Policy Analysis, 17*(3), 305–322. Retrieved from http://www.jstor.org/stable/1164509

McKnight, C. C. (1979). Model for the Second International Mathematics Study, *SIMS Bulletin, 4,* 6–39.

Metz, M. M. (1990). Real school: A universal drama amid disparate experiences. In D. E. Mitchell & M. E. Goertz (Eds.), *Education politics for the new century* (pp. 75–92). London: Falmer.

Murray, C. (2007, January 16). Intelligence in the classroom. *Wall Street Journal.* Retrieved from http://www.opinionjournal.com/extra/?id=110009531

Murray, C. (2008, May). The age of educational romanticism. *The New Criterion, 26,* 35.

Murray, S. E., Evans, W. N., & Schwab, R. M. (1998). Education finance reform and the distribution of education resources. *American Economic Review, 88,* 789–812.

Myth. (2011). In *Merriam-Webster Online Dictionary.* Retrieved from http://www.merriam-webster.com/dictionary/myth

National Academy of Sciences. (2002). *Learning and understanding: Improving advanced study of mathematics and science in U.S. high schools.* Executive summary. Committee on Programs for Advanced Study of Mathematics and Science in American High Schools, National Research Council. Washington, DC: National Academies Press.

National Center for Education Statistics. (2009). *The nation's report card: Mathematics 2009.* (NCES 2010-451). Washington, DC: Institute of Education Sciences, U.S. Department of Education.

National Center for Education Statistics. (2010). *The nation's report card: Grade 12 reading and mathematics—2009 national and pilot state results.* (NCES 2011-455). Washington, DC: Institute of Education Sciences, U.S. Department of Education.

Obama, B. (2009). Obama in Philadelphia. [Transcript]. *The New York Times.* Retrieved from http://www.nytimes.com

Ogden, C. L., Lamb, M. M., Carroll, M. D., & Flegal, K. M. (2010, December). *Obesity and socioeconomic status in children and adolescents: United States, 2005–2008.* (NCHS Data Brief, No. 51). Washington, DC: U.S. Department of Health and Human Services, Centers for Disease Control and Prevention, National Center for Health Statistics.

Orfield, G., & Lee, C. (2004). *Brown at 50: King's dream or Plessy's nightmare.* Cambridge, MA: The Civil Rights Project, Harvard University.

Parker, T. H., & Baldridge, S. J. (2004). *Elementary mathematics for teachers.* Okemos, MI: Sefton Ash.

Parker, T. H., & Baldridge, S. J. (2008). *Elementary geometry for teachers.* Okemos, MI: Sefton Ash.

Pekkarinen, T., Uusitalo R., & Kerr, S. (2009). School tracking and intergenerational income mobility: Evidence from the Finnish comprehensive school reform. *Journal of Public Economics, 93*(7–8), 965–973.

Peske, H. G., & Haycock, K. (2006, June). *Teaching inequality: How poor and minority students are shortchanged on teacher quality.* Washington, DC: The Education Trust.

Philippon, T., & Reshef, A. (2009, January). *Wages and human capital in the U.S. financial industry: 1909–2006.* (Working Paper No. 14644). Retrieved from the National Bureau of Economic Research website: http://www.nber.org/papers/w14644.pdf

Porter, A. C. (1989). A curriculum out of balance. *Educational Researcher, 18*(5), 9–15.

Porter, A. C. (1991). Creating a system of school process indicators. *Educational Evaluation and Policy Analysis, 13*(1), 13–29.

Porter, A. C. (1993). School delivery standards. *Educational Researcher, 22*(5), 24–30.

Porter, A. C. (1995). The uses and misuses of opportunity-to-learn standards. *Educational Researcher, 24*(1), 21–27.

Porter, A. C. (2002). Measuring the content of instruction: Uses in research and practice. *Educational Researcher, 31*(7), 3–14.

Porter, A. C., Archbald, D. A., & Tyree, A. K. (1990). Reforming the curriculum: Will empowerment policies replace control? *Journal of Education Policy, 5*(5), 11–36.

Porter, A. C., Floden, R. E., Freeman, D. J., Schmidt, W. H., & Schwille, J. R. (1986). *Content determinants.* East Lansing, MI: Institute for Research on Teaching.

Porter, A. C., Floden, R., Freeman, D., Schmidt, W. H., & Schwille, J. (1988). Content determinants in elementary school mathematics. In D. A. Grouws, T. J. Cooney, & D. Jones (Eds.), *Effective mathematics teaching* (pp. 96–113). Reston, VA: National Council of Teachers of Mathematics.

Porter, A., McMaken, J., Hwang, J., & Yang, R. (2011). Common core standards: The new U.S. intended curriculum. *Educational Researcher, 40*(3), 103–116.

Porter, A. C., Polikoff, M. S., & Smithson, J. (2009). Is there a de facto national intended curriculum: Evidence from state content standards. *Educational Evaluation and Policy Analysis, 31*(3), 238–268.

Promoting educational success forty-five years after "Brown." (1999). Special Issue on Education. *Southern Changes, 22*(1).

PROM/SE. (2006). *Knowing mathematics: What we can learn from teachers* (Research Report Vol. 2). East Lansing, MI: Michigan State University.

PROM/SE. (2008). *Dividing opportunities: Tracking in high school mathematics* (Research Report Vol. 3). East Lansing, MI: Michigan State University.

Raudenbush, S. W. (2009). The *Brown* legacy and the O'Connor challenge: Transforming schools in the images of children's potential. *Educational Researcher, 38*(3), 169–180.

Ravitch, D. (1985). *The schools we deserve: Reflections on the educational crises of our times.* New York: Basic Books.

Ravitch, D. (Ed.). (1995a). *Debating the future of American education: Do we need national standards and assessments?* Washington, DC: Brookings Institution.

Ravitch, D. (1995b). *National standards in American education: A citizen's guide.* Washington, DC: Brookings Institution.

Ravitch, D. (2010a). *The death and life of the great American school system: How testing and choice are undermining education.* New York: Basic Books.

Ravitch, D. (2010b). Why public schools need democratic governance. *Phi Delta Kappan, 91*(6), 24–27.

Remillard, J. (2005). Examining key concepts in research on teachers' use of mathematics curricula. *Review of Educational Research, 75*(2), 211–246.

Reynolds, A. J. (1991). The middle schooling process: Influences on science and mathematics achievement from the Longitudinal Study of American Youth. *Adolescence, 26*, 133–158.

Reynolds, A. J., & Walberg, H. J. (1992). A structural model of science achievement. *Journal of Educational Psychology, 83*(1), 97–107.

Reys, B. J. (Ed.). (2006). *The intended mathematics curriculum as represented in state-level curriculum standards: Consensus or confusion?* Charlotte, NC: Information Age Publishing.

Rice, J. K. (2003). *Teacher quality: Understanding the effectiveness of teacher attributes.* Washington, DC: Economic Policy Institute.

Richardson, V. (Ed.). (2001). *Handbook of research on teaching* (4th ed.). Washington, DC: American Educational Research Association.

Roemer, J. (2004). Equal opportunity and intergenerational mobility: Going beyond intergenerational income transition matrices. In M. Corak (Ed.), *Generational income mobility in North America and Europe* (pp. 48–57). Cambridge, UK: Cambridge University Press.

Rothman, R., Slattery, J. B., Vranek, J. L., & Resnick, L. B. (2002, May). *Benchmarking and alignment of standards and testing.* (CSE Technical Report 566). Los Angeles: National Center for Research on Evaluation, Standards, and Student Testing. Retrieved from http://www.achieve.org/files/TR566.pdf

Rowan, B., Camburn, E., & Correnti, R. (2004). Using teacher logs to measure the enacted curriculum: A study of literacy teaching in third-grade classrooms. *Elementary School Journal, 105*(1), 75–101.

Rowan, B., Harrison, D. M., & Hayes, A. (2004). Using instructional logs to study mathematics curriculum and teaching in the early grades. *Elementary School Journal, 105*(1), 103–127.

Sawhill, I., & Morton, J. E. (2008). *Economic mobility: Is the American dream alive and well?* Washington, DC: Economic Mobility Project, Pew Charitable Trusts. Retrieved from http://www.economicmobility.org/reports_and_research/

Saxe, G. B. (1985). Effects of schooling on arithmetical understandings: Studies with Oksapmin children in Papua, New Guinea. *Journal of Educational Psychology, 77*(5), 503–513.

Saxe, G. B. (1988). The mathematics of child street vendors. *Child Development, 59,* 1415–1425.

Saxe, G. B. (1990). The interplay between children's learning in school and out-of-school contexts. In M. Gardner, J. G. Greeno, F. Reif, A. H. Schoenfeld, A. Disessa, & E. Stage (Eds.), *Toward a scientific practice of science education* (pp. 219–234). Hillsdale, NJ: Lawrence Erlbaum.

Scafidi, B., Sjoquist, D. L., & Stinebrickner, T. R. (2007). Race, poverty and teacher mobility. *Economics of Education Review, 26,* 145–159.

Schmidt, W. H. (2011). The cumulative effects of middle school tracking: How content coverage varies. In G. Gueudet, B. Pepin, & L. Trouche (Eds.), *From text to "lived" resources: Mathematics curriculum materials and teacher development* (pp. 143–160), (Vol. 7 of Mathematics Teacher Education Series). New York: Springer.

Schmidt, W. H., Blömeke, S., Tatto, M. T., Hsieh, F.-J., Cogan, L. S., Houang, R. T., . . . Schwille, J. (2011). *Teacher education matters: A study of middle school mathematics teacher preparation in six countries.* New York: Teachers College Press.

Schmidt, W. H., Cogan, L. S., & Houang, R. (2011). The role of opportunity to learn in teacher preparation: An international context. *Journal of Teacher Education, 62*(2), 138–153.

Schmidt, W. H., Cogan, L. S., Houang, R. T., & McKnight, C. C. (2011). Content coverage differences across districts/states: A persisting challenge for U.S. education policy. *American Journal of Education, 117*(3), 399–427. doi: 10.1086/649213

Schmidt, W. H., Cogan, L. S., Houang, R. T., & Wiley, D. E. (2008). *Relationship of tracking to content coverage and achievement: A study of eighth grade mathematics.* East Lansing, MI: Michigan State University.

Schmidt, W. H., Cogan, L. S., & McKnight, C. C. (2010). Equality of educational opportunity: Myth or reality in U.S. schooling. *American Educator, 34*(4), 12–19.

Schmidt, W. H., & Houang, R. T. (2007). Lack of focus in the mathematics curriculum: Symptom or cause? In T. Loveless (Ed.), *Lessons learned: What international assessments tell us about math achievement*. Washington, DC: Brookings Press.

Schmidt, W. H., Houang, R., & Cogan, L. S. (2011). Preparing future math teachers. *Science Magazine, 332*(6035), 1266–1267. doi:10.1126\science.1193855

Schmidt, W. H., Houang, R. T., & Cogan, L. S. (in press). Preparing primary teachers in the United States: Balancing selection and preparation. *ZDM—The International Journal of Mathematics Education*.

Schmidt, W. H., Houang, R. T., Cogan, L. S., Blömeke, S., Tatto, M. T., Hsieh, F. J., ... Paine, L. (2008). Opportunity to learn in the preparation of mathematics teachers: Its structure and how it varies across six countries. *ZDM—The International Journal of Mathematics Education, 40*(5), 735–747.

Schmidt, W. H., Houang, R. T., McKnight, C., Cogan, L. S., & Jakwerth, P. M. (1999). *Facing the consequences: Using TIMSS for a closer look at U.S. mathematics and science education*. Dordrecht, The Netherlands: Kluwer.

Schmidt, W. H., Houang, R. T., & Shakrani, S. (2009). *International lessons about national standards*. Washington, DC: The Thomas B. Fordham Institute.

Schmidt, W. H., Jakwerth, P. M., & McKnight, C. C. (1998). Curriculum-sensitive assessment: Content *does* make a difference. *International Journal of Educational Research, 29*, 503–527.

Schmidt, W. H., Jorde, D., Cogan, L. S., Barrier, E., Gonzalo, I., Moser, U., ... Wolfe, R. G. (1996). *Characterizing pedagogical flow: An investigation of mathematics and science teaching in six countries*. Dordrecht, The Netherlands: Kluwer.

Schmidt, W. H., & Maier, A. (2009). Opportunity to learn. In G. Sykes, B. Schneider, & D. N. Plank (Eds.), *Handbook of education policy research* (pp. 541–559). New York: Rutledge for American Educational Research Association.

Schmidt, W. H., McKnight, C. C., Houang, R. T., Wang, H. A., Wiley, D. E., Cogan, L. S., & Wolfe, R. G. (2001). *Why schools matter: A cross-national comparison of curriculum and learning*. San Francisco: Jossey-Bass.

Schmidt, W. H., McKnight, C. C., & Raizen, S. A. (1997). *A splintered vision: An investigation of U.S. science and mathematics education*. Dordrecht, the Netherlands: Kluwer.

Schmidt, W. H., McKnight, C. C., Valverde, G. A., Houang, R. T., & Wiley, D. E. (1997). *Many visions, many aims, volume 1: A cross-national investigation of curricular intentions in school mathematics*. Dordrecht, The Netherlands: Kluwer.

Schmidt, W. H., Raizen, S. A., Britton, E. D., Bianchi, L. J., & Wolfe, R. G. (1997). *Many visions, many aims, volume 2: A cross-national investigation of curricular intentions in school science*. Dordrecht, The Netherlands: Kluwer.

Schmidt, W. H., Tatto, M. T., Bankov, K., Blömeke, S., Cedillo, T., Cogan, L., ... Schwille, J. (2007). *The preparation gap: Teacher education for middle school mathematics in six countries* (MT21 Report). East Lansing, MI: Michigan State University, Center for Research in Mathematics and Science Education.

Schmidt, W. H., Wang, H. C., & McKnight, C. C. (2005). Curriculum coherence: An examination of U.S. mathematics and science content standards from an international perspective. *Journal of Curriculum Studies, 35*(5), 528–529.

Schoenfeld, A. H. (2004). The math wars. *Educational Policy, 18*(1), 253–286.

Schwille, J. R., Porter, A. C., Belli, G., Floden, R. E., Freeman, D. J., Knappen, L. B., Kuhs, T. M., & Schmidt, W. H. (1983). Teachers as policy brokers in the content of elementary school mathematics. In L. Shulman & G. Sykes (Eds.), *Handbook of teaching and policy* (pp. 370–391). New York: Longman.

Sears, J. T. (with Carper, J. C.). (Eds.). (1998). *Curriculum, religion, and public education: Conversations for an enlarging public square.* New York: Teachers College Press.

Shepard, L. A., & Dougherty. K. C. (1991, April). *Effects of high-stakes testing on instruction.* Paper presented at the annual meeting of the American Educational Research Association and the National Council on Measurement in Education, Chicago, IL.

Shulman, L. S. (2005, February). *The signature pedagogies of the professions of law, medicine, engineering and the clergy: Potential lessons for the education of teachers.* Paper presented at the Math Science Partnership (MSP) Workshop, Hosted by the National Research Council's Center for Education, Irvine, CA.

Shulman, L. S. (1983). Autonomy and obligation: The remote control of teaching. In L. S. Shulman & G. Sykes (Eds.), *Handbook of teaching and policy* (pp. 484–504). New York: Longman.

Shulman, L. S. (1985). Paradigms and research programs in the study of teaching: A contemporary perspective. In M. C. Wittrock (Ed.), *Handbook of research on teaching* (3rd ed., pp. 3–36). New York: Macmillan.

Smeeding, T. M. (2005). Public policy, economic inequality, and poverty: The United States in comparative perspective. *Social Science Quarterly, 86*(Supplement s1), 955–983.

Smith, B. (2002). Quantity matters: Annual instructional time in an urban school system. *Educational Administration Quarterly, 36*(5), 652–682.

Stein, M. K., Remillard, J., & Smith, M. S. (2007). How curriculum influences student learning. In F. K. Lester (Ed.), *Second handbook of research on mathematics teaching and learning* (pp. 319–370). Charlotte, NC: Information Age.

Stigler, J. W., Gonzales, P., Kawanaka T., Knoll, S., & Serrano, A. (1999). *The TIMSS videotape classroom study: Methods and findings from an exploratory research project on eighth grade mathematics instruction in Germany, Japan, and the United States.* Washington, DC: National Center for Education Statistics.

Stille, A. (2011, October 23). The paradox of the new elite. *The New York Times,* pp. SR1, SR6.

Strauss, V. (2010, June 3). *What common core state standards are—and aren't.* Retrieved from http://voices.washingtonpost.com/answer-sheet/national-standards/what-the-common-core-standards.html

Strum, P. (Ed). (2002). Brown v. Board of Education: *Its impact on education, and what it left undone.* Washington, DC: Woodrow Wilson Center.

Suter, L. E. (2000). Is student achievement immutable? Evidence from international studies on schooling and student achievement. *Review of Educational Research, 70*(4), 529–545.

Taylor, C. (1979). What's wrong with negative liberty. In A. Ryan (Ed.), *The idea of freedom* (pp. 175–193). Oxford: Oxford University Press.

Ucelli, M., Foley, E., & Emdon, T. (2002). *First steps to a level playing field: An introduction to student-based budgeting.* New York: Annenberg Institute for School Reform at Brown University.

U.S. Department of Education, National Center for Education Statistics. (1998). *Pursuing excellence: A study of U.S. twelfth-grade mathematics and science achievement in international context,* NCES 98-049. Washington, DC: U.S. Government Printing Office.

U.S. Surgeon General. (2001). *Overweight and obesity: Health consequences.* Retrieved from http://www.surgeongeneral.gov/library/calls/obesity/fact_consequences.html

Valverde, G. A. (2002). Curriculum, international. *Encyclopedia of Education.* Retrieved from http://www.encyclopedia.com/doc/1G2-3403200168.html

Valverde, G. A., Bianchi, L. J., Wolfe, R. G., Schmidt, W. H., & Houang, R. T. (2002). *According to the book: Using TIMSS to investigate the translation of policy into practice through the world of textbooks.* Dordrecht, The Netherlands: Kluwer.

Walker, L. H. (2004, Summer). *Brown* after 50 years: Looking for equality and raising expectations. *New Coalition News & Views.* Retrieved from http://www.newcoalition.org/Article.cfm?artId=15015

Weinert, F. E. (1999). *Konzepte der kompetenz. Gutachten zum OECD-projekt "Definition and selection of competencies: Theoretical and conceptual foundations (DeSeCo)"* [Concepts of competence. Expertise on the OECD project "Definition and selection of competencies: Theoretical and conceptual foundations (DeSeCo)"]. Neuchatel, Switzerland: Bundesamt für Statistik.

Weinert, F. E. (2001). Concept of competence: A conceptual clarification. In D. S. Rychen & L. H. Salganik (Eds.), *Defining and selecting key competencies* (pp. 45–66). Göttingen, Germany: Hogrefe.

The White House. (2004). *Educating America: The president's initiatives for high school, higher education and job training* [Executive Summary]. Retrieved from http://www.whitehouse.gov/infocus/education/20040513-educating-america.html

Whitehurst, G. J. (2002, March 5). *Scientifically based research on teacher quality: Research on teacher preparation and professional development.* Paper presented at White House Conference on Preparing Tomorrow's Teachers, Washington, DC.

Wiley, D. E., & Harnischfeger, A. (1974). Explosion of a myth: Quantity of schooling and exposure to instruction, major educational vehicles. *Educational Researcher, 3*(4), 7–12.

Willie, C. V., & Willie, S. S. (2005). Black, white, and brown: The transformation of public education in America. *Teachers College Record, 107*(3), 475–495.

Wilson, W., & Youngs, P. (2005). Research on accountability processes in teacher education. In M. Cochran-Smith & K. Keichner (Eds.), *Studying teacher education: The report of the AERA Panel on Research and Teacher Education* (pp. 261–308). Mahwah, NJ: Lawrence Erlbaum Associates.

Wu, H.-H. (2011). *Understanding numbers in elementary school mathematics.* Berkeley, CA: Author.

Young, M. F. D. (1998). *The curriculum of the future: From the "new sociology of education" to a critical theory of learning.* Philadelphia: Falmer.

Zehr, M. A. (2009, November 6). *States slow standards work amid "Common Core" push*. Retrieved from http://www.edweek.org/ew/articles/2009/11/11/11standards_ep.h29.html

Zhang, Y., Mizunoya, S., You, Y., & Tsang, M. (2011). Financial inequity in basic education in selected OECD countries. *International Education Studies, 4*(3), 3–22.

Zhao, Y. (2009). *Catching up or leading the way: American education in the age of globalization*. Alexandria, VA: ASCD.

Zuckerbrod, N. (2007, March 8). Bill Gates: Remove limits on H1-B visas. *The Washington Post*. Retrieved from http://www.washingtonpost.com/wp-dyn/content/article/2007/03/08/AR2007030800890.html

# Index

A letter *f* or *t* following a page number refers to a figure or table, respectively.

# About the Authors

**William H. Schmidt** received his undergraduate degree in mathematics from Concordia College in River Forrest, Illinois, and his PhD from the University of Chicago in psychometrics and applied statistics. He carries the title of University Distinguished Professor at Michigan State University and is currently co-director of the Education Policy Center, co-director of the U.S.–China Center for Research, and director of the NSF PROM/SE project. He holds faculty appointments in the departments of Statistics and Educational Psychology at MSU. Previously, he served as national research coordinator and executive director of the U.S. National Center, which oversaw participation of the United States in the IEA-sponsored Third International Mathematics and Science Study (TIMSS). He has published in numerous journals, including the *Journal of the American Statistical Association, Journal of Educational Statistics*, and the *Journal of Educational Measurement*. He has co-authored eight books, including *Why Schools Matter* and *Teacher Education Matters*. His current writing and research concerns issues of academic content in K–12 schooling, assessment theory, and the effects of curriculum on academic achievement. He is also concerned with educational policy related to mathematics, science, and testing in general. He was awarded the honorary doctorate degree at Concordia University in 1997, received the 1998 Willard Jacobson Lectureship from the New York Academy of Sciences, is a member of the National Academy of Education, and is an American Educational Research Association (AERA) Fellow.

**Curtis C. McKnight** is emeritus professor of mathematics at the University of Oklahoma. He has his PhD from the University of Illinois. He served as national research coordinator and executive director of the U.S. National Center for the Second International Mathematics Study (SIMS). He served as the senior mathematics consultant to the U.S. Research Center for TIMSS. He is the author of more than 100 publications and papers. His specialties include cross-national comparative studies, cognitive studies of mathematics learning and performance, and curriculum policy studies such as those involved currently in U.S. calculus reform curricula. He has received more than 20 research grants and served as a consultant on many other projects.